Nov 19, '97

Sleeping with the Mayor

SLEEPING
WITH
THE MAYOR

A TRUE STORY

John Jiler

Hungry Mind Press
SAINT PAUL, MINNESOTA

Published by Hungry Mind Press
1648 Grand Avenue
Saint Paul, Minnesota 55105

9 8 7 6 5 4 3 2 1
First Hungry Mind Press printing, 1997.

Library of Congress Catalog Card Number: 97-73315
ISBN: 1-886913-14-5

Printed in the United States of America

Book Design: Wendy Holdman
Typesetting: Stanton Publication Services, Inc.

For my wife Elizabeth and my son Jake, who are my home.

TO THE READER

This is a true story. Because there is still a stigma to homelessness, some of the characters' names, as well as those of their family and intimate associates, have been changed. Information that might identify them has sometimes been disguised. Additionally, some minor characters have been combined to form composites, and not all conversations are verbatim; the author takes the occasional liberty of interpolating dialogue.

Acknowledgments

All my debts of gratitude pale in comparison with the first three, the people who have gotten *Sleeping with the Mayor* into print. My agent Eric Simonoff, at Janklow and Nesbit, continues to define friendship and integrity in a professional relationship: fortunate indeed is the writer who has such a collaborator. My editor, Charles Flowers, was nothing less than a full artistic partner. And lastly, the people at Hungry Mind Press—Margaret Wurtele, Nicole Baxter, Dallas Crow, David Unowsky, Pearl Kilbride, Page Knudsen Cowles, and Gail See—they gave me an experience all writers should have: the hands-on passion of a vibrant small press.

Since *Sleeping with the Mayor* is largely an oral history, its first obligation is to acknowledge the conversations that brought it to life. The following people gave me hours and hours of their time, and finally allowed me to understand their world, and the complexity of the problem to which they have given so much of themselves: finding people a place to live.

They are: Mike Amadeo, Michael Avrimides, Stan Brezenoff, Bonnie Brower, Lloyd Casson, Paul Dickstein, John Engel, Bill Green, Ryan Fitzpatrick, Alberta Fuentes, Abe Gerges, Peter Harris, Jim Haughton, Victoria Hernandez, Kim Hopper, Ed Koch, Jenny Laurie, Leon Lane, John Luce, Sidney Leader, Steve Leader, Connie Lessold, Ed Logue, George McDonald, Ruth Messinger, Lora Nelson, Beverly Neufeld, Yolanda Rivera, Peter Rubinstein,

Roy Parker, Nelson Prime, Norman Siegel, Teresa Skehan, Tom Sligh, Henry Stern, Joan Tappen, Alair Townsend, Daniel Weisz, Lou Winnick, Larry Wood, and Kathy Wylde.

For a work of this nature one constantly depends on research facilities, and New York's came through for me brilliantly: the Municipal Archives, and its remarkable director Kenneth Cobb; the Municipal Reference and Research Center, particularly the tireless Devra Zetlan; Aimee Kaplan at the LaGuardia and Wagner Archives; Barry Moreno at the Ellis Island Immigrant Museum; the Bronx Historical Society; the Bronx Building Department; the Schomburg Center for Research in Black Culture; and of course, the New York City Public Library.

For my own personal education in the field I absorbed the books, periodicals and films of some of the best chroniclers of New York, and of the issues raised by this book: Jim Baumohl, Barry Bearak, Gordon Berlin, Elizabeth Blackmar, Bill Brand, Robert Caro, Christopher Gray, Clifton Hood, Kim Hopper, Christopher Jencks, Ed Koch, Jonathan Kozol, Michael Lerner, William McAllister, Rob Rosenthal, Jennifer Toth, Cornel West, Talmadge Wright, and a host of talented writers in publications as far ranging as *City Limits*, *The Village Voice*, *Street News*, *The New York City Bar Association's Report on the Homeless*, *The New York Times*, the plethora of information published by the New York City Department of Housing Preservation and Development and the astounding *Encyclopedia of New York City*, edited by Kenneth T. Jackson.

I am thankful to the members of my family who have read over parts of the manuscript, Elizabeth and Scott Hovey, and particularly Fran Hovey, who pored over it with passion and precision. My gratitude also to Terry Johnson, Ross Wetzsteon and David Herndon, my editors at *The Village Voice*.

Lastly, and mostly importantly, there are the men and women of Kochville, without whose heroism and perseverance there would be no story to tell. Besides Duke York and Larry Locke and

Marc Greenberg, for whose devotion to this project I will always be grateful, there are many, many more. I cannot give their last names, but they know who they are: Abby, Al, Angel, Annie, April, Ben, Beverly, Carla, Chris, Connie, David, Deanna, Dennis, Edwin, Edmond, Eric, Ernesto, Fritz, Heavy, Horace, Jesse, Jim, Joe, Keith, King of Kings, Lamont, Laura, Lee, Leonard, Lonnie, Luther, Martin, Mary, Mike, Nelson, Nina, Patricia, Princess, Rasta, Reynard, Roger, Ron, Sebastian, Sergio, Shep, Slick, Sonny, Stan, T, Tamara, Tom, Tony, Tracy, Vern, and Vicki. Wherever they are, I hope they have a roof over their heads tonight.

Preface

On a summer morning in 1988, I took my newspaper and a cup of coffee into City Hall Park, which is my custom. I live a block away, and the place is an island of peace in the madness of Lower Manhattan. To my surprise, the lawn was dotted with sleeping human beings. There were about fifteen of them, and they had sprung up overnight, like mushrooms.

At the time I did free-lance work for *The Village Voice*, and I was intrigued. I approached them and learned that they had been rounded up from street corners and places like Penn Station for an "all-night vigil" protesting homelessness. Now that morning had come, however, the organizers had gone home. The homeless, having no home, remained. The trees were high and leafy, and the old park cool and serene: certainly more so than the floor of Penn Station or the dreaded city shelters.

I shivered a little. When Ed Koch got to work, this was the first thing he'd see. The mayor was a complicated man, and not always a kind one. Homelessness was his Waterloo. When he took office in 1978, there was only Skid Row, the timeless cluster of Bowery drunks. Now, ten years later, New York was the Calcutta of the modern world. According to the mayor's enemies, it was all his fault. He had allowed cronies like Harry Helmsley to build their glittering towers with no thought to the dispossessed. The streets were now full of them. Here was a village of fifteen, right outside his window—his own chickens come home to roost.

Whether or not that was a fair assessment, the little encampment figured to enrage him and I wanted to see what happened next.

Sure enough, the mayor arrived and immediately tried to get rid of them. But the move backfired badly. As Sanitation Department trucks dismantled the little village, the City Hall press, bored to numbness by the minutiae of government, poured down the steps to cover it. "Kochville," as they called it, delighted them, and the mayor had to back off.

My own dispatches to the *Voice* were gleefully inflammatory. The American Left was passionate about the housing issue, and no scenario could have pleased my editors more: a taut little cat-and-mouse game between the fuming mayor and the trembling village of the poor.

But the more time I spent in the camp, the less all that seemed to matter. Now thirty people were living on a lawn—in starvation and chaos. As much as they needed to eat, they needed rules for living. But where were the homeless to learn about government?

City Hall sat right in front of them. By day they would sit in air-conditioned galleries and observe the City Council meetings, by night they would emerge and apply the rules to the government of Kochville.

I was spellbound. Democracy was forming from the ground up.

At first, infatuated with the idea, the men held their midnight meetings with a simple rule—anybody who had anything to say stood up and said it. But there are mentally ill among the homeless, and one night one of them stood up and hallucinated for hours on end about laser beams and giant sexual organs and the spinning moons of Venus. Clearly he had to be muffled. So the government veered the opposite way, towards absolute tyranny. Thus democracy struggled to define itself. Jefferson must have been through all this; the Athenians too.

I was riveted. I didn't want to go home at night, for fear that the tiny government would experience some new upheaval or that the mayor would wipe them out altogether. Finally, on August 1, I gave in to my obsession. I sublet my apartment and moved into Kochville.

My family and friends were horrified. Surely I would be raped or murdered. But I already knew my hosts better than that. Though I was one of the few white men there, I was treated with courtesy and an utter lack of racism. Many of them respected the craft of writing, and some even aspired to it. Presided over by a half-dozen Vietnam veterans, the security in the camp was impregnable; at every moment of the day and night, hawk eyes protected us from incursions from the outside world. In the clear night air, I slept blissfully.

Through the end of summer, the camp's notoriety grew. As the mayor sizzled, Kochvilleans were invited to talk shows and political fund-raisers, to fashionable cocktail parties, dinner parties, and even into boudoirs. I was shocked by how easily I took to homelessness. I had no keys, no schedule, nothing to protect. When the sensuality of it all was good—when the sun was out, when the belly was full—there was a profound sweetness to things. As office workers trudged about, we contemplated the larger issues.

But I would soon learn what the rest of Kochville already knew: how quickly and brutally it all turns. You sleep with one eye open, and there is no true rest. Frayed bare, the emotions change like traffic lights. There is only the next meal, the prayer that the day will not be monstrously hot or cold, that it will not rain, that the rats will not find you edible. By October, the open air is not sweet or intoxicating, nor the lack of keys something to celebrate.

Sleeping with the Mayor is not about a white man romanticizing homelessness. It is about the strength of dreams. For most of Kochville, the idea of "home" existed only as a shadow of childhood or as a long shot in a bleak future. But the dreams of the desperate are powerful things. They are also mythic, profound, dangerous, demented, sweet, and finally fragile.

Kochville wound finally to its dramatic conclusion, years passed, and I became a husband and a father. Administrations changed, and New York changed: the homeless began to seem less visible and less aggressive. But as I was creating my own home, the men and women of Kochville began to populate my dreams. Many of them, I knew, were dead. Yet with time the dreams grew more vivid, not less. Finally, I had to revisit the story and write it.

Ten years ago Ed Koch was the villain of the American Left, a braggadocio, a betrayer of New York. When he received me in his law office last winter, I found an aging, complicated man who felt the darkness all around him—no less so than the people of Kochville. Ten years ago, when he was in office and I was a ragamuffin out on the lawn, we could not have had our dialogue.

Finding the key players of Kochville was considerably harder. Where do you look for a homeless man? You get a tip on a recent sighting, you go to that neighborhood, you spend day after day stalking the same twenty-block strip. If it is January, you sit in a coffee shop with a view of the street, ready to bolt when you see your man, silently praying he is not emaciated beyond recognition. You go broke giving dollar bills with your phone number on them to homeless people you see, hoping that one of them will pass the information along. Finally, at four o'clock on a winter morning, the phone rings and it's him, the one you need. Over a series of long dinners, you help each other remember Kochville.

It will not be long before the reader realizes that one of the major characters in *Sleeping with the Mayor* is made out of brick and mortar. The more I sought out the housing experts of New York (and what a vast, byzantine domain is theirs!), the clearer did the reality become; there is hardware here. As surely as the word homeless contains the word home, so does Manhattan contain thousands of empty buildings. Each one of them has a story no less heartbreaking or complex than the people that inhabit them . . . or fail to.

But one does not take a building to dinner. To learn the life story of a place like 850 Longwood Avenue, you spend time among the dusty archives, handling blueprints that crumble as they are touched. You seek out the living who remember, like the remarkable Victoria Hernandez, and the writers who hear the breathing of these old places, like Christopher Gray of *The New York Times*. Finally, you stand in silent, cold corridors and imagine.

The homeless have not vanished. Visitors to New York marvel at the new orderliness, but the truth is that the current administration has taken a more cosmetic approach. Indeed, in 1997, whenever there is a demonstration in City Hall Park, the strip of land that once was Kochville is cordoned off as a buffer zone, a staging area for squadrons of police. The desperation of the poor no longer shocks us, nor do attempts to conceal them. New York housing remains a giant game of musical chairs—when the music stops, there are only so many places to sit, and more left standing than ever.

But the dream of home dies hard. A robin weaves its twigs and mud. A vagrant looks for a warm grate. Even the legions who arrive daily craving New York's freedom and anonymity—even they wish at some point only to turn a key and close a door behind them.

For most of the men and women of Kochville, the dream of home will not come true. Many lie in early graves, others wander about in semimadness: foul-smelling, larcenous, saintly, meek, violent, self-destructive or self-deceiving. But I still see them in my dreams. They sit in the lobbies of first-class hotels, smoking fine cigars, or for those who prefer it, behind picket fences with adoring wives. This is fraud and fantasy, but that is my prerogative, as the dreamer.

New York, May 1997

Sleeping with the Mayor

One

Jamaica Bay made the man sing.

There comes a point, riding the New York subways to the outer boroughs, when you emerge from the tunnels and burst into light. Then, even Brooklyn and the Bronx glow for a moment like a sweet dream. And when your destination is the largest borough of all, when the A-train has rushed south and east through twenty miles of darkness and suddenly explodes into the daylight of Queens, you're on your way to the promised land. First you endure endless streets of low two-family homes, then the hulking grandstands of Aqueduct Racetrack, then the sad canals of Howard Beach. But then all of it falls away, and the train runs out over a trestle to . . . Jamaica Bay!

Late on the afternoon of June 1, 1988, a large black man named Duke York got himself out between the cars and took it all in. Smell of the open sea. Last sun glinting off the marsh. Big birds on the wing. The song jumped out of him. "Is it an earthquake, or merely a shock . . ."

The first time he had sung it to Diane she absolutely swooned. Lord, could he get over with the Cole Porter! "Is it that good turtle soup, or only the mock . . ." The woman GREW WEAK! "Is it an illusion that I'm dreaming of . . ." She watched him tame the song, take its power into his body, stroke it, then release it to roam like a beast.

He knew he was giving her something she got nowhere else,

not from the morons she worked with or hoodlums she grew up with. "Or is at long—last—love!!! . . ."

CCRRANNKK! The A-train agonized around a turn, jerking him out of the memory. The train was leaving Jamaica Bay behind, and the small houses of Rockaway Beach were coming into view, the end of the line. It was late in the day, and on the way back, Jamaica Bay would be in the dark. Then would come Howard Beach again, an ill omen for any black man, especially one whose nerves have been frayed bare by three days on the A-train. A couple of years ago, an unfortunate Negro had had car trouble in Howard Beach, and he finally rode out of there in a hearse. He had been chased onto the Belt Parkway by some Italian punks and mutilated by a half-dozen automobiles travelling at sixty miles an hour. By the time the famous case died down, Howard Beach had become a synonym for "Keep moving, boy."

And keep moving the A-train did, right back out of Rockaway, right past the murky dark of Jamaica Bay, right past Howard Beach, right past Aqueduct Racetrack, dim and dumb in the last light, right through southern Queens and back down into the dark tunnel.

That was enough for Duke York. There was no reason to ride the loop again, either the A-train to Washington Heights or the loop in his mind. Diane was gone. That's what these three days in purgatory were for: to get the hell over her. And Jamaica Bay in the dark was no different from Nostrand Avenue, which was above him now in all its grimness. Three days was enough. This time around, he was getting out.

He rode the width of Brooklyn one last time, with its interminable teenage chatter ("So I says to him, 'Nigger, you got to be *crazy!!* I'm married to your brother, and you think you gonna get some pussy off of me!!?'") He felt the serenity that always came to him when the train dove under the East River. Everyone felt it, and the whole car went quiet. And then, Manhattan! The rock! The train pulled into the Broadway-Nassau stop, and he bolted from his seat and into the mob. It was the tail end of rush hour, and every secretary and file clerk and chunky junior executive in a bad suit was heading home. He fought through them and climbed up to the street and gulped the air—sweetness itself after three days in a tin can. Unfortunately, the promising dusk of Jamaica Bay had undergone a transformation during Duke's ride underneath Brooklyn. It was raining. Not much, but enough to make him duck into a little Greek place and drink a cup of coffee. What about a toilet? he inquired.

An old Greek took him in with narrow eyes. "Is only employees," he said. Duke checked himself in the mirror. Three-day beard, wrinkled shirt, probably a bit of a smell. He could be mistaken for a vagrant, a homeless person. There was nothing to indicate that he was a gifted man, that he had performed on three continents, that Cab Calloway himself had pronounced him an "interesting talent." No, there was no evidence of that now, save for a swedish krona in his pocket, left over from his last tour. Clearly it wasn't going to get him into the Greek's crummy toilet.

"Finish now?" the Greek was saying. "Not yet," Duke snarled back, protecting his cup of coffee with both hands. He was a gentle soul, but you had to have a tough sheen in New York.

He needed to think swiftly and clearly. A bad night was coming on. He had left Diane's with very little money, certainly not enough for a decent room. He could call his friend Craig, but he'd stayed with Craig last week, for two nights actually, and his welcome might be lukewarm.

It was at this moment that the face appeared. It was not an extraordinary face, but he recognized it instantly. To some this is a mystical event in New York, the spotting of a familiar face in the crowd. What are the odds, in a city of ten million? Others maintain that it's an ordinary occurrence, that given the never-ending parade, you're almost *bound* to see a familiar face now and then. But *this* face was too much!

It had begun with Diane, as all things did. She and Duke and their two daughters were living in Queens, happily, he thought. Then she started seeing another man. When Duke found out about it it broke his heart . . . for the last time, he vowed. The cat was a saxophone player, a *bad* saxophone player with a dashiki and an extremely smooth line of bullshit. Diane said she wanted Duke to be friends with him, wanted them all to get to know each other. Friends!? How could she even suggest it?!! Didn't she have any idea the size of the passion Duke was carrying around for her? She said she wanted the two men to play music together! What music!? The cat played the lamest horn Duke had ever heard!! Supposedly they were African sounds, cheetahs wailing in the high hills of Kenya, or some such crap. It was an insult. Duke was a true artist, this man was a pretentious dilettante.

It all came to a head on Staten Island. Diane moved out there with the girls to get away from their jealous father. Duke found out where they were and one night, when he knew she was up in her apartment with the horn player, he appeared downstairs and rang the bell. When she wouldn't let him in, he lost his equilibrium completely. "I know that nigger's in there," he began to scream. His two little girls hid behind curtains. Neighborhood cats and dogs trembled. "I KNOW THAT NIGGER'S IN THERE," he continued to bellow, finally picking up a two-by-four and pulverizing the door with it. The thought of her with another man pitched him down into a dark, terrifying hole.

By this time, somebody had called the police. He heard sirens and took off through a series of side streets to the ferry, which he rode to lower Manhattan. After a night of the kind of hell into which only Diane could pitch him, he found himself on the train platform at Queensboro Plaza. He still doesn't remember how or why, but he suddenly leapt down onto the tracks and began to run. Someone spotted a man on the tracks, so the electricity of the third rail was turned off and all the trains stopped dead. The rush hour travellers were livid. Duke raced wildly along the trestle, out towards the Queensboro Bridge. As he got out over the water, the sounds of the angry people faded and all he could hear was the din of traffic and the river rushing below.

Then he threw himself off.

But in midair, he changed his mind and grabbed wildly for the bridge, digging his fingers into a splintered plank. There he dangled, his two-hundred-pound hulk blowing in the wind. Dear God, I take it all back!! Let me live and love again and play my music and see my beautiful little daughters and cook a meal and watch the moon rise!

That was the moment he saw the face: pink, beefy, and Irish. The guy was a member of some crack city police unit, some kind of SWAT outfit, and he did this kind of thing all the time. "Grab onto me," the guy was saying, "one arm at a time." This was crucial information. Never let go with both hands. Duke did as he was told, and the young Irishman pulled him to safety.

And now, outside this Greek place a month later in a rainy dusk, here was the guy again. There was no mistaking him. Much had intervened, including a few days on a mental ward and a brief, miserably failed reconciliation with Diane. And the Irishman was wearing not the official windbreaker of his unit but his street clothes, and he looked like an ordinary guy—with the *Daily News* sticking out of his back pocket and a glazed look on his face.

Before Duke could think what to do, to thank him, to curse him, whatever, the guy's face joined the never-ending stream and was gone. That's New York. Give you an unsettling image and let it settle in while a million people mill around you.

"Wanting close up now," the Greek was saying, grabbing the cup out of Duke's hand and throwing a wet rag on the counter.

Duke stepped outside to a dark sky spitting rain. The rush hour was thinning out. He started to walk up Broadway, aimlessly but rapidly. Maybe if he found one of those all-night movies he could sleep in a seat for a few hours. Times Square was miles away, but he was a walker.

The secretaries were all back home in Brooklyn, but now an-

7

other throng of people was clogging the streets. Duke rubbed his eyes and squinted. Some kind of yellow glow was coming off them. It was otherworldly, possibly a hallucination born out of the booze and sleeplessness. He got up closer, and that's when he saw the candles in their hands. A religious event of some kind was taking place. This he didn't need. He looked to find a way to move past them quickly. Then he heard the sound.

As a musician, he thought he'd heard all the sounds there were, including phony African saxophones. This was clearly the sound of a horn, but the rawness of it was new to him. It twisted his insides around somehow, in the way Charlie Parker or Miles could blow something so deep it would ream you out, cleanse you.

Now he was in the middle of the crowd. The night was foggy, and the candles seemed to light up the air itself, like one big cloud. And now he could see the cat with the horn. It was more like a horn of plenty, a big old bent thing, and the cat blew it again and it got right inside Duke, and dredged a tear out of his bloodshot eyes.

Now he was walking beside a white woman. She was holding one end of an oilskin banner and having trouble keeping her candle lit. Duke pulled his knife out of his pocket, deepened the wick's well, and drained it. It was the kind of thing he used to do when he was making love to Diane and wanted the candles to burn through the night.

"Thank you," she said.

Duke realized it was the first moment of kindness or civility he'd had with any human being since he'd boarded the A-train three days earlier.

"You're entirely welcome," he said, and he could feel the sleek bullshit begin to ooze out of him, which it did so easily when he was feeling himself. The woman was a bit too old for him, but she had a pleasant face, sharp features that Duke thought might be Irish, and big intense blue eyes catching the candlelight. She said her name was Ellen and explained that the group was on its way to City Hall Park, where they intended to spend the night. What on earth for? Duke asked. Well, said Ellen with a slight edge, in case he didn't know it there was a big housing problem in New York. By simply being in front of City Hall all night, singing songs and saying prayers, they hoped to influence the city budget hearings that were to begin in the morning. Duke peered at the sodden banner, which read "Interfaith Assembly on Homelessness and Housing."

He looked around him. Even as he studied the faces, they were vanishing. The rain was coming down hard, and every few minutes someone else withdrew, mumbling apologies. Since the time he had joined them, Duke estimated that their number had dwindled from a hundred to less than fifty. The faces that remained were a strange mixture of the holy and the profane. There seemed to be religious people of every stripe, in Catholic nun's habit and flowing Buddhist robe. But the *other* faces, the ones clearly not priests or gurus, were the most intense. Almost all were black. Drenched to the bone, the skinniest of them were like skeletons with huge, glaring eyes, scared to death of whatever would happen next.

"Who are these people?" Duke finally asked Ellen.

"They're the reason we're here," she said. "They're the homeless."

Duke tightened up. He did not like the term, first of all. It implied desperation. Everyone without a roof over his head on a given night was not necessarily some terminal, pathetic waif. Some of them were just having a run of bad luck. Temporarily, like himself. But *these* people! Where the hell had they been dredged up? They looked like the Third World come begging, the living dead.

His first instinct was to get the hell out of there. But then another thought came, as it always did when he was around liberal white people. At the core of his being he believed everyone was alike, and he held no deep resentment towards the white man for

9

the enslavement of his great-great-grandfather, or any of that. But the truth was that white people had the money, and the guilty ones would eventually give it to you. So why not take it? At some point in this strange enterprise, there would be a hot meal or a few dollars or a warm bed. Especially the latter. Because surely if the rain continued, these white people were not spending the night in front of City Hall, soaked to the bone.

Now the odd horn blew again, and Duke was close enough to see who was doing the blowing: an old man who didn't look like a musician. "What is that thing?" he said to Ellen. "I think it's something Jewish," she said, "but you'd have to ask Marc." She pointed to a intense-looking young white man whose immediate passion seemed to be keeping the group together. The rain was torrential now, and people were defecting in droves. Duke sidled up to the man, and when there a break in the pep talks, Duke asked him about the horn.

Marc turned and burned a couple of intense brown eyes into him and said, "Welcome."

Duke took a moment, vaguely uncomfortable at the warmth of the greeting. A love-in he did not want. Nevertheless he had to admit that the word "Welcome" washed pleasantly over him, as did the concept.

"I wondered about the horn," he repeated.

"It's called a shofar," replied Marc. "It's a ram's horn. The Jews have been blowing it for five thousand years. Moses blew it to get the attention of the people when he came down from the mountain."

An image came to Duke's head from his youth, from the little church in St. Albans, Queens. Moses had gone to the mountaintop to talk to the Lord. While he was gone, the revelers went wild, praying to golden statues, screwing virgins, drinking like there was no tomorrow. Then, suddenly, the trumpet blast!! They turned around, and there was Moses, the Man!! He had the stone tablets with him, into which the Lord had burned the Ten Commandments with his eyes, *burned* them in with lightning bolts from his fingernails. Wait . . . eyes or fingernails? He forgot which. One was Charlton Heston, the other was the Bible. Either way, Duke had always been partial to the Old Testament. Mountains trembled, water parted, cities burned.

"And this is the same horn?" said Duke.

"The same," said Marc, and moved off to stop another rain-soaked priest from going home.

Duke fell back to Ellen and told her what he had learned ". . . and this is the *same horn*!!"

"I doubt that it's the same, exactly," said Ellen gently. "I'm sure Marc meant that it's the same *kind* of thing. A ram's horn, or whatever. The Jews are very big on symbols."

Duke trudged in silence a while. Fooled again. Familiar feeling. He had believed Diane's lies, he had believed the Jew about the horn.

Now the group, or what was left of it, proceeded into a park. There was immediate relief from the rain under the rich June growth of the elm trees. In front of them stood New York's City Hall, lit up in the imperial style from below, like something out of ancient Rome. Duke would soon learn that it dated from 1803, and that Lincoln's coffin had once rested in the big rotunda for a few days. That apparently was *not* bullshit. The man who freed the slaves had actually been laid out here.

By now the man named Marc had drawn the group around in a circle. Duke counted a paltry nineteen—four white church people, including Ellen and Marc, fourteen of the homeless, and himself. Marc said a few things that Duke ignored, having been inoculated now against the man's bullshit. Then Marc introduced Annie. A huge black woman from Georgia, Annie said she had been brought north to be a maid forty years ago, and had since been through a string of misfortunes that defied belief. They included rapes, abandonments, incarcerations and the deaths of children. She asked everyone to join hands; then she closed her eyes and began to testify. "Lord, we ask you tonight to hold back the rain, like you did when you finally decided Noah's tribulations be at an end. Lord, we ask you to touch the mayor's heart, Lord we ask you to touch the governor's heart; we ask you, Lord, to turn stone to flesh . . ."

The woman was good. She found a rhythm, and her big jelly body trembled with the cadence. Then Marc stepped forward again and laid something in the middle of the circle. It looked like a brick, but you'd have thought it was the baby Jesus the way Marc stared at it, gathering inspiration to speak.

"The brick is used to build," he began. "We come to you naked, Lord, and we ask you to build us a house out of the bricks we bring—our memories, our souls, our sweet devotion . . ."

Duke had to concede it, the cat was not bad either. He was letting each thought take him to a new place, and trusting it would lead to the next thought. Blind faith. He was testifying. Very few white men could do it.

"Take us in your sweet sheltering embrace, Lord, and look at us. We're wet but we're happy, because we know we stand at the threshold of your house, and inside is the warmth that only you can make us feel . . ."

Duke looked around at the faces. Lit now by only a couple of pathetic, spitting candles, the group was holding hands. Strangers had connected. Duke was embarrassed by the sweetness of it, but there it was. The white boy had brought it off. The buzz they were feeling, modest as it was, was as real as the cocktail glows or cocaine highs in the glittering towers around them.

Marc finished, and everyone looked at each other. Of course, the planned schedule was off. To sit around singing folk songs in this downpour was lunacy. Duke hoped for a Plan B involving a hotel room. Instead, the consensus was to unroll the sleeping bags and try to fall asleep while still dry and not totally miserable. Unfortunately, the sleeping bags brought by the clergy were already wet and useless, and the homeless had no equipment at all.

At this point, a small homeless black man named Art took over. Art had given six years of his life to the United States Army, most of it crawling on his belly through the jungles of Vietnam and Cambodia. He was a Forward Point Operative; he informed everyone. His job had been to give the coordinates of a target, and then wait for the big guns behind him to slam it. "Let's say we was goin' for that there," said Art, pointing to City Hall. "I call it in, light me a cigarette, and watch them take it out about thirty seconds later. Blammmm!! Be nothing left of the motherfucker at all."

Everyone absorbed the thought a while, then Art set to work. He took several cardboard crates out of the trash, cut them up with Duke's knife, and lined the underside of a row of park benches.

"Learned this from an old man on the Mekong Delta," said Art. "They call it a kubi hut."

Duke knelt down and peered into it, a long low tunnel. The cardboard roof, double thickness under the wooden slats of the benches, which was keeping out the rain, which was already deflected by the trees. It wouldn't hold nineteen bodies end to end, but if they dovetailed, then they could fit . . . face to kneecap right on down the line.

And so the nineteen of them entered this strange wet intimacy, new to some and deeply familiar to others. Everywhere were sodden clerical collars, rosaries, and plastic bags with half-eaten sandwiches from yesterday's soup kitchen. Duke was about dead center, wedged between an old black man and a Catholic priest. Very shortly, as rain pounded the top of the kubi hut, he drifted into a deep sleep.

≡

The next morning was nearly perfect. The storm had cleared the air, and there was a great crispness to things. One felt as if one's windows had just been washed.

For a passenger travelling alone in the backseat of a Lincoln Town Car, this was literally true. The automobile's windows were cleaned daily with ammonia and a dash of lemon juice for sparkle. Nothing less would do for the mayor of the City of New York.

As the car joined the stream of traffic heading south on FDR Drive, Edward I. Koch set down his reading matter and gave himself over to watching the river. Of this pursuit he never tired. The odd mélange of Roosevelt Island, with its futuristic housing developments and little Victorian churches (Dickens once stayed there, someone had just told him), then the low sprawl of Queens, then the smokestacks of Greenpoint—the prelude to Brooklyn. Dozens of ethnic neighborhoods in the vista, a hundred thousand chattering tongues, and he felt protective and fatherly to them all. And in turn, he felt secure in their love. On their most recent trip to the polls, in November 1985, they had returned him to office with one of the highest pluralities in the history of New York City politics. Yes, Fiorello La Guardia and Robert Wagner had also been re-elected for a third term . . . but not with 80 percent of the vote!!

So utterly had the mayor dominated the body politic that politics itself had seemed to change its nature. From the very beginning, there was no caution about him. He behaved as if he didn't care whether or not he was re-elected, and it seemed to free him. He said whatever he felt like saying. Habituated to blow-dried politicians who measured their every word, the public adored him. It got to the point where he couldn't alienate them even if he tried. His enemies had become exhausted and exasperated. By the end of the second four-year term in 1985, Ed Koch was as loose as a pool player on a magic run. Shortly before the last election, the city had experimented with a street sweeper that announced itself with a recording of the mayor's voice. "Get out of the way, I'm spraying water!" it would shriek as it came down the street, and passersby, smiling warmly at the familiar nasal bleat, would step aside.

But on the magnificent morning of June 2, 1988, there was nothing smug about Ed Koch. Not now, nor at any time in the recent past. Though he was a member of an Orthodox temple, the mayor was not a strictly observant Jew, and only a casual student of the Talmud. Yet he had the ancient wisdom in his bones. God disliked arrogance. He did not like to be upstaged. Acts of overweening pride on the parts of humans were dealt with quickly and rudely.

And so it was with Ed Koch. No sooner was his history-making triumph secure, no sooner had he stood on the flag bedecked platform outside City Hall and taken the oath of office for his historic third term in January 1986, than the whole thing fell apart. That very same week it was revealed that the highest-ranking members of his political coalition, many of whom could be seen in the official inaugural photograph, were thieves.

Thieves.

The blow was almost mortal. Later the mayor would admit that one night during those first awful days, he searched Gracie Mansion for a gun. Had he found one, he would have blown out the mayoral brains.

This would have been hari-kiri, the death of honor, because this was an honorable man. No one believed that Ed Koch was crooked, not even his worst enemies (and many could vie for that title). But the mayor had been guilty of terrible, terrible misjudgment. He had disregarded the warnings of W. B. Yeats, one of his favorite writers, who said "I have seen more men destroyed by the desire to have wife and child and keep them in comfort than I have seen destroyed by drinking and harlots." In other words, all crooks didn't slink around in silk suits and dark glasses. Lester Shafran, one of the minor figures in the scandal, had taken his first bribe to pay for his son's bar mitzvah.

It all came to an agonized head a month later, when Donald

Manes, the Queens Borough president and a lieutenant in the vast white middle class Koch coalition, committed suicide in his basement. He was acting out the mayor's darkest fantasies. The mayor sank into what seemed a terminal depression. He stopped eating, a troubling symptom for the gormandizing Ed Koch. At his worst moments he would speak longingly of Manes being "out of it all now," and at his best moments he was merely listless. The government of New York stopped. Oh, the busses ran . . . barely. As for anything energetic or innovative, forget it. Democratic Party officials hoped only that the damaged man could somehow limp to the finish line and turn the reins of government over in 1990 to someone else . . . hopefully a Democrat.

But the Old Testament god that Ed Koch believed in was apparently not done with him. In the summer of 1987, riding to an event in the back of his town car, the mayor felt faint and dizzy and ordered the car to Lenox Hill Hospital. He had suffered a stroke. The city, which had grown so used to this odd, avuncular man, held its breath. Miraculously, he was released the next day with no "medical deficit," as the doctors put it. That meant no damage . . . no paralysis. Ed Koch took it as a miracle on a grander scale. He was being summoned back to life. He was being told that even the nightmare he had undergone in the past year was trivial, a distraction from the greater mission, which was to live . . . to watch the tugboats from his Gracie Mansion window, to discipline his dog Archie not to urinate on the mansion antiques, to dip his considerable nose in one of those fabulous martinis at Lutece. "Shmuck," God was saying to him, "LIVE!!"

He threw himself back into government with a hot, thrilling passion. Having no family, he created a family of 10 million, and saw to their daily affairs with care and precision. And even the event at which he would shortly arrive, the normally monumental pain-in-the-ass budget hearings, even this would be high adventure. For he had regained his love for the battle. Everyone in creation would be squeezing something out of him, or making him feel guilty about something, or just breaking his balls in some general way.

"Let them come!!" said the mayor to his startled driver as they arrived at the steps of City Hall. The mayor of New York pulled his plum-shaped self out of his car, and with several aides huffing behind him, ran up the steps to work.

≡

Marc Greenberg was the first to extricate himself from the kubi hut and his eighteen water-logged companions. He sat on a park bench, stretched, and luxuriated in the clear morning light.

Now Greenberg had another reward: the pomp and spectacle of the mayor's arrival at City Hall. As he watched the mayoral buttocks jiggling up the steps, Greenberg reached in his pocket and pulled out the thing that would have gotten him through the night even had there been no kubi hut: a beautiful old wooden flute. Within a few seconds, he had quietly improvised a playful, loping melody for the bouncing mayor . . . something like the theme of the duck or the bear—the more playful animals—from *Peter and the Wolf.*

Truly, Marc Greenberg found it hard to hate Ed Koch. As an advocate for the homeless, he knew he was supposed to. But there were times, looking into the mayor's hazel eyes even as he was spewing his usual venom at a press conference, that Greenberg thought "fundamentally, this is a mensch." That is a Yiddish word meaning, very roughly, "good, kind, caring person—one of us— a regular—a big lovable, sometimes cranky but always reliable—a kind of—hell, just a mensch!!"

Of course most people in the housing movement did not view Ed Koch that benevolently. This was 1988, and the hard focus of the American Left, narrowed over a bitter century of war, race, disease, disenfranchisement, and poverty, had come together on one issue—housing. The streets were full of people. During the Reagan years, selfishness had become a virtue, and the result by some

17

estimates was a million Americans with no place to go. Nor did they *deserve* a place to go, according to the thinking in vogue. They had somehow failed to measure up, and since we were all now blessedly relieved of the stupid, soppy obligation to take care of each other . . . well, let them wander.

But the profile of the American vagrant had changed since the Bowery bum, usually white, sat philosophizing on a curbstone sipping a pint of Old Sidewinder. Now the wandering army of the homeless was overwhelmingly black. They were not people "down on their luck," who had "fallen from grace," because they had been never been *in* grace. To the concerned advocates, they were the flotsam of an America grown monstrously heartless and racist.

For all of this the homeless advocates held Ed Koch every bit as responsible as Ronald Reagan. To all appearances, the mayor had turned City Hall over to the real estate tycoons. He had allowed them to build their glittering commercial towers anywhere they pleased, and given them enormous tax breaks to do so. He had invited the realtors to take over the old rooming houses that once held the poor, turn the places inside out, line the bathrooms with marble, and resell them as subdivided mansions. And only after losing several lawsuits had the mayor grudgingly built shelters—vast, hangarlike warehouses of the poor—to cram the poor devils he had dispossessed.

Manhattan was a rock with only so much space on it, and space had become the precious commodity, like gold in the Yukon. And as drooling realtors trampled each other in the gold rush, the homeless advocates felt, Ed Koch had become their errand boy. In return for making it easy for them, the realtors tipped him in the form of campaign contributions that allowed the son of a bitch to stay in office.

Of course, Marc Greenberg knew it wasn't that simple. For one thing, Ed Koch was no errand boy. He was an extraordinarily complex creature, personally and politically. Nor was Greenberg interested in making a villain out of anybody. He was coming at the whole thing from a completely different point of view, well personified by the handsome, wiry woman just emerging from the kubi hut.

"Good morning, Ellen," he said.

"Good morning, Marc," she replied.

Indeed, Ellen McCarthy was one of those people, Marc often thought, who vexed New Yorkers. You looked at the intense blue eyes, the cheekbones that belonged on a *Vogue* cover, circa 1965, and you said to yourself, "What the hell is her angle?" and the answer was . . . none! She was exactly what she appeared to be—someone who had wiped her heart and soul clear of all agendas but one: to do God's work on earth. Fine, fine, but WHAT WAS HER ANGLE!?

Greenberg knew only the slightest outline of her life. She had grown up in New Jersey and suffered through a meaningless marriage. She had sought out the only philosopher she knew, the local priest. Where could she put herself to some use? she asked him. Where was the greatest need? "Among the homeless in New York," shot back Father Martin with not a moment's hesitation. And so here she had come, to a place where she had never been before except to shop and have lunch and see a Broadway matinee with her girlfriends. Now she spent her time ministering to the poor in lice-ridden city shelters and murderous crack dens.

Greenberg stared at her as she sunned herself: erect, lean body, hands clasped on her lap. The real thing.

By now the kubi hut had disgorged most of its inhabitants, who were stretching and greeting the new day. The morning rush hour was beginning, and City Hall Park, such a wild, remote outpost the night before, was becoming a thoroughfare. In a moment they would be swallowed by the vast moving human sea of New York.

Marc Greenberg shouted for everyone's attention. In past years, he announced, when the overnight vigil was over everyone went home. This year, with homelessness finally grabbing headlines, they had all been invited to the City Council building for morning coffee.

They looked around at each other. They were a mess. Even the clergymen who had begun the night with neatly pressed vestments were wrinkled beyond belief. As for the homeless . . . forget it. Taken as a group, you wouldn't want them greeting the plumber, let alone the City Council. Nor were they inclined to. "Just as soon be moving on," said Duke York, squinting at the new day.

But Greenberg was not to be denied. It wasn't the whole City Council they were meeting, he explained, just a few of the most sympathetic ones. A disheveled state would be nothing to apologize for. To the contrary, it would be expected of them.

Greenberg had the golden tongue, no doubt about it, and within a few minutes they were all headed out of the park and across lower Broadway. Bringing up the rear was Duke York. He would make his decision when the time came to enter the building. Nobody dictated to him. The "homeless cause" was nothing that particularly interested him anyway. Much of it was bullshit, in his opinion. Many of the homeless people he knew were crackheads, boozers, or just plain lazy.

However, he had nowhere else to go. The very thought of Diane was too painful to entertain for a second. To be wandering around town feeling that pain all by himself would demand an anesthetic. Duke's anesthetic of choice was vodka by the pint. A healthier choice might be to divert himself with these people for a while.

By now they had entered the building, shuffling into a huge elevator en masse. The smell grew very game very quickly, and Duke took a perverse pleasure in the discomfort of their fellow passengers. Soon they reached the twenty-third floor and were ushered into a room where a few politicians lounged over coffee and croissants and mountains of papers. Everyone rose and greeted the homeless brigade respectfully. Greenberg had been right. Suddenly it was as if they didn't smell.

No one knew how to begin. The purpose of the meeting, as Marc Greenberg had explained it, was to "have a dialogue" and "set agendas," and several other terms that no one understood on a practical level. One of the council members began to talk about the need to "reach out" to each other. But it was all too vague and subtle for the homeless, who were astonished merely to be indoors.

Annie Howard, the large woman who had said the prayer the night before, made her way to the food table and began cramming croissants into her mouth, flakes flying everywhere. Another man, slight, light-skinned, with rather feminine features, lit up a cigarette. None of the council members seemed to notice.

Or rather, they all noticed, but no one said anything. This was what generally bothered the hell out of Duke York about white people. Obviously, smoking was against the rules in this room. Nevertheless, everyone was afraid to say anything to the poor homeless man. It was as if two hundred years of slavery and another hundred of racism could be compensated for by letting this poor bastard have a cigarette where it was forbidden.

The homeless didn't need to be coddled, in Duke's opinion. They needed to be slapped around a little, grabbed by the throat, dangled over the edge of a building and told "Wake the hell up!" But since there was going to be smoking, he leaned over and whispered in the ear of the light-skinned man, "Got a cigarette, brother?"

The man reached into his pocket and pulled out a virtually brand new pack of Newports. Heaven on earth!! Duke took one and squeezed it. Perfect! Soft as a baby's bottom. This was fresh tobacco, the meaning of life. He rummaged for a match, lit up, and his head filled with a sweet narcotic cloud. It had been a full four days since he'd found a decent-sized butt in his shirt pocket before boarding the A-train.

By now most of the politicians had vacated the room, apologetically murmuring "committee meetings." Only two remained. One was an extremely attractive, dark Jewish-looking woman who identified herself as Council Member Ruth Messinger. The other was a lanky bespectacled man named Abe, whom Duke immediately associated with Lincoln, the only other tall skinny politician he knew of.

"What are you going to do now?" said Ruth Messinger. The question caught everyone by surprise. First of all, it contained the word "now," a refreshing tonic in the so far formless dialogue. Secondly, the woman sat there as if she really expected an answer.

"Well," said Marc Greenberg, "we thought we'd sing some songs, which we didn't get to do last night because of the rain, and then go to our various—"

"What about the rest of you?" she asked, interrupting him.

Duke bristled. It was kind of a rude, stupid question, rudely put. Where else would these people be going? Gambling in the Caribbean? Obviously, the poor devils were going back to Penn Station, or the Atlantic Avenue Shelter, or wherever the hell else they had been rounded up.

"Why go anywhere?" she snapped, answering her own question.

"Well, as I said," Greenberg stammered, "we'd be singing songs. Angry songs. Songs about—"

"I'm not talking about music!" she barked. "I'm talking about staying here. The budget hearings go on for a month, not a day."

Greenberg was at a loss. "We hadn't thought of . . . staying."

"Why don't you think about it now?"

Greenberg was being dominated. Curled up in a corner with his smoldering Newport, Duke was embarrassed for him.

"What are they supposed to eat?" Duke said suddenly, surprised at the sound of his own voice in the formal room. "They supposed to eat the leaves?" He was proud of himself for standing up to the bitch. He wished he could stand up to Diane as easily.

"What are you eating now?" Messinger shot back.

"First of all, it's not 'me' we're talkin' about here," said Duke, stung.

"We've got to stop thinking about it that way," said Ruth Messinger. "As them and us."

This was too much. This bitch was on her way back to Park Avenue somewhere. "What do you know about it?" Duke shot back.

"As much as you do," she replied. "And you can put out that cigarette."

They stared at each other. No backdown. He liked it. The bitch was an actual human. He dropped the cigarette in an empty bottle of Evian water. The homeless braced themselves to be thrown out, which is what usually happened when voices were raised in places with roofs.

Instead Ruth Messinger left.

"I've got a meeting," she said, standing. "Think it over." And she was gone.

"Ruth can be abrupt," said the remaining politician, with a weak smile. He revealed that his name was not Abraham Lincoln but Abraham Gerges, a council member from Brooklyn. "But she really believes in the cause." And then he, too, left. Once he was gone, the homeless party stuffed the remaining fruits and croissants into their pockets and exited the large meeting room.

Riding down the elevator, Greenberg tried to think clearly and quickly. His ego was battered to a pulp, which was no surprise. Ruth Messinger was a heavyweight. And of course she was right. If the idea was to try to prick the consciences of the budget makers as they shuffled in and out of City Hall all month, why *not* just stay there?

Because, thought Marc Greenberg, surveying his ragged troop at a traffic light, there was such a great fragility to the homeless. There were thugs and murderers among them, to be sure. But for the ones Greenberg had come to know best, their fundamental flaw was their delicacy; they just didn't have the get-up-and-go, the chutzpa, the "Fuck you too!!" or even "Pardon me, you're standing on my foot," to exist in New York. They were dogs who had been kicked too many times. That was a pretty good reason right there not to leave them out in front of City Hall, at the mercy of a brutal cadre of the New York Police Department.

Besides, Ruth Messinger had her own agenda. It was no secret that she, as well as many of her colleagues on the City Council, would do almost anything to discredit, damage, embarrass, or otherwise piss off Ed Koch. Next year was an election year, and Koch, who had been deeply gored by the scandals in his administration, was vulnerable. Messinger herself was considering a run at citywide office. What could be more humiliating to the mayor, who claimed the homeless problem was "exaggerated," than to have a bunch of them sitting outside City Hall day after day after day?

They reached City Hall Park, and returned to the little row of benches where the kubi hut had been built the night before. The morning rush hour was over, the noon lunch hour had not yet begun, so they found themselves more or less alone. It was the moment of decision for Marc Greenberg. He handed out the sheet music for the folk singing. Perhaps they would sing a few tunes, and see what happened next.

Two

The mayor's father, Louis Koch, was a Polish Jew who came to America at the age of fourteen, part of the vast immigration from turn-of-the-century Eastern Europe. As a boy, Louis had followed his own father around the south of Poland peddling goods off a cart. When young Ed Koch once asked his father what he had done for fun in the old country, Louis Koch had said, "Come in from the cold."

The Jews from Russia, across the Carpathian Mountains, were fleeing not only poverty but the brutal pogroms, the ethnic cleansing of the late nineteenth century. Russian Jews fell into two categories—those who waited for the ax to fall, and those who anticipated it. One of the latter was Albert Brackman, a distant relative of Louis Koch and a Moses of the modern diaspora.

In 1875, at the first sign of trouble, at the first sneering, mumbled insults by the young officers lounging in the town square, Albert Brackman understood that bad times were coming. Like Louis Koch he was a proud man, and his threshold for disrespect was low. One night in the early spring Brackman boarded a train with his wife and daughter and headed south from his village in the Ukraine. At Odessa they got a ship, and a month later sailed past the barren sand spit of Bedloe's Island. Albert Brackman had even beaten the Statue of Liberty to New York.

So far in the vanguard of immigrating Jews was he that the famous shtetl of the Lower East Side was not yet fully defined. So

Brackman settled well to the south, in what was truthfully the only neighborhood he could afford. But "Five Points," so named for the five grim little streets that converged where the New York courthouses now sit, was a living hell. It was as much Irish and Negro as it was Jewish, and in fact the Brackmans' immediate neighbors were a trio of Ethiopian drug addicts and a mother-daughter prostitute team named Murphy. The building itself had seen several tuberculosis deaths in the prior year, and the outhouse could be reached only by descending five flights of stairs and crossing a yard.

Clearly Brackman had to get his family out of there. He found employment in the district's biggest industry: pleasure. He became a bartender at Shea's Tavern, a temple of bawdiness and violence. A man of delicate sensibilities, he was now obliged to watch at close hand the excesses of New York's lower classes. When there was no other reason to fight, the blacks and the Irish would get drunk and resurrect the bitterness of the Draft Riots, when many of New York's Irish had refused to fight in the Civil War. "What do I care if some nigger works himself to death in a field somewhere," said the Irish in 1860, and they said it again in Shea's fifteen years later, just for the sake of argument. Bottles would fly, teeth would clatter to the floor on a ribbon of blood, and Albert Brackman would pour the drinks.

But Shea's had other moods. Sometimes on quiet afternoons the Irish politicians, the patriarchs of Tammany Hall, would stop by on their way home from the courthouses. There came the famous—George Washington Plunkett and the aging, fugitive Boss Tweed—and the obscure. Some of them took notice of the young bartender. Clearly here was a man of dignity and intelligence, a rare presence behind the long wooden bar at Shea's. Albert Brackman, grateful for the civilized companionship, became a friend, peer, and the traditional bartender-confidant.

After several years, Brackman acquired some capital and made plans to move his family out of Five Points and up to Hester Street. New York was defining itself: like Darwin's finches, each group was finding its niche. The newly arriving Jews were pouring into the Lower East Side, and soon blacks would be flooding north into Harlem, an old Dutch farming village. The high heat was being turned down on the melting pot. Of course, Albert Brackman would find the conditions on Hester Street not much better, but at least he would be among his own people.

His Irish friends counselled him otherwise. At that very moment, they assured him, the engineering miracle of the age was taking place. A system of subterranean trains was being planned for New York, and the tunnels were being dug right underneath them as they spoke. At the moment, the plans called for the trains to run only the length of Manhattan. But if and when they expanded, the real estate opportunities in the outlying areas would be phenomenal. Brackman took it all in, skeptically. The outer "boroughs," as they were now called, seemed so remote. But he had grown to believe what these men told him about city policy, since they dictated most of it from the back booths at Shea's.

Even more than economic promise, Albert Brackman was seduced by the idea of filling his lungs with clean air. Five Points had left him contaminated, physically and morally. Yes, on Hester Street he would be among Jews, but before he was a Jew, he was a father and a husband. No, even *that* was not his primary identity. He was a man—a solitary man with a need for dignity that was insulted daily by the sheer density of the mob. In the little village in the Ukraine, where you walked down country lanes and greeted your neighbors by name, life had been of an infinitely higher quality. He wanted that again, not only for his wife and growing daughter, but for himself. Perhaps he might actually be able to ply the trade his father had taught him—a builder of houses.

One morning shortly thereafter he did not report for work,

but instead boarded a steam locomotive bound for a distant area known as the Bronx. Had he wished, he could have made the journey by horse-drawn trolley, but that would have taken the better part of the day. The huge locomotive, belching smoke as it trundled along its elevated track, would get him there in a couple of hours.

The first part of the trip was over ground he had already covered, on expeditions with his family to Central Park. Then, when the train got past the few buildings that lined the park's west side, among them the Dakota (so named because it was so remote it might as well have been a thousand miles away), the vista widened. Here and there were little Irish shantytowns, with thatched roofs and laundry fluttering in the wind. Beyond them could be seen the geological sweep of Manhattan Island. Across an endless meadow lay Manhattan's western ridge, rising to greet its sister palisades across the Hudson. Huge outcroppings of hard gray rock protected its flank, making Brackman wonder how subterranean tunnels could ever penetrate all this. Then the locomotive curved to the east and descended a long slope and across a brackish meadow to a terminal. Here, Brackman was obliged to take another train across the Harlem River into the Bronx.

He consulted his silver-cased pocket watch, a gift from his maternal grandfather, long dead in a Russian winter. He didn't have all day. He had a family who would begin to wonder about him, so he got off at the first stop across the river.

This was the Bronx. The only road he could see was more like a path that descended into a wooded area, so he followed it. After a time, he was swallowed up by a forest. No sound penetrated. Lush hickory trees blocked out the sky, and songbirds flitted around him. Soon he came upon a brook, sat on a rock, and took off his shoes and socks. He let his feet trail in the cold clear water and turned his face to the dappled sunlight. Huge groups of muscles and nerves uncurled in his body, and tears came to his eyes.

It was many hours before Albert Brackman returned to his family, but when he did, it was with the news that they were moving.

In the Blue Room of City Hall, Ed Koch was consuming a cup of coffee, his third of the morning, though the hour had not yet struck ten. The whole month figured to be like this. State law required that the budget be in place by the first of July, so that meant that all the haggling, the compromises, the bitching, the kvetching, the accusations, all of it had to be compressed into thirty days. That meant coffee.

It also meant a carnival sideshow. Ed Koch's immediate goal was to reach the graceful curved staircase that led to the second floor. From this he was separated by only twenty feet of distance, but also by a hundred lobbyists, all of them with frenzied, heart-rending agendas, some of them in costumes. To his left were six fat women in fire hats, protesting the closing of a firehouse in Brooklyn. Directly ahead of him were a trio of extremely angry women, all with photographs of dead babies, protesting the lack of prenatal care for the poor. The ACT UP people, demanding money for AIDS, could always be counted on for theatricality. This year they had brought in a gaunt, lesion-studded young man on a litter. Swathed in a black caftan, he reminded the mayor of a photograph he had once seen of Sarah Bernhardt playing Medea.

By the time he finally reached the staircase, Ed Koch had been branded a murderer a half-dozen times by almost as many organizations. His unspoken reaction, even as he took it all in with a pained, sympathetic look, was "Screw all of you." This was not necessarily cruel. Far from it. As the mother pig, you have only so many nipples, and there are countless gaping, open mouths. You can say yes to everyone, of course, and everyone will love you for a few weeks, until the city goes broke and everything goes down the toilet.

Ed Koch considered his greatest political talent the ability to say "No." He had balanced ten consecutive budgets and was about to balance his eleventh, dead babies notwithstanding. That was what he got paid for, what he was famous for, and what had saved New York.

When Ed Koch had run for mayor for the first time, in 1977, the city was in the worst financial mess in its history. Businesses were leaving New York in droves for the Sun Belt. The banks would no longer lend the city money, and the feeling was that the whole place would soon become like Detroit, an empty shell of an inner city, a place where people worked in the daytime and then abandoned after dark to the whistling wind and packs of roaming hairless dogs. New York!! Where Joe DiMaggio had fumed as puffs of air blew Marilyn's skirt in the air, where victorious armies had marched down Broadway, where playboys had eaten caviar off the belly buttons of chorus girls. The city of the United Nations, of Ziegfeld, of Jimmy Walker! What had turned it into a place everybody wanted to leave?

The seeds of the city's money troubles had been planted far earlier. There had been great costly public works during the twenties, followed by an easing of real estate taxes during the thirties to bolster a depression economy. The city's coffers had been dangerously low even before World War Two. The postwar years gave the illusion of prosperity, but economists noted with quiet horror the slow disappearance of manufacturing jobs. Every time an artist took over a 3,000-square-foot loft in Soho, it meant that a hundred seamstresses had lost their jobs.

It was at this point, say economists, that the great villain in the drama stepped forward, well-camouflaged as the handsomest mayor ever. When John V. Lindsay was elected in 1965, many people thought the voters were trying to resurrect Jack Kennedy. Indeed Lindsay had the patina of Camelot about him: a sheen of glamour and a liberal enthusiasm that seemed to be saying, "There's enough for everyone."

There wasn't. His welfare programs were presided over by a man the wags dubbed "Come and Get it" Ginsburg. Viewed in the most cynical terms, Lindsay "shipped truckloads of cash up to Harlem, basically to keep them from rioting. But he didn't want to tax his rich friends to pay for it, so he got the money from the rest of us." So said a political enemy, but even Lindsay's supporters, while insisting on the purity of his idealism, thought him financially naive. The City of New York floated huge bond issues to pay for Lindsay's largesse, and the economy staggered.

When the Democrats finally regained City Hall in 1973, they were horrified by what they found. According to Harrison Goldin, the new city comptroller, "There were big cartons of blank checks standing in the middle of a corridor. They had no numbers! No sequence! The way bills got paid in New York City was that a clerk—and there were hundreds of them—just reached into a box and wrote a check whenever a bill came in. Wait! You haven't heard the worst!! . . . When the bank statements came in at the end of the month—remember, there were no numbers on the checks—the clerks would just put rubber bands around them and throw them in a corner! That's where I discovered them. There wasn't even an attempt made to go over them. Do you get the picture!?"

Besides Lindsay, there were plenty of people to blame. A free-spending Congress, which included Ed Koch, had gone hog-wild in the sixties. The whole country had. But now that Lindsay himself was gone, the heat fell squarely on his successor, the diminutive Abe Beame, the first Jewish mayor of the City of New York. He was on the defensive from the beginning. He had been Lindsay's comptroller during the last term and had to take some of the responsibility for the sheer disarray of it all. But it was far more than bad accounting. Unemployment was by now sky-high, and the city's credit rating had been suspended. New York, in essence, was bankrupt.

They say that voters vote their pocketbooks, and that notion goes a long way towards explaining Ed Koch's unexpected success in 1977. The maverick, gangling congressman was considered a long shot in a field that included heavyweights like Mario Cuomo and Bella Abzug. But Koch was not to be denied. His theme, referring directly to his predecessors Lindsay and Beame, was "After eight years of charisma and four years of the clubhouse, why not try competence?" He traded on the fierce pride of New Yorkers, who had been deeply offended by the implications that they were helpless fools who could no longer manage their own affairs.

Koch won the election and went immediately to Washington, where he used his old connections to float some bonds and raise some cash for New York. Having done that, the next step was elocution: learning how to say the word "no." He became the stern parent, and the message to his 10 million children was clear: tighten your belt, and for the good of everyone, satisfy yourselves with a bowl of porridge for the time being. It seemed to bring out some deep yen for austerity, and the people bought it. With the smallest, leanest budget in years, the city was on its way back.

Of course, not everyone was eating porridge. The other prong of the mayor's attack was to stimulate the economy, and this he did by encouraging the business community in sometimes shameless ways. It was an echo of the trickle-down theory of economics, with which Republicans were perennially enchanted, and it made liberal economists squirm. But there could be no quarreling with the immediate results; by using tools like tax abatements, the mayor encouraged an enormous boom in Manhattan building. The skyline was transformed daily. Be they glass and steel office towers zigging and zagging at modernistic angles into the sky or renovations of decaying grand old buildings into brand new co-ops, they were potent symbols of rebirth. The big town was on its feet again.

Even the mayor's enemies were impressed. To Daniel Patrick Moynihan, with whom the mayor rarely agreed, "He gave us back ourselves. After all the horror of the seventies, he took over and marched down the middle of Broadway, thumbs up. It was a huge, intensely personal achievement."

Paul Dickstein, the budget director, stood at the head of the curved City Hall staircase and waited for the mayor to finish his ascent. One of the fat women protesting the closing of the Brooklyn firehouses had thrown herself in his path, like some Roseanne Barr cum Mahatma Gandhi. Relaxed and amused, Dickstein smiled wanly. Remarkably, budget time was a fairly easy time for the budget director. The work was done, the fundamental plan was all drawn up, and all that remained to be seen was how much could be chipped off or added on by the fat women from Brooklyn or the gaunt men with AIDS from Manhattan. Truly, thought Dickstein, there was so much the public didn't understand about the process.

That also went for the whole notion of Ed Koch as the savior of New York. There was a cyclical nature to these things, and poor Abe Beame had been in the wrong cycle. It was hardly his fault that manufacturing jobs had dwindled to nothing and that the great service boom of the late seventies had not yet kicked in. When that finally happened, Ed Koch just happened to be the lucky stiff standing around. No, although Dickstein loved his boss and thought him a great leader of men, he never bought the "savior of New York" routine. The pendulum simply swung, and whoever was mayor was a fly on the pendulum. Whether pushing or pulling, he was merely along for the ride.

By now the mayor had reached him, and they conferred briefly on a number of small matters. An event was going on outside, and the mayor was straining to get out there. Miss Puerto Rican New York was being crowned, and any tardiness would be perceived as a slight. The Latin personality was tricky, but the mayor felt he had a good handle on it. In fact, his success among Hispanics was a strong thread in his remarkable political coalition. Among the most important things he had learned was this: they did not wish to be lumped in with blacks as "people of color," as some politicians made the mistake of doing. They wished to be perceived as white ethnics, like Italians or Irish, people with a culture that was basically European, and therefore to be venerated and respected. In practical terms, it meant that the mayor could treat them as part of the vast white middle class and assuage their fears of taxes and crime. The same strategy worked with the black middle class, as long as the mayor was careful to distinguish them from the proletariat . . . and of course from the Hispanics. It was tricky, but that's what got him where he was and that's what kept him there.

Outside City Hall, a crowd of a hundred people had turned out for the crowning of Miss Puerto Rican New York. The aspirants, dark beauties in taffeta and tiaras, sat chatting among themselves on a platform. Puerto Rican flags snapped in the pleasant breeze, and a power salsa band rocked the premises.

At the moment he was expected, and not a moment later, the mayor of New York emerged to respectable applause from the crowd. Taking the microphone in both hands, he said *"Te amo."* This means "I love you," the only phrase the mayor knew in Spanish.

In English, he proceeded to acknowledge the Hispanic dignitaries present, particularly Bronx Borough President Fernando Ferrer and the old warhorse Herman Badillo. Then he turned his attention to the lovelies on the dais, whom he compared to orchids from Havana. This was no speechwriter's turn of phrase; the mayor had made it up himself. Then he drew a deep breath and allowed a moment of silence as a prelude to another thought. This would be the meat of the speech, as veteran Koch watchers knew. The year before an election year there was no such thing as a merely ceremonial appearance for Ed Koch.

In the moment of silence, however, another sound filled the air. "Kum-ba-yah, my Lord, Kum-ba-yah . . ." It was a song that Ed Koch recognized from his youth, but it wasn't on the program.

Ah well, he thought, probably young Hispanic men serenading their princesses—but with rather rude timing. Koch's instincts told him to wait it out, make a joke about hot-blooded Latins, and then resume his remarks. ". . . Someone's starving, my Lord, Kum-ba-yah . . . someone's starving . . . Kum-ba-yah." Wait a minute. This was not a love song.

Now several heads swung around to the source of the singing. Beyond the trees, fourteen people, mostly black men, were holding copies of sheet music. They were being led in song by a white man, and the intent was clearly to interrupt the program. "Someone's homeless, my Lord, Kum-ba-yah . . ." One of the black men held up a crudely lettered sign saying HOUSE THE HOMELESS, and it became clear to all that this was some sort of political demonstration.

For the Hispanic men in the crowd, many of them in ruffled finery, this was behavior typical of the despised *negrito*, and under certain circumstances might have warranted stern, chivalrous measures, like a bullet in the head. From the podium itself, the reaction was not hot but cold. Ed Koch merely stared at Marc Greenberg and the fourteen homeless people he led in song.

It was at this moment that Canon Lloyd Casson entered City Hall Park. Casson, a civil rights-era clergyman, was still a prime player in New York's racial politics. He had just been named the first black vicar of old Trinity Church on Wall Street, and in fact had hosted the beginning of the candlelight march to City Hall the night before. He had been looking forward to the folksinging this morning. It would be like the old days of the movement.

Clearly, though, he was too late to participate. But he was not too late for the dramatic climax. Casson had seen this look in Ed Koch's eyes before. The mayor did not like to be humiliated. When he was, he felt as if something had been taken from him, and he never forgot it.

After several more moments, it became clear the folksingers were not going to stop. The mayor signalled the salsa band, and they resumed playing at a thousand decibels. The sounds of gentle folk songs disappeared, pulverized. The mayor turned and re-entered City Hall. The event continued, and Miss Puerto Rican New York was eventually crowned. But Ed Koch's closing remarks had not been heard. And for that, Lloyd Casson knew, there would be a price to pay.

As a teenager, Marc Greenberg had hung around the fringes of antiwar demonstrations, tossing eggs. There was a certain thrill in taunting the beast you knew could maul you. But at this moment he was responsible for these people, and he was almost glad when the salsa band drowned them out.

It was time to end this. The Interfaith Assembly of Homelessness and Housing was his baby. It was made up of clergy who believed that in this day and age, when it was fashionable to despise the poor, religion ought to translate into action. To this end they organized, they fed, they clothed, and to a modest degree they sheltered the homeless. And thanks to Greenberg, they had fashioned a political arm and had begun to lobby for laws to help the poor. That was what the vigil was all about. It was not about putting people in a position to get their skulls crushed.

Lloyd Casson arrived as Greenberg was collecting the sheet music. This seemed providential. Casson was one of the wise old heads in the movement.

"Lloyd, we're getting out of here."

"I assumed as much. The vigil's over, isn't it?"

Greenberg told him about the meeting with Ruth Messinger. "She's got a point," said Greenberg, "but I'm not interested in getting anybody hurt out here."

Casson digested it for a moment. Then he pointed to the homeless. "They're men, aren't they?"

"Well . . . yes."

"Then why don't you let them do what they want?"

Greenberg was surprised, and Casson even more so to hear

himself say it. Obviously the young Jew was right. It *was* dangerous for them to stay out here. Casson knew that better than anyone, because he knew Ed Koch. But at a certain point, it bothered
the hell out of him when Jews kept telling black people what
to do.

As a disciple of Martin Luther King, Casson remembered lying
across bridges with men wearing yarmulkes. It had seemed like
such a natural alliance: the two races who had endured the unendurable—slavery and the Holocaust, to say nothing of the
perennial abuse of bigoted Americans. But something had gone
very wrong, and over the last twenty years Jews and blacks had
begun to seem like natural enemies. Currently, no more odious
anti-Semitic rhetoric existed than what came out of the mouth of
Louis Farrakhan, high priest of the black Nation of Islam. And no
more thinly disguised racism could be found than that of Meyer
Kahane, head of the Jewish Defense League.

At Casson's last position, as vicar of the grand, Waspish National Cathedral in Washington, he had sought to right the situation. He went to a B'nai B'rith meeting and described in brutal
detail the Middle Passage, the voyage of the slaves to America. In
this fashion he had sought to establish common ground. When
he finished, he was met with cold silence. *Nothing* compares with
the Holocaust, he was told. Do not insult the memories of our
dead ancestors by even suggesting it. So this was how hopeless it
had all become. They were competing for martyrdom.

Casson felt he knew how the problem began: with just the
kind of kvetching Marc Greenberg was doing right now. Throughout the Civil Rights movement, wonderful Jewish lawyers had
protected blacks and filed their briefs and bailed them out and
done everything but change their diapers. Finally it became time
to say ENOUGH! Thanks, but no thanks. We have to do it ourselves. Some of the Jews understood, but many more slunk away,
rejected.

"Just don't worry about it, Marc," said Casson, more gently

37

now. "You feel guilty every time somebody sits on a piece of gum in the subway. Leave it alone."

Greenberg mulled it over. Maybe he did get stuck in moral quagmires. The Ruth Messingers (and the Ed Kochs) of the world just *acted*. If they were wrong, if some dreadful hell was visited upon somebody because of it, well, that was the price of action. Slowly and uncertainly, Marc Greenberg gathered up what was left of the sheet music and moved off through the park.

Casson watched him go. He liked Greenberg. No, liked was too mild. He was *inspired* by Marc Greenberg. There was something messiah-like about the young Jew when he stood up and talked in front of weary, broken-spirited black men. Nothing less than that was needed, in Casson's opinion.

As an intelligent, educated black man, Casson had tasted much of the white man's bounty—even the luxury of psycho-analysis—and what it had taught him was this: worse than the Middle Passage, the fire hoses, the police dogs or the crosses burned on lawns was the abuse the black man heaped on himself once he bought the idea, rammed home from childhood, that there was something wrong with him. Not superstardom or even a lifetime of quiet achievement could rectify it. And the best proof of that was the psychiatric bills of Lloyd Casson.

He surveyed the dozen or so black men lounging on benches around a long cardboard hut. These homeless events always brought out a streak of guilt in him, especially since his return to New York from Washington. Trinity Church, his new employer, had once been the most merciless landlord in New York. When that was pointed out to them, they simply got out of the business. It never occurred to them to get involved in housing in a positive way. That was often typical of the church, thought Casson. Turn the other cheek, turn and look away.

But guilt would not help the homeless. Frankly, Lloyd Casson didn't know what the hell would. Should people like him move back to the ghetto, and be role models at close range? Why? He had climbed out of the nightmare, why should he climb back in? Catch a bullet outside a 7-11 in Brownsville?? After the journey *he'd* been on? No thanks. He did far more than most, anyway, as a committed, creative clergyman. Maybe in the end, that was all you could do for the poor—get down on your bony knees and pray for them.

"Morning, Father," said Duke York. Lloyd Casson looked at the dark-skinned man with the crooked smile and the odd look about him. What on earth were the prospects for a creature like this? "Good luck, son," said Casson finally, and walked slowly away.

Duke watched him for a moment, admiring his robes, and resumed his conversation on the park bench. Duke was now on his second cup of coffee, and he was settling into a disturbing truth. He didn't seem to be leaving. At the moment, smoking a huge fragrant cigarette butt, he actually felt a pang of sympathy for the office workers who scurried around him. Heads down, attaché cases cocked, they seemed grim and unhappy, and not at their leisure to contemplate the larger things in life, as he was now doing.

He stepped over a black iron railing and lay on his back and looked up at the blue sky. It was early June and the Park's magnolia and apple trees had deposited their blossoms on the ground. The tulip beds had been planted with a remarkable breed, deep blood-red tulips striped with vermilion. A tiny breeze that had found its way off the East River was keeping the morning from becoming hot, and a young mother with an old-style perambulator was sitting on a bench nearby. Duke thought of his youngest daughter, who had had such an infancy: untroubled, among flowers. She had been named Shianna, after the actual sound of the summer wind.

DRRRRRAANNNGGGGG!!!!! Suddenly a monstrous sound jerked him out of his daydream. A huge green truck was about ten feet away, making a churning, unbearable noise.

This was the retribution that Lloyd Casson knew would come

from City Hall. It was a Sanitation Department garbage crusher, and it was designed to devour and pulverize whatever parks workers threw into it, from trash to tree limbs. "Big Mouth," one of the homeless immediately dubbed it. And what Big Mouth was devouring was the kubi hut that little Art had constructed the night before. Everyone in the crowd took a step backward and watched Big Mouth do its thing. Duke noted the body language of the homeless. There was a kind of collective shrug that seemed to say, "It always happens sooner or later."

One of them, however, did not step back. Instead, he took a step forward and began to glare at the truck and the workers. Everyone took notice of him. The parks people did not stop feeding the debris of the kubi hut into Big Mouth, but they lost the calm of a moment before.

Duke was struck by the man's face, which was new to him. He had not been there the night before, in the rain, nor had he participated in the folk singing that morning. Duke would have remembered, because the face was unlike any he'd ever seen. The man had a big, strong jaw, a wide mouth and flared nostrils, commonplace negroid features. But in what Duke's high school acting teacher called the "mask area"—the upper nose, the eyes, the brow—there was something else . . . a dignity and a crude, frightening quality.

Then everyone was startled by a bright flash of light. They turned to see a stylishly dressed woman with a camera. She began to ask questions. What was going on? Well, said Duke, these people . . . they just were kind of sitting here . . . and . . .

"The mayor was offended," said a voice behind him. It was the man with the strange features. His voice was quiet, but it commanded attention. "These are poor people who wanted to make their needs known to the mayor. Many of them, including myself, are veterans of the Armed Forces of the United States."

The woman devoured it. Very soon she was joined by a couple of other people, also with cameras. One of them explained to

Duke that they were reporters and that the budget hearings were legendary among the press for their sheer, stupefying dullness. So when they heard the noise of Big Mouth and all the hubbub, they poured down the steps of City Hall to see what was going on.

But by now, the sound of Big Mouth had stopped. The first flashbulb had prompted one of the parks workers to pick up a walkie-talkie. Now he and another man were looking in the direction of City Hall. Though the naked eye could perceive no movement in any of the windows, the parks men seemed to see a signal. The big green truck was put in reverse, and soon the park lawn was empty of all but one thing—the few remaining shreds of the kubi hut, adorned by a set of U.S. Army dog tags. This pathetic little piece of nothing was then photographed, over and over again, by the major newspapers of New York.

Three

$$\equiv$$

About a month after his transformation in the deep woods of the Bronx, Albert Brackman loaded the family possessions onto a series of horse-drawn wagons and left the hell of Five Points behind. Within a week they were settled into a wooden clapboard house in the Bronx village of Springhurst. Not long after that, the shingle was hung outside the door: "Albert Brackman—Builder."

But Brackman was not immediately welcomed into paradise. He was among the first Jews to arrive in the Bronx, and there was an emotional price tag to the lanterns, the tobogganing in winter, and the squadrons of meadowlarks in summer. He had invaded a rural community of Irish and German people who didn't like Jews, particularly those who had schemes to build and attract other Jews.

So from the beer gardens and roving German singing societies, the culture of the Bronx, the Brackmans were excluded. For the younger generation, the hostility was more direct. Brackman's daughter, now twelve, was attacked by peers wielding the weapon of choice, sockfuls of ashes and cinders. Sometimes at school her classmates would delight in slipping slices of ham into her lunch and watching her mortification when she discovered she had violated the dietary laws of Judaism.

Nor was Brackman's business going well. To accomplish things, he needed architects, bricklayers, carpenters, and plumbers. Most of them were German or Irish, and if they agreed to work for the Jew at all, it was in their spare time, with leftover materials, and at very high prices.

Finally, in despair, Brackman returned to his old Manhattan neighborhood for advice. He never thought he would enter Shea's again, but there he was, smelling the familiar bouquet of beer and sweat and vomit. Boss Tweed was dead and many of his cronies were in jail, but at last Albert Brackman espied a familiar face: an insurance salesman from his old building. Insurance was primarily a racket in the slums of Five Points; for twenty-five cents a week you bought burial insurance so that at least when you succumbed to TB or cholera, your relatives could pay for a box to put you in. But insurance agents were also the closest thing to social workers. They read complex city forms to illiterates and generally interpreted the bewildering new world.

And there at the corner of the bar sat Jimmy Morgan, the benevolent, slightly larcenous Prudential Insurance man. Brackman sat beside him and got immediately drunk and poured out his heart. The Irish in Manhattan had been such nice people; why were they so cruel in the Bronx? Morgan said that country people were narrow-minded. Then he held out a sliver of hope to Brackman. He had a cousin who was an architect in the Bronx, and a rather well-known one. He had just designed some houses for Henry Morgenthau, a big-time Manhattan builder. So perhaps he was sympathetic to Jews.

Then he told him the name, and Brackman almost fell off his stool. James Meehan?! James Meehan was his next-door neighbor, for God's sake! The Brackmans often peered enviously into the Meehan's huge yard, dominated by succulent yellow cherry trees.

With a letter from Morgan, Albert Brackman returned to the Bronx and stood outside Meehan's gate the next day. As he prepared a speech, the gate swung open. It was Meehan himself, holding a pair of pruning shears. He had watched Brackman's mental contortions from the vantage point of a cherry tree.

After only a few moments of conversation, the young Jew

struck a chord in the Irish architect. Most builders were looking for the bare minimum; three- or four-story brownstones of the dullest variety. Brackman was an idealist with grand visions. That was seductive to the talented James Meehan. But did the threadbare, immigrant Jew have the bankroll? Brackman gave Meehan a brief account of his holdings, and they were pathetic.

Meehan agreed to sleep on it. On a practical level, it was madness. Being undercapitalized and running out of money in the middle of a project was a disaster and a career-threatening humiliation. And yet an actor wants to play Hamlet and an architect wants to build something bold. And what Albert Brackman had in mind was a six-story building.

The next morning, the Irishman knocked on the door of his neighbor's modest cottage. Was he aware, Meehan wanted to know, that six-story buildings were now required by law to have elevators? Virtually no one in the Bronx had ever seen an elevator, much less contemplated building one.

There was going to be an elevator, said Albert Brackman, and not just because the statutes demanded it. He shared a story with Meehan that he had told no one else. On a dark night several years earlier in Five Points, while climbing the four stories to their flat from the outhouse, Brackman's wife had slipped down the stairs and had a miscarriage. It had been the bitterest moment of their time in the New World.

Meehan nodded slowly. Yes, there had to be an elevator.

There was more. Brackman wanted a courtyard. Not an air-shaft as required by law, not an open yard to separate the house from some dreadful outhouse, but a courtyard JUST FOR THE SAKE OF HAVING A COURTYARD! It was indulgent beyond belief. Just something to gaze upon!! Or sit in, and read a book! And everything proceeded from there: the best porcelain china for the bathrooms, marble pillars for the entrance, fire escapes of limestone with filigreed iron grillwork, and huge bay windows for the hopefully fashionable shops that would occupy the ground floor.

With each new idea, Meehan frowned and his stomach tightened. Even if such a building could be built, nobody in the Bronx could afford to live in it!! Then, late at night, Meehan would digest the ideas and take secret delight in drawing up the plans. He had waited a long time to show the world he was capable of this kind of thing.

Between the disturbance of Big Mouth and the noon influx of office workers with sandwiches and suntan oil, Duke York had had enough of City Hall Park. As he tried to decide what to do next, his eye fell upon, indeed could not avoid, the twin towers of the World Trade Center. A lifetime New Yorker, he'd never been to the top. Why not be a tourist for a day? Especially since no other course of action was clearly indicated.

Lacking the entrance fee for the observatory, Duke found an empty pizza box and took the elevator to an office on the 102nd floor, posing as a delivery man. He found a quiet window and looked around. From this vantage point, much of the journey of his life could be surveyed. Beyond the glut of midtown office buildings were the lowlands of Harlem. There Duke had led a troubled childhood, somewhat brightened by an intellectual curiosity rare in his circle of friends. And it led him to a rare pursuit: stealing books from the Columbia University library. In fact, it was there that he had perfected his phony pizza delivery routine. It was easier for a little boy. Furthermore, it was hard for the librarians to imagine that a black child would have any motivation to steal books. When he was done, he always returned them, leaving them on the steps of the library in the middle of the night. If a security guard spotted him, he took off down the bluffs of Morningside Heights back into Harlem, where no huffing Irish cop would ever follow him.

After his parents' marriage failed, he was sent to live with his grandmother in a mixed middle-class area of Queens. It was thought that exposure to white kids would stabilize him. Just the opposite proved to be true. Duke fell immediately into the white counterculture, smoking hashish, dropping acid, and worshipping The Jefferson Airplane. He grew wilder. The good thing to be said for Cardoza High was that it encouraged him musically. He had a naturally smoky baritone voice, and by the time he was a senior he was the dominant talent in the school. He played the leads in *Brigadoon* and *My Fair Lady* opposite white girls, to the consternation of their parents.

". . . Help you?"

Duke turned to find an attractive black woman, a secretary.

"Just, you know . . . lookin' . . ." He tried to be cute and boyish, but she wasn't having it.

"I'll have to ask you to leave the office," she said, not moving until he stood up. He felt like a spanked child. When he was feeling vulnerable on account of Diane, every rebuff was painful, even the small ones. When he was feeling most sorry for himself, Duke thought it probably had to do with his glass eye, the result of a bad infection as a young man. "Either get rid of it now," a surgeon had told him about the diseased eye, "or the poison's going to flow into the other one." Whether or not that was true, they did the procedure, and it was a lousy job. Duke knew it gave him kind of a wild look. Sometimes it scared people, and often it repulsed them. In his worst moments, he blamed the little colored glass bead in his head not only for Diane's philandering but also for his failure in show business.

By the time he had taken the elevator back down, the evening rush hour was beginning. Duke headed south to the Battery, swept around the point, and stopped to gaze a while at the Statue of Liberty, still blushing from the hoopla of her centennial celebration a couple of years earlier. Finally he headed back up the East Side, past the South Street Seaport and the Fulton Fish Market. Here the combination of darkening skies and streets fetid with fish oil turned him inland, and he found himself once again facing the illuminated City Hall, this time in a clear, gorgeous dusk.

He entered the park and made his way to the central pathway, where last night's demonstration had taken place. The weather was so different it hardly seemed like the same place. The stars were out, and every detail of the huge Woolworth Building was visible. This was truly the Cathedral of Commerce, as it unashamedly announced on a plaque out front. Old man Woolworth, the five-and-dime king, had spared no expense bringing artisans from all over the world to crawl over his building, chiseling cornices and gargoyles. Looming over the park against a sky of deep dark blue, it seemed medieval, part of a child's dream.

Several people were sitting on benches, and Duke was surprised to recognize some faces from the night before. There was big Annie, and next to her the delicate, light-skinned man from whom Duke had bummed a cigarette. Apparently sheer inertia had prevailed, and these two had simply plopped back down in the park. Duke bummed another cigarette and sat between them to smoke. A white man emerged from the dark and introduced himself as Dave from Wyoming. The cat was wearing a cowboy hat! He explained that he was an ironworker and that the word had filtered all the way out west that New York's Williamsburg Bridge was crumbling and that there might be work on it. Apparently opportunities in the trade were so few that Dave had been motivated to travel the two thousand miles on the rumor. Unfortunately, he had underestimated the amount of cash reserve he'd need to set himself up, and he had soon been forced to move into a city shelter. Immediately his tools were stolen. It was a rude introduction to New York for someone who didn't particularly look like he could take it.

Duke found the story interesting, but quite frankly he needed to think more about his own story; that is, the next chapter. A chilly night was coming on. Bumming yet another cigarette (he did his best thinking while smoking), he moved to another bench.

47

Within a minute he was drawn into another conversation. A frail young black man, teeth already chattering from the cold, was telling Duke that he had AIDS. Duke immediately slid off to the end of the bench and did his best not to let the man breathe on him. The story was impossible to listen to. The poor devil was brain damaged in some way and had been too simple-minded to protect himself from the legions of men who had enjoined him to have sex with them. All of this had apparently taken place in the city shelter system, which now seemed to Duke, with each new tale, a nightmare out of the middle ages. From time to time, said the young man, he would glimpse his own father in one of the shelters.

Duke stood to leave. It was dangerous to spend time with hopeless people, especially when your own grip was so frail. He would call Craig, perhaps risk imposing, but at least get a bed and a shower and a fresh start on a new day.

The chattering of the sick man's teeth was now the most audible sound in the night. Even after walking several yards toward the street, Duke could still hear it . . . or thought he could. His big heart began to ache. Duke was a man who could not pass a dead pigeon without removing it to a patch of grass where it could decay in peace. He might even say a word over the corpse to hasten its path to heaven. Duke cursed this instinct in himself and felt it was somehow connected to his eternal misery over Diane.

But he could not simply walk away from these people. Fortunately there was wood on the ground, jetsam of the Dutch elm disease that was attacking trees all over New York. Duke gathered some of it up, then tore a little bark off a dogwood, begging its forgiveness. He found a trash barrel with a healthy bed of paper, arranged the bark for kindling, and on top of it placed the elm wood. One match later, it all roared into being. He led the man with AIDS over to it and watched him smile at the sheer warmth. Soon the others were up and around the fire, and Duke surveyed their faces. Lit from below, they were a bohemian photographer's gallery of the poor. Big Annie's fleshy face looked almost maniacal, and the delicate light-skinned man, whom everyone called Fritz, was almost deathlike. Even the innocent cowboy from Wyoming, boyish and chunky as he undoubtedly looked by day, took on the aspect of a devilish imp.

But it was the face directly across from him that riveted Duke York. It was the man who had stepped towards the garbage crusher earlier in the day, seeming almost to intimidate it, and then spoken so authoritatively to the reporters. This image of the face—intermittent, licked by flamelight—would endure long after Duke had grown to know the man very well. It looked like it belonged only by a fire and nowhere else. When the flames leapt at a particular angle, the face looked murderous.

Someone began to sing. Any notion that Duke had of being on his way now vanished utterly. His repertoire, which ranged from Gilbert and Sullivan to James Brown, was inexhaustible. But he was not leading tonight, he was following. Around the fire were at least a half-dozen strong black voices, including a female one, and so they sang from the canon of rhythm and blues. They began with a version of "Poppa Was a Rolling Stone" that lasted about twenty minutes and had Duke gasping for breath at the end. The harmonies were lush, eternally unfolding, lapping at each other like waves. It was hard to imagine that anything better was going on at the Apollo Theatre.

Now big Annie Howard took control and practically induced epilepsy with "Shop Around," the tumultuous old Mary Wells song about cautious love. When that was over, Duke had to leave the fire to cool off. To his amazement, he had to fight his way through a second tier of people. Yes, they were two deep around the fire, even three in some spots. Where the hell had they come from? By now Duke was suspecting that these homeless people had some kind of communications network like the animal kingdom . . . songbirds passing along a note from one valley to the next.

But why were they here? No one was passing out free food, and the night was growing colder. Nevertheless, as the hour grew later, still more people arrived. In shifts, people left the fire and tried to sleep. The park benches, with railings in the middle, seemed designed to prevent this, but many curled up anyway. Little Art reappeared and constructed something even more sophisticated than the kubi hut, made out of plastic and wood. It was intended only for one, however, and he soon disappeared inside it. A couple of other makeshift shelters were created, also by Vietnam vets.

Duke moved to an empty bench at some distance. He wanted to doze a while. Before he drifted off, his eye was caught by the man on the bench opposite him. This was the man whose brooding presence had hovered over Big Mouth and over the fire. He was still brooding. With a blanket wrapped around him, he was staring at the Woolworth Building but somehow beyond it, as if in contemplation of something vast and disturbing. In this pose, blanket on shoulders, the features that had baffled Duke earlier—the eyes, the brow, the nose—struck a chord. The man had Indian blood. Cherokee, Sioux, something like that. Duke would have bet his life on it. It was a face out of the Old West, with a thousand creases in it. So the man was part African, part Indian, and all American, judging from the army fatigue jacket he wore, with the word LOCK on it . . . whatever that meant. But if he was a veteran, he was not bivouacking in a cardboard tent, like his comrades. Instead he sat erect, and his eyes remained clear and open.

Marc Greenberg was almost asleep when the picture came on the *Eleven O'Clock News*. At first it was just a disconnected image—army dog tags dangling from a piece of wood. But when the camera drew back in a long shot, Greenberg recognized City Hall and practically hit the ceiling. Within a minute he was behind the wheel of his van, tearing down downtown.

"Kochville," the evening news had called the homeless clustered around the remnants of the kubi hut in City Hall Park. For a housing activist, for any political creature, it was too good to be true. You couldn't buy publicity like this. It was worth ten parades down Broadway.

Greenberg's van lurched along Chambers Street until he found a parking spot. He leapt out and hurried toward the tiny encampment in City Hall Park. From a distance he saw about thirty people. Clearly they were homeless, but something about them was different. He could tell just by the silhouettes. They were erect, not slouching around.

When he got there, he recognized only a few faces. Several kubi huts had been re-erected on the lawn, and a fire had been lit in a trash can. Taking a seat on a bench, he picked up a newspaper and began to read it as a way of blending in. By the licking light of the fire, it revealed itself not as a newspaper but rather a mimeographed newsletter called *Voices to and from the Street*. Greenberg had never seen it before. "LIPOSUCTION!!" screamed the headline. "While you grovel for food in garbage cans, the rich are having their excess fat *surgically removed!!*"

The thing was absolutely inspired. In addition to tips on dealing with hypothermia, it suggested where to find the best soup kitchens, which of them served the best egg salad, tuna fish, etc., as if it were giving epicurean reviews on the finest restaurants in Manhattan. Then, in a final ironic flourish, the newsletter advised that red shoes at Charles Jourdan (one of the most obscenely expensive boutiques in New York) were 10 percent off. Greenberg was impressed by the sheer wit and vitriol.

He was starting to pick up snatches of conversation now, and the tone was markedly different from anything he was used to hearing in the shelters. Usually, the homeless recited the litany of their complaints with a sort of sigh. Now, there was steam underneath it.

"I heard in Tucson, man, they turnin' German shepherds loose in the park, to get people outta there."

"Indianapolis is worse, man. You try to get you some food out of a dumpster there, forget it. They puttin' bleach in there so you can't eat it. Can you imagine the motherfuckers doin' that?"

"Heard about a cat in Washington Heights, man, fell asleep in a dumpster to keep hisself warm. They come by with a trash compactor and crushed the cat up into a ball . . ."

"Forget Washington Heights, man," said a large man with a gold chain around his neck. "I was in the damn Kenton right up here on Third Avenue last night, man, and you know they done? They give us pills after dinner, and some cat said it was Thorazine. That's a damn *tranquilizer*, man. They tryin' to put us to sleep!"

Then one man called for silence, as if he had the biggest news of all to deliver. Slowly, a smile crossed his face.

"Seen in the paper this mornin'," he said, "the roof fell in at the damn Helmsley Palace Hotel. Crushed these people from Australia right in their beds, man. Crushed 'em *dead*. Motherfuckin' room cost *two hundred dollars a night*!!"

And with that there was whooping and hollering. Greenberg was horrified. But who could deny them their celebration? They had such terrible anger toward the world, yet yearned so much to be a part of it. Greenberg had seen them weep when people hurried their children past them on the street.

They were all around the trash fire now, exuberance filling their throats. Greenberg got to his feet, then climbed up on one of the green benches. All the squeamishness he had ever felt about putting the frail homeless in harm's way seemed stupid and timid. This was the moment—seething, singing, hot. It could not be stopped any more than the fire could be stopped from burning. "Excuse me . . . Could I have your attention . . . everybody . . . please. The reason we all . . . please . . . excuse me . . . could I . . . could I . . ."

They weren't even looking at him. Why should they? He was just a strange white man flailing around in the darkness.

"Yo!! Listen to me, you all. Yo!!"

The booming voice stopped all conversations. It was Duke York, mustering his theatre basic training and projecting to the back of the house, or in this case, to the elms along Broadway. "Yo, this man been here since last night, in the rain. He brought everybody here in the first place. So show him some respect. Go ahead, brother."

Greenberg felt the silence and the respect, recognizing now the powerful black man with the glass eye.

"I'm glad you're all here," he began. "God has given us a chance . . ." No, not God. This was no prayer meeting, and these were not the ordinary hangdog homeless. They were waiting to hear something new. "I . . . hope that . . . I . . . I want to try to . . . I want . . . I . . ." No use. He was drying up. There was no worse feeling. Expectant faces were looking up at him, and his face was turning red, and he was saying nothing. The first and worst time it had ever happened was at his bar mitzvah. After he had said all the Hebrew things perfectly, he began the personal remarks about being on the threshold of manhood, and drawn a complete blank.

"Just talk, man. Go ahead." The voice was firm and calming, and Greenberg turned towards it. It was another man, with American–Indian features. Something about the look in the man's face immediately relaxed him. Miraculously, the thoughts began to flow more easily into Greenberg's head and out his mouth.

"What I mean is, you have as much right to be here as anyone else." Good. That was a sentence. He tried another. "People are inside that building all day long complaining to the mayor, asking for money. If they can do it in there, we can do it out here."

There were a few murmurs.

"Doctor King walked across a bridge once and set out on a

53

long road, and it led through many places through many years, and now it runs right down the middle of this park."

He could feel the crowd quieting down and listening to him. Even Duke York could see that the white man had found his rhythm. He was testifying pretty well, like he had last night.

"That man over there," Greenberg went on, "caused trouble in this park two hundred years ago." Heads swivelled to the left, where Greenberg's finger was indicating an old statue. "His name was Nathan Hale, and his freedom was more important to him than his life. When the British caught him, they decided to hang him, and they asked him if he had any regrets. 'You're goddamn right I do,' he said. 'I regret that I can only die once fighting you bastards.'"

This was a slight distortion of Hale's famous speech, but it played well. Greenberg had them now. But as he reached his crescendo, he was interrupted.

"That's enough for now," said a clipped voice from around the fire. It was the man with the Indian face again. "We need to get some sleep." It was if he had given Greenberg the power to speak and now was taking it away.

Watching him next to the fire, Duke York was convinced now that this man named Lock had as much Indian as Negro blood. He looked like Geronimo giving a command to a thousand braves. He had that kind of authority. His voice was slow and soft, but everything stopped, and everyone waited for his next thought. He was a center of gravity. He was someone you watched.

But for now, Lock was through talking. Turning his back to them all, he continued to warm himself by the fire. His meaning had been clear. There would be no more speeches tonight.

Instead, smaller groups broke off, and intense conversations crackled. Marc Greenberg stepped down from the bench, not knowing if he'd had any effect at all. Perhaps it was too overblown to compare these men to historical figures. But maybe the more important point had been made: that the homeless, as foul, larcenous, lame, and muddled as they might think themselves to be, were also human.

⸻

Ed Koch was alone at last, and City Hall was almost empty . . . thank God. After eleven years in office, the mayor had become protective of the ornate old building. The budget hearings, with hordes of angry people tromping about, were like having the relatives over for a month. You counted the silverware when they left.

But late at night, City Hall was glorious. Sounds resonated in the empty marble hallways. Somewhere a cleaning woman was singing a ballad from the old country. Suddenly, there was the click-click of heels in a distant corridor. He loved the elegant desolation of it all.

Tonight, however, did not afford the usual peace. From where he stood at the south window of the Blue Room, the mayor could see the flickering light of the trash barrel fire in the park. An hour earlier, he had seen the *Eleven O' Clock News*. Clearly, it had been a mistake to move so swiftly against these people.

He could imagine the newspaper stories. He could have written them himself. "The mayor's huge ego has been gored again," they would say of the Miss Puerto Rican New York episode. Then there would be heart-wrenching photos of the homeless, including at least one of an old woman pushing around a mammoth shopping cart. And so Ed Koch would once again be the villain.

He was sick of it. He had given his life to public service and put his ass on the line many, many times for the public good. He had dodged bullets in France during World War Two, and he had outrun white southern farmers who wanted to beat the crap out of him for registering black people to vote. And after running the City of New York for eleven years, with all the agony and madness that implied, tomorrow morning he would be taken to task by a bunch of liberal reporters fresh from the Ivy League.

What simplistic point would drive their stories? That he, Ed Koch, was somehow responsible for homelessness? Never mind that Ronald Reagan, the emperor of the me-first era, had slashed the federal housing budget to almost nothing. It was still cheaper to buy a subway token and protest at City Hall than it was to take the Metroliner to Washington, so everyone came here and crucified Ed Koch for caving in to the real estate barons.

First of all, he thought, what was he supposed to say to the Harry Helmsleys and the Lew Rudins of the world? Fuck you? *Don't* build anything here in New York? These were the men who bailed New York out, for God's sake, when the city was bankrupt! Where did everyone think that money for welfare came from, anyway? It came from taxes. Expel the rich from New York and there wouldn't *be* any goddamn taxes. There wouldn't be any *streets*, for God's sake. The infrastructure of New York was a crumbling Victorian nightmare. Who was going to pay to fix it? Old women pushing shopping carts? Didn't anyone understand this!?

Apparently not. The left wing of the New York Democratic Party (and there didn't seem to be another wing to it) would accept nothing less than complete orthodoxy to a point of view that was already exhausted when Lyndon Johnson was in the White House. Welfare and affirmative action were the sacred cows. The latter, in particular, infuriated Ed Koch. Nobody had given him special privileges when he was a Jew trying to break into a Wasp, white shoe law firm. Ed Koch asked no quarter, and he gave none.

"Grow up!!" he wanted to say to them all.

He had begun his career as the most uncompromising liberal of all. In the late fifties, Greenwich Village was a head-spinning mélange of bohemia. It was the time of Jack Kerouac, of skinny, pubescent Allen Ginsberg, of outrageous Off-Broadway theatre, of endless arguments over espresso on MacDougal Street. Gangling Ed Koch and every other ambitious young politico had the same idol, and his name was Adlai Stevenson. None of them could believe that such a giant intellect and a sensitive soul actually stood on the brink of national power. They worked passionately for him, and they dedicated an organization to him that endures to this day: the Village Independent Democrats (VID).

"They exhausted themselves in arguing," remembers an observer of the VID. "They would seize on a point of politics and stay up all night screaming at each other and were too exhausted the next day to do anything about it. But they loved the life."

No one was more heady or self-righteous than Ed Koch. New York politics was ruled, among other people, by Carmine De-Sapio, the living symbol in the 1960s of Tammany Hall—the collective name for the ward heelers, pimps, mountebanks, and scoundrels who had run the Democratic political machine since the days of Boss Tweed. In the world of Tammany Hall, people voted six times and were rewarded with lifeguard jobs at Jones Beach . . . even if they couldn't swim.

The idealistic young Ed Koch sought to change all that. He took on DeSapio, who presided over his Greenwich Village district in a silk suit and a pair of dark glasses. The lines were cleanly drawn; the skinny young Jewish lawyer with an armload of position papers and the sleek politico with an ever present envelope of cash, from which he would tip hatcheck girls and aldermen with equal grace.

Koch based his campaign on the rights of folksingers to perform all night in Washington Square Park. That alone would have been enough to doom him to defeat in the conservative Italian election district. But on top of it he piled other impossibly liberal agendas, until his platform collapsed under the weight of them. The "SAD" campaign, as the wags dubbed it, stood for Sodomy, Abortion, and Divorce (without grounds). Naturally he was squashed and humiliated. But he had learned a critical lesson.

The next time around, Koch's defense of sodomy disappeared. That was to be expected. What no one expected were certain other compromises that fellow VIDs considered nothing less than betrayal. Suddenly, Ed Koch was railing against the intellectuals making noise all night in the tables outside the Café Figaro. They were disturbing people's sleep, complained Koch. His friends were aghast at the hypocrisy. Ed Koch was *one of those people*, for God's sake, slurping espresso and yapping all night long about Mississippi, or Algeria, or any of the other things roiling around in his big egghead.

But it worked. The Italians appreciated the gesture, and it put Koch over the top. To his friends, Koch explained the obvious: to defeat a monster like DeSapio, you couldn't go into it like Rebecca of Sunnybrook Farm. You had to get tough and make compromises and take some of his constituents away from him.

But by the time Ed Koch was elected to the United States Congress in 1968, the VID had forgiven and forgotten his transgressions. He was the most passionate liberal of his era. No one was more outspoken on Vietnam or civil rights. But then, in the early seventies, came another incident that enraged Koch's critics and resurrected the cries of "Betrayal."

Mayor John Lindsay, at the dizzying height of his liberal mandate, was integrating New York by urban planning design. By placing scatter-site public housing throughout the city, Lindsay sought to stitch poor blacks into white middle-class neighborhoods. To New York liberals it seemed a good idea, the final, natural fruit of a progressive era. And Ed Koch, veteran of those summers in Mississippi, ought to have led the applause.

But he didn't. To everyone's surprise, Koch condemned the scatter-site housing in Jewish Forest Hills. "Why should a stable neighborhood be shredded?" he asked. "Shredded?!" the liberals shrieked. It was being *integrated*. Koch disagreed. The people of Forest Hills, many of them poor immigrants, had spent a lifetime creating a healthy middle-class community. Why should it be wiped out with one stroke of an urban planner's pen?

Ed Koch called the moment his Rubicon. That was the river Julius Caesar had crossed into Gaul committing Rome to war. For Koch, Forest Hills was a final commitment to a life of political independence and integrity. For the liberals, it was the most cynical brand of sellout. Koch had crossed a river, all right—the East River into Brooklyn. He would spend the rest of his political life pandering to the prejudices and fears of the Italians and Irish and Jews who were terrified of blacks and would vote for anyone who would keep them from trampling the streets of Bensonhurst and Canarsie and Sheepshead Bay.

Idiots, thought Ed Koch. God forbid that anyone should ever disturb the sanctimonious fantasies of these liberals either with facts or with compassion for working-class people trying to make a living. Had he travelled a distance from the days of railing outside the Café Figaro over espresso? Of course he had. All thinking people evolved. What the hell was wrong with that?

He returned his gaze to the dark mass of City Hall Park, still faintly etched with the light of a trash can fire. Case in point: the homeless—poor victims of a heartless world. What unmitigated bullshit!! First of all, most of the homeless were either drug addicts or mentally ill, or both. That was fact. The liberal fantasy was that they were productive average joes, just like you and me, who had been turned into the streets by the Simon Legrees of New York, who had then reamed out their simple little cottages and turned them into gaudy pleasure domes.

What a delusion! And the liberal solution to this was the wildest fantasy of all. There were thousands of empty buildings in New York, many of them the property of the city through tax delinquency. There were a hundred thousand homeless people walking the streets. Why not simply put the people into the buildings? Why not train them to fix up the buildings themselves, thereby giving them a skill on top of a home?? Brilliant! Ed Koch had to listen to prattle like this all day long!!

Did anyone have any idea how much it would cost to fix these crumbling buildings up? Or even worse, to try to *train* homeless derelicts to do it? To say nothing of the incredible, ball-breaking hassles and howls that would then emanate from the building unions?

Put the homeless into the empty buildings, eh? Just *put* them there? Why? Reward them for what? Because they exist?? Because they breathe?! What kind of message did that send to people clinging to the bottom rung of society, trying to eke out a living? Let go? Just give up, and the city will take you in its loving arms and put you in a penthouse??

NO!! Not on my watch, said Ed Koch to himself, sweeping out of the Blue Room and down the empty marble hallway to the big front door of City Hall.

≡

Lock rolled out his United States Army blanket in the northeastern corner of City Hall's front lawn, the spot where in winter the city erects its sixty-foot Norway spruce Christmas tree. It was far enough away from the noise to give him a little peace.

The activity around the fire was dying down, but Lock had lost interest in it anyway. He didn't sing much. The speech of the white man had excited some people, but that didn't interest him either. He wasn't from New York City, like most of the others. He came from a place where people liked to talk, but in long, loquacious, slow-rolling waves. That rhythm was still with him. Here the talking was too fast. You had to tense up to follow it, so why bother?

He tucked the plastic sheeting up around the corners of his blanket and rolled his jacket into a makeshift pillow. Underneath it he placed a knife. This was a general precaution he took in New York City. Here in the park it had an additional, more specific purpose: to prevent the rats from fucking with him. They'd be out tonight, even though it was cold. Too cold for early June. He thought briefly of his father. This kind of weather would worry his father just about to death, fearing that the tobacco buds would not survive it.

Lock took a last look around him and that's when he saw the odd-looking figure on the top of the City Hall steps. Lock was not a man who kept up with politics, but you'd have to be from outer space not to be familiar with Ed Koch.

The mayor motioned to a car idling at the bottom of the steps. Wait a while, he seemed to be telling it. No doubt, thought Lock, the soft, pampered man has fallen in love with the night. Nights like these were ordinary in the South, but rare up here. The evening air was cool, but sweet enough to eat. The magnolias had been late and abundant this year, and their ghost essence still curled through the darkness.

After a few moments, the mayor slowly descended the steps of City Hall, and his town car swung around in readiness. Its headlights lazily strafed the shadows of the park and for an instant caught the eyes of Lock. The two men stared at each other like a pair of jackrabbits in the bush. Then, just as quickly, the moment passed. The mayor proceeded down the steps, and Lock completed the journey to his blanket on the ground. As the mayor put his hand on the car's door handle, the patch of grass in front of City Hall was as quiet as it had been a thousand years ago, when the smoke of an Algonquin campfire was the only movement in the night.

SCREEEEEECH! The peace was interrupted by the sudden, noisy arrival of a New York City taxicab. The doors flew open and out bounded two expensively dressed women, the sort of people the mayor had encountered last week at a Waspish women's civic club. What did they want? How could they know he was still here at this hour? The Wasps were slowly but surely becoming his political allies, but he had a sense of them only at a great distance; the distance, say, from the Lower East Side to East Hampton. What he truly knew about them he had basically culled from F. Scott Fitzgerald's novels. Were these women here on some sort of empty-headed fling, some Jazz Age bit of excess? Were they going to jump into the fountain?

The real explanation was not as exotic. A gap in the mayor's knowledge of Wasps was their sense of noblesse oblige. The women had been at a reception honoring the family whose colt had just won the Belmont Stakes. Their husbands (both generous Koch campaign contributors) were out of town, and the women had been sitting around the party feeling rather gay and useless and finishing off the last of the champagne. Then someone flicked on the *Eleven O'Clock News*. Watching the report about the valiant homeless group in City Hall Park, the women were seized by the heroic instincts that characterized their families' histories. The appetizer trays were still three-quarters full and undoubtedly to be thrown out in the morning. In an exhilarating, Robin Hood-like bolt of instinct, they grabbed the food and went downstairs to find a cab.

And here they were, holding the trays—now hooded with tin-foil—and staring into the darkness. What adventure!! They either did not notice or did not acknowledge the presence of the mayor of the City of New York. With a look at each other, they girded their spirits and moved cautiously into the wooded glen, carrying hors d'oeuvres to the poor.

The mayor slowly pulled open the door of the town car and climbed in. As the driver pointed the car east through the darkness of lower Manhattan toward the FDR Drive, he tried to engage the mayor in conversation. He did not succeed. Instead, the mayor opened the window, watched the dark river roll beside him, and felt the night air rush against his dry, tight cheeks.

Four

On an April morning in 1906, Albert Brackman piled his wife and daughter into a horse-drawn buggy. Once there had been a matched pair of horses, but one of them had been sold, along with virtually everything else Brackman owned, to pay for building materials.

Family and surrey then clip-clopped along the main street of Springhurst, crossed the bridge over Leggett's Creek, and rode up the hill to the corner of Prospect and Longwood. A crowd was already gawking at the structure that stood before them. Triangular in shape, marble pillars gleaming, it was as grand as a palazzo. On a balcony stood James Meehan, the architect, wearing a silk hat. Soon Brackman, more modestly dressed, clambered up to join him. Together they cut the ribbon of 850 Longwood Avenue, the first elevator building in the Bronx.

The skeptics in the crowd (and there were as many of these as admirers) smirked that the two men would never find tenants for a building so grand. Brackman found them almost immediately.

By this time, the masses of the Lower East Side were beginning to differentiate themselves. Not all of them sold rags from pushcarts. There were doctors, lawyers, and business executives among them, and they wanted out. Now that they were making a little money, why should they raise their families on a "lung block," as they referred to places like Rifkin Street, where tuberculosis lived in the air?

In Albert Brackman's building at 850 Longwood Avenue, not even the marble trappings were the important thing. There was light! There was space! There was silence! You could breathe the air without worrying what germs were riding on it. You could sit in a room and hear nothing, nothing at all for hours.

You might decide to while away the early evening in the library. Not the public library, like the pathetic, musty, crowded building back on Hester Street, but the library IN YOUR OWN HOUSE, for Albert Brackman and James Meehan had laid out the seven-room apartments to include libraries and parlors and dining rooms—all separate from each other! On the very top floor, the master bedroom of the Zulutoffs held the jewel of the crown: a curved oval window, like an elegant monocle in the eye of a rich man. And from this remarkable window could be seen, on a clear day, the bluffs of Manhattan past the hill of Kelly Street.

All this luxury, and a short walk would have you in the country. Once you got past the tavern and the general store and crossed the bridge over Leggett's Creek, you were in a different universe. If it was Monday, wash day, you might even see a German hausfrau stirring a pot of clothes in a giant kettle, a wood fire crackling underneath. The countryside was dotted with white clothes snapping on lines. A little farther on, it was sheer green. If you were a boy, it was paradise. You broke into a dead run, and once you got down to the Bronx River, you stripped off your clothes and dove in. You swam until your lips were blue, and then you climbed out and dried in the sun, or if evening was coming on, you made a bonfire in a field and stood around it and told tales of the Lower East Side or of the old country, if you remembered it, though very few did. Then you realized what time it was, and you raced home to Longwood Avenue. At the front steps, your family's servants waited nervously for you. They grabbed you by the collar and hauled you upstairs to your father, who sat in the library after a long day in Manhattan and a long trip home on the elevated locomotive or the horse-drawn trolley. He forgave you, and the whole family repaired to the dining room, where the cook had laid out another feast in a long season of feasts.

And so it went for a few wondrous years for the residents of 850 Longwood, for the Freunds and the Zulutoffs and the Lubins. Even the anti–Semitism of the Bronx abated, once the natives realized what bounty the Jews were bringing to the tradesmen and the artisans. And it wasn't so bad to have Dr. Goldberg a few hundred yards away when little Billy O'Doul came down with whooping cough. On a spring day in 1908, the final symbolic stroke was made with a mason's trowel. On Prospect Avenue, the cornerstone was laid to a synagogue by a rugged Irish laborer named McGraw.

<hr />

The midnight visit of the two socialites to the City Hall Park homeless had a seismic effect. The women did not make a grand gesture of their generosity, nor did they seek displays of gratitude. They just put down the hors d'oeuvres and left.

It was as if a spaceship from Venus had paid a brief visit to a small family farm.

For one thing, the two women had the most amazing odors about them. After only a moment's presence, they left behind a wake of peach lotion, of Oil of Shalimar, of Chanel Number Five. As the men watched them go, instant erections sprang to life under grime-caked trousers. The women were not dressed lavishly or seductively, but their linen dresses and simple pearls suggested that to hold them, just for a moment, would be like a month in a fine hotel.

Marc Greenberg also took notice. Beyond the dreams of a shiksa goddess that bedevil many Jewish boys, often to their ruin, Greenberg was thinking bigger. A corner had been turned in the public mind. After their initial revulsion, perhaps people were now willing to look the homeless in the eye.

He was emotionally played out, but he didn't have the energy or the inclination to drive home. He wanted to miss nothing. He curled up on a bench and stared into the clear night sky.

He was truly on the brink of history, he felt. That had not been an empty pep talk about Nathan Hale. For him this night was the culmination of a journey that had begun long ago, when he left his Long Island hometown as a teenager. Like many members of his generation, he had idealism but no concrete ideas. So he began to drift and search. He wound up in the deserts of New Mexico, where he immersed himself in the culture of the purple plains. He took peyote with old Indians and participated in birthing rituals on mountaintops. He meditated for days by dry riverbeds.

Unfortunately, while carrying a large amount of peyote from one place to another, Greenberg was caught and arrested. To pay for his defense, he had to borrow a large sum of money from his father, who had a business in the garment center of New York. Young Marc got off with probation, but in order to pay his father back he was obliged to go to work making ladies' clothes.

For years, his spiritual development was in abeyance as he rode the Long Island Railroad into work everyday. Fortunately, his father was an enlightened man. The elder Greenberg was not punishing his son but teaching him responsibility. To seek the spiritual life was fine. You just had to be prepared to pay the price if in the process you were caught with a suitcase full of hallucinogenic drugs.

He began to give his son Wednesdays off to think about the next step. Greenberg drifted around town, sampling the bewildering cultural menu. One night he found himself at a concert in St. John the Divine Cathedral, a huge, astonishing place that affected him the moment he walked in the door. When the music (by a man named Paul Winter) began, it was all manner of strange sounds, from conch shells and hollow pieces of wood to bizarre arrays of gongs, bells, and chimes. Suddenly Greenberg felt his journey picking up where it had left off years before in the mountains of New Mexico.

The metal was white-hot, and the next day it was shaped. He went with a friend to see a movie about the Mahatma Gandhi by a British filmmaker. It was a full-color action adventure not many cuts above the standard movie biography, but what a life it celebrated! With fascination, Greenberg watched Britain knuckle under to the Mahatma, who sat naked on the floor with all the power on earth. Not long after that, Greenberg began befriending the clergy around St. John the Divine and trying to goad them into social action. Within a couple of years, he had widened his net to include most of New York's religious community. Old priests and social workers looked on in amazement. With the sheer force of his personality, the passionate young Jew had created something called the Interfaith Assembly on Homelessness and Housing.

The sky above City Hall was now pitch-black and starless. The last of the voices had died down around the campfire. No longer resisting, Marc Greenberg drifted off to sleep.

Only a couple of people were still up, Duke York among them. Despite his immense exhaustion, Duke would not have been able to sleep had he been led to a featherbed. Greenberg's speech was still ringing in his head. Duke knew there was a danger in getting lathered up by some idealistic notion. You crashed and burned when you discovered it was all a lie. This feeling had its roots not only in the tortured romance with Diane but also in the books he'd stolen from the Columbia library as a kid. One time he'd gotten all worked up about being an astronaut. He read voraciously, he collected decals, he even left several unanswered telephone messages for Alan Shepard, the first American in space. Then he got a little older and figured out what the chances really were of a one-eyed Negro being allowed to fly to the moon.

But Duke was a creature of passion, and when he got ahold of an idea that inflamed him, it took extremely harsh evidence to make him let it go. And at the moment, the idea was justice.

Even though he did not consider himself a homeless person, and even though he still believed most of them were lazy bastards with only themselves to blame, Duke never doubted that the system was out to screw them. A few feet away, a pregnant woman dozed on a bench. Her name was Princess, and she had apparently been denied health services by the city for the first seven months of her pregnancy. She'd been told that when the baby came, she'd get all the help she needed. This was clearly bullshit, as far as Duke was concerned. He had two daughters and might have had three except for a miscarriage Diane had suffered when she was three months along. So *that* was the delicate time. Instead, Princess had spent her first two trimesters on the street, smoking crack and hustling. She had become so habituated to the life that she preferred it. God only knew what kind of a baby she was going to give birth to—any day now, from the looks of her.

In all of this Duke read dark things; the darkest was that the city was willing to be careless with the health of black mothers. If she had an uncomfortable pregnancy, fine, and if the black race vanished altogether, so much the better. No. He drew back from that thought. He could not allow himself to believe, even for a second, that there was that much evil in the world.

"Got a cigarette, partner?" Duke looked up at the man who stood across from him at the fire. His name was Lonnie, and he had arrived sometime during the endless night. He was one of the few white men in the camp, a classic gap-toothed cracker from Tennessee. Duke had felt the instinctive fear of southern white men almost immediately. But to all appearances, Lonnie was as mellow as a grove of dogwoods. He almost hypnotized with his homespun primer for survival. "Fingernail polish'll stop a carburetor leak faster'n anything known to man," he would drawl. "Dump a lady's purse in my lap and I'll drive you halfway across the country on it."

If Lonnie was to be believed, he had been drafted into the army from a little hollow deep in the Tennessee mountains, where he was a legendary crack shot, even as a boy. But after a few months of basic training in jungle warfare, Lonnie deserted. He was caught, and the ensuing year in an army stockade was enough to give him a lifelong hatred of America and all its formal institutions.

"Took to the brush then," said Lonnie. "Survived on the game I could kill. Then I got to know the animals in the woods and come to like 'em more than people. Started eatin' vegetation instead."

Lonnie's rap was smooth, and it led to a noble conclusion. "You give me the power," he told Duke across the fire, "and I'll end the damn homeless problem in this country. I'll force the rich to skill the dumb. Man, you publicize the price of an aluminum can, you get every alkie in the South up here crawlin' through garbage cans. Clean up the goddamn world."

By this time Lonnie had water boiling in the battered saucepan he was holding over the fire. He tossed in a few leaves, then poured half the mixture into a paper cup and handed it to Duke. "Holly tea. Cure any of the problems of the seven vital organs as the Greeks define 'em."

The tea was pungent and hot, right on time for the first deep chill of evening. Yet for all that was soothing about Lonnie, Duke felt a vague discomfort. As Lonnie droned on with his hillbilly wisdom, Duke was riveted to the man's wrist tattoo, which was a picture of a coiled snake above the legend LOVE TO FUCK YOU. There was a crudeness about him that belied the sweet talk. He had, for example, been the only one openly rude to the socialites with the hors d'oeuvres.

"Damn AIDS thing got me scared to death," he had said audibly as the women laid down their gifts. "Never live to a million if I stick my tongue into all the pussies I'd like to." Whether or not the women had actually heard him was almost beside the point. Lonnie didn't care. And then, when a black man had put a hand on his shoulder to chasten him, Lonnie had whirled and put him instantly in a crippling hammerlock. Duke got a feeling of deadly violence from the man, all the more so because you couldn't tell when it was coming.

Clutching his tea, murmuring thanks, Duke drifted away from the fire. Exhaustion was muddling his thoughts, but he was clinging to the manic crystalline high of the night: what if it was all true? What if these thirty assorted losers and derelicts *could* change the world? Why should pregnant black women be lurching around the streets in a cocaine haze? Why should an old cracker from Tennessee be sleeping under a tree? True, the thirty of them were illiterate and didn't know the Constitution from a take-out menu, but so what? Didn't Jesus change the world, and wasn't he born in a barn, his parents freezing their asses off on a night even colder than this?

Perhaps this was all too grand. But at least it was a clear thought in a positive direction, the first he'd had after many, many months of circular, consuming misery over Diane.

He went over to the sleeping form of Marc Greenberg and shook him awake.

"I got to talk to you, man . . ."

". . . Huh . . . ?" Greenberg had been unconscious for about twenty minutes.

"You think we can make something happen here?"

". . . Uhhh . . ."

"I want you to be straight with me, now."

". . . Why wouldn't I be?"

"Because you lied to me before, about the horn."

"The . . . ?"

"The ram's horn, man. That the cat was blowin' last night, when it was raining. You told me the thing was five thousand years old. You told me Moses blew the thing when he come off the mountain."

"He did blow a ram's horn."

70

"But not the same horn, right? Not the exact same horn?"

"No . . ."

"So then you was lyin' to me."

"I wasn't trying to mislead you. Maybe I didn't understand exactly what you were asking."

"Maybe you didn't," said Duke York.

There was a silence.

"All right," Duke said. "That's over with. So what I'm askin' you now is, you think we can do anything out here?"

"I think we can have an effect," said Greenberg.

"You think we can make it so all people have a place to sleep at night?"

"That's what we're trying to do."

"But I'm sayin', you think we can do it?"

"I think we can make the world hear us."

The phrase made a hot current run along Duke's body. Heard By The World.

The men sat a while as the first light started to appear in the eastern sky. Then an engine kicked to life in the shadows beside City Hall: Big Mouth, the garbage crusher, was back.

A dozen heads snapped awake on the lawn. Duke York leapt to his feet.

"They comin' for us again?"

"I don't know," hedged Greenberg. He did know this: at some point, the city would definitely be coming for them again. And now was a discreet time, before the reporters arrived for work.

"So what're we gonna do?" said Duke York.

Greenberg wasn't sure what to do, but maybe something could be talked about. He strode off into the shadows, disappearing from Duke's view. Several minutes later he re-appeared beside City Hall, talking to whoever was in the cab of Big Mouth.

"Time to pick up the trash again, huh?" said a voice behind Duke. It was Lock, the man with Indian blood.

"I don't know," said Duke York.

"Well, we'll see, won't we?" said Lock, smiling and moving away.

Duke watched him. The man had the gait of a wolf.

"Wait a minute," said Duke.

Lock stopped and turned to him.

"You think anything gonna come out of this?" Duke asked him.

Lock did not respond but simply looked at him. Duke could not interpret the look, but it went on far past the point of comfort. Finally he had to turn away. He felt certain by now that Lock was a man with great spiritual powers. Whether he used them for good or evil was not clear.

At last he sensed that Lock had gone, and he turned his head and indeed saw nothing but a dark empty thicket. At that moment, Greenberg arrived back from his conversation with Big Mouth.

"What'd he say?"

Greenberg paused. He wasn't sure how candid to be. "We're going to see about it later."

"Yeh? How?"

"I'm going to see the parks commissioner."

"You want me to come?" said Duke York.

". . . Uhhh . . ." Greenberg was thrown off balance by the offer.

"So we can show him who we are out here," said Duke. "Like a sympathy thing."

Greenberg considered it a moment. The one-eyed man was indeed a pathetic-looking creature. But whether that would help or hurt was not clear.

"And I know who else we can take," said Duke York.

Before Greenberg could reply, Duke was over by the bench occupied by the pregnant, sleeping Princess. He nudged her awake.

"What you want?"

"Just want you to come with me," said Duke York.

She put her brown hand on his crotch. "Cost you five dollars."

"Just get up," he said.

Soon they were back standing in front of Marc Greenberg. "I figured we could appeal to the man as a human," said Duke York, pointing to Princess's huge belly.

When people called Parks Commissioner Henry Stern an odd duck, they meant many things, not the least of which were his companions in his Central Park office. Ducks. Dozens of them. Rubber, porcelain, velvet, windup, oil paintings, hanging mobiles, even a duck phone that quacked instead of ringing. Stern was a quixotic man with a visual sense of fun, and he celebrated the natural world of which he was, in New York City, the emperor. His very conference room was dominated by an old Central Park Carousel wooden horse.

To his admirers, and there were many, Henry Stern was the ultimate marriage of man and job. To his detractors (and there were plenty of those too) he was an eccentric, remote man more at home with plants than people.

About his huge, devouring intelligence, there could be no debate at all. Henry Stern was the ultimate fruit of the New York City Public School system. He had excelled at Bronx Science, at City College, and then the hometown boy made good in a big way, graduating at the top of his class at Harvard Law School. Then he returned to New York and hurled himself into the public arena, where he served with a piercing, lean integrity.

He began by working under Bess Myerson at the Consumer Affairs Department, and woe to the shoddy or unethical businessman who came under his scrutiny. Then he ran for city councilman-at-large. He brought to his campaign a first-class liberal pedigree; like his good friend Ed Koch, he had worked in the South registering black voters. And once in office, he made good on his promises. He was the councilman who could not be bought or bullied.

"More rat inspectors, not movie inspectors," he had said as campaigner, and as councilman he delivered, eviscerating censorship statutes. "Truth in dying," he demanded, and exposed the legion of New York funeral directors who preyed on the grieving.

When the position of councilmember-at-large was eliminated by city charter in 1981, Henry Stern was thought to have a great palette of opportunities in front of him. Many thought him a potentially greater mayor than the current one, Ed Koch. It was to everyone's surprise, then, when Stern accepted Koch's appointment as parks commissioner. With the exception of Robert Moses, who had used the job to augment his stranglehold on the city's physical plant, Parks had been mainly a perch for socialites and lightweights. Their tuxedos were in a state of perpetual drycleaning.

Henry Stern preferred to ride a Land Rover all day, identifying trees and spotting new rock outcroppings. He was a natural for the job, and a naturalist in the job.

Nor did he stop going after the bad guys. When a Queens developer cut down a dozen trees to make way for a building, Stern tore into him. Coining the term "arborcide," Stern arranged to have the man's building permit revoked and charged him $100,000 per tree to get it back.

But the skeptics persisted. They saw a kind of odd vassalage in Stern's relationship to Koch, who was the godfather of Stern's oldest son. Stern made many enemies in the Liberal Party by bolting it and supporting Koch in his doomed campaign for the governorship in 1982. Even before that, in the early seventies, when Koch crossed his "Rubicon" by opposing the housing projects in Forest Hills, Henry Stern was silent. According to form, he should have been outraged. Instead, he adhered to some strange loyalty.

"Sir . . . ?" It was the intercom on the parks commissioner's desk.

"Yes?"

"The people from City Hall Park are here."

"Send them in."

He had been waiting all morning for this. He scrutinized the three visitors as they crossed his threshold. Only Marc Greenberg was familiar to him: the two men had worked together on a hunger project years before. The idea was that no food should be wasted in New York City, but it had proved impossible to execute. It was fine to suggest that the leftover burritos from a Mexican restaurant in Queens should feed a homeless man in Brooklyn. How to do it was another question. It had been the intellectual, logistical challenge that appealed to Henry Stern and the opportunity to save the world that appealed to Marc Greenberg. The project fizzled, but each man carried away indelible impressions of the other. Greenberg was an impossible dreamer, Stern amused himself with intellectual brainteasers.

"Good to see you again, Marc."

"You too, Commissioner. This is Duke York, and this is Princess."

Stern was taken aback for an instant by the large black man with the glass eye, then quickly took Duke's beefy hand in his own. Then he turned to greet the woman. To the dismay of Marc and Duke, Princess had spotted the old carousel horse in Stern's conference room and was already riding it. This meeting of some gravity would have a surreal backdrop: a pregnant woman-child atop a wooden horse shrieking "Go horsey!" It was a reaction Stern was used to—from visitors under the age of five.

"What can I do for you, Marc?"

"Well, you know we're out there in the park."

"Yes, how did the event go?"

"Wonderfully. Thank you. So we decided to stay a while."

"So I'm told. Your permit was for one night."

"We thought that since the budget hearings go on for a month, maybe we could stay a little longer . . ."

"I can't allow that, I'm afraid. No one can live in the park."

"There are lobbyists in City Hall all month, aren't there?"

"Yes, Marc, but they go home at night."

"These people don't have a home."

"That's not my fault."

"Whose fault is it?"

"Homelessness is a complicated problem, Marc."

"That's why we want to solve it . . ."

"But you can't stay in the park all night."

"Why not?"

"Because the park is for people."

"Aren't we people?"

"GO HORSEY!!"

"Commissioner, I know the mayor is angry . . ."

"It has nothing to do with the mayor!" It infuriated Stern when people assumed he acted merely at the bidding of his superior. "It has to do with the law. You can't build structures on the lawn. You can't live there. No one can!"

Duke York had rarely seen people argue this well. They were fighting with their minds. Duke admired that. Most arguments in his experience were physical, even between white people. You'd see a couple of Italians in Queens shouting at each other at a traffic light, and pretty soon they'd be out of their cars beating the crap out of each other. This was different. Duke was following both lines of argument clearly and was tempted to jump in himself, but was too timid.

Finally, Greenberg and Stern stopped talking and shook hands, although no agreement had been reached. Greenberg said they were staying in the park, and Stern said if that happened he would do what he had to do. On the ride back downtown, Duke asked if it had gone well. Marc Greenberg had to be honest. "I don't think I budged him."

When they returned to the park, Greenberg's worst fears were confirmed. The lawn was empty. Here and there was a piece of plastic or cardboard and a couple of half-dismantled kubi huts. But no people. Either the midday heat had scattered them, or

Stern had moved with brutal swiftness and already wiped them out.

Greenberg felt as if he'd been kicked.

Then he heard a voice behind him. "Are you Marc Greenberg?"

He turned to find an attractive blonde woman in what must have been a sweltering outfit of velvet and sequins. Next to her was a small boy.

"Yes . . . ?"

"My name is Olga Mathiessen," she began. She went on to tell an extremely long story that fascinated Duke but only irritated Greenberg, whose mind was now racing on another subject: how to reconstruct Kochville.

Apparently Olga Mathiessen was a Scandanavian who had last been employed as a bareback rider in the Viennese Circus. She had fallen in love with a travelling American who then brought her to New York and dumped her, along with her ten-year-old son, Leif. So here she was with no papers, no home, no money, and no skills except the ability to do acrobatic stunts on a bare-backed horse. But it was June, and there was nothing left of the Barnum and Bailey Circus but the elephant droppings. She had apparently heard of Kochville on last night's news and come here as a last resort.

At this point in her tale, she collapsed into convulsive sobbing. Leif, meanwhile, was throwing balls of dirt at Greenberg, hitting him squarely in his sweating temples.

"Look," said the exasperated man, functioning on no sleep. "Go to the Austrian embassy or go to YWCA. I can't help you."

"They said you could."

"They?"

"The men who were just here."

"The men who . . . where did they go?!"

"In there, I think," she said, pointing to City Hall.

Greenberg sprinted toward the big building and raced up the steps, pulling in his wake Duke, Princess, Olga Mathiessen, and

Leif. "Anything going on in here today?" he asked the guard breathlessly.

A large, red-faced Irishman looked up from a swivel chair and eyeballed them. Greenberg could feel his own anger rising. Administrations could come and go, Ed Koch or Malcolm X could be the mayor, and the political machine would still have some rude, incompetent slob sitting at the doorway to City Hall.

"POMP meetings in the Board of Estimates," the man finally snarled into his newspaper. Greenberg pulled his people behind him and raced down the hall. The POMP hearings! He'd forgotten all about them!

POMP (Private Ownership Management Program) was a huge issue among the housing advocates. It was a scheme under which dilapidated city-owned buildings were given away to private people, just as the advocates had always wanted. The only trouble was that they were not being given to poor people, or to community groups, but to the worst kind of landlords—slumlords, or worse still, high rollers who would eventually turn the places into expensive condos. POMP, to the advocates, was an outrage. Camouflaged as a progressive measure, it actually set things backward.

This afternoon there was a public hearing on the matter in front of the Board of Estimates. In a sense the hearings were futile, because the Board was the original fox watching the henhouse. It consisted of the five borough presidents, the comptroller, the president of the City Council, and the mayor—all of whom had been financed in their recent election campaigns by real estate interests.

When Greenberg and his entourage got to the room, he spotted the homeless immediately. They were in a corner of the gallery, under an oil painting of old Dutch New York. All thirty of them were fast asleep.

Marc Greenberg had only to close his own eyes and hear the faint hum to know why. The air-conditioning was superb. They had come in to beat the heat. And once here, free of heat and rats and all other discomforts and dangers, they had fallen blissfully asleep. Sleep was what the homeless craved, more than food, money, or sex. And unlike public libraries, which threw you out the minute you dozed off, City Hall seemed almost to encourage it. Much legislation could be snuck past a snoozing public.

A landlord from Brooklyn was standing at the podium speaking on the bill. Arrayed behind a huge, curved desk were the members of the Board of Estimates, looking vaguely distracted. Greenberg knew the look well: the meeting was a formality, a rubber-stamp operation. The POMP legislation would be passed, hopefully soon, and the politicos would be free to go to their late lunches or early cocktails.

"Are there any other speakers to be heard on Bill 34446?" droned a clerk who looked as if he'd had the job for a thousand years.

"I got something to say."

A few heads turned lazily toward Duke York, who had spoken the words.

"Does this relate to Bill 34446?" said the clerk.

"This relates to the cradle that rocked me," said Duke.

Now a few more spectators took notice. After an afternoon of numbingly dull speeches, this might be different.

"I was born in New York and I'm gonna die here. Dig me a hole in that graveyard right beside the Brooklyn-Queens Expressway." The words were pouring easily. Greenberg was impressed by the man's poise.

". . . But until I die," Duke continued, "I need a place to live." Since the meeting with Stern he had been consumed with what he could have said and should have said. Since Greenberg's speech last night, in fact, everything had been building to this.

"I got two beautiful daughters, and one of them ain't much older than that little one there." Duke pointed to a small black girl squirming in the arms of a woman across the gallery. "Do you think we ain't human? Do you think your children are any better than ours?"

He swivelled his gaze to the board, as did everyone else. The politicians began to fidget with guilt, embarrassment, and irritation. This odd-looking black man was carrying on about things that had nothing to do with the pending legislation. And yet to muffle him would be a mistake. The press was present, and they were already whispering among themselves.

Duke York was a man with many hundreds of hours of stage time, as actors like to say. Comfortable in front of an audience, he knew how to reach the back row without shouting. That was critical. He didn't want people tuning him out. He was setting his thoughts out clearly. And when he had done that, when he had laid the groundwork, then he had the right to wail. And that's what he intended to do. Duke York intended to wail on his instrument like the meanest horn player on Basin Street.

"I can't go home to my daughter and tell her there's no money for this and no money for that," he said. "She don't want to hear it. Anymore than your daughter wants to hear it. So I say to you, what do we say to God when he says 'Bless the children?' We gonna say 'No?' We gonna say 'There ain't enough money?' You don't say that to God, and you don't say that to my little girl."

A ripple of 'yeahs' and 'amens' and 'tell its' ran like a current along the gallery.

"God *is* my little girl," said Duke York.

The mother held her child aloft.

"He made her perfect, and he sent her forth into the world, and what happens to her is more important than what happens to this building and every damn piece of paper in it."

Roars now from the gallery. No one was asleep anymore. None of the homeless had ever seen anyone remotely like themselves speak in a public place. The reporters were scribbling furiously, having made the connection between the man at the podium and the Kochville story which had so amused them yesterday.

"So I want to finish up now by sayin' to you 'I Love New York.'" Duke held up a souvenir pin he'd gotten somewhere, with the little heart. "But New York, you got to love me back!"

Bedlam. With the exception of the board members themselves, everyone was on their feet, clapping and stomping. The weary look on the face of Claire Shulman, the Queens borough president, said it all: even though the black man's diatribe had nothing whatsoever to do with Bill 34446 or any of the complex issues it raised, he had won the day. Passion sometimes did in this building.

The final agreement was more or less down the middle. Of the ten potential POMP cases before the Board, half were rejected. The advocates were buoyant. It was a victory they had never expected. The citizens of Kochville were exhilarated . . . but only for the moment. Now that the meeting was over, they had to leave the building and face the heat. The good news was that the heat had broken. The bad news was that it had been broken by the worst thunderstorm of the summer.

The mayor was at the health club when he got the news. Usually he did not tolerate interruptions when he was on the treadmill, but every so often his personal trainer took the liberty, just to end the torture. Her torture. The mayor exercised with a Sony Walkman and earphones, listening to the Barbra Streisand tune "The Way We Were." Often he sang along. The mayor had a sort of whining high tenor, aggravated by severe pitch problems.

He took the interruption, and the news, very badly. The POMP thing had gotten fucked up!? How?? If anything, POMP was a *concession* to the housing advocates. The dilapidated buildings were being returned to private ownership. Wasn't that what everyone wanted? All right, so the new landlords weren't all Boy Scouts. All right, so some of them were scumbags. But at least the damn buildings would be off the city's books and back in the hands of someone who could run them.

81

It was a puzzlement to Ed Koch why the housing issue in particular was the cross to which he was so consistently nailed. The truth was that he understood the crisis of New York housing better than anyone, because he had lived it. He remembered, as a child in the Bronx, riding the subway all the way to the Lower East Side of Manhattan with his father Louis. There they would visit grandmother Koch, who still lived in a five story walk-up on Rivington Street. One of their main activities was bathing her. Eddie had to go and fetch buckets and buckets of water from the common pump and then pour them into a huge metal tub in the kitchen. Grandmother Koch was an enormous woman, and she wore a shift for modesty as her son Louis sloshed water over her and scrubbed her. Afterwards there would be a great mess that father and son had to clean up.

The mayor never forgot those sessions. Not long afterwards, the Depression forced his family to leave their home in Crotona Park in the Bronx and move in with his Uncle Howard in Newark. They slept three to a room, and Howard was a bastard who made them acknowledge every crumb of his so-called largesse. He even made them work the hatcheck concession in his Newark dance hall, the whole family crammed together in a cloakroom. So tell me about housing and space, thought Ed Koch to himself as he exited the gym.

The truth was that there was only so much housing to go around, and housing was not free. The advocates liked to sentimentalize about the sanctity of the hearth, but the truth was that housing was a commodity, like bananas or automobiles. It cost money to build and maintain and somebody had to pay for it. And if you couldn't afford it, you shouldn't get it. That was the truth about housing, and truth was Ed Koch's currency.

Of course, every so often it cost him dearly. When he ran for governor in 1982, his compulsive truthfulness did him in. In a *Playboy* interview a year earlier, he had been asked about the suburbs. "The suburbs?" the mayor said. "The suburbs are a joke.

They're full of housewives in gingham dresses running to Sears for their big thrill of the week."

During the campaign, the remark was widely quoted upstate and virtually killed him. What finished him off was the smart alec reporter who asked him, at a campaign stop, what county he was in. "Uhh . . . Oneonta . . . no, Oneida . . . is that a county? Wait . . . uhhh . . . I have no idea."

In retrospect, Ed Koch had no regrets. He would have been miserable in Albany. Are you kidding? he asked friends. With three movie theatres and a choice between McDonald's and Bob's Big Boy for dinner? He retracted none of the *Playboy* interview; in fact, he believed it more than ever. His only regret was that he even pretended, for a second, to care which hayseed county he was in that day.

Ed Koch had consciously lied only twice in his life and both times were for the best possible reason, the *only* acceptable reason: to spare someone's feelings. One incident he regretted, the other he did not.

The first had occurred forty years earlier, when young Ed Koch was a soldier in the United States Army as it moved cautiously from the Brittany coast toward Germany. The tide had turned, Hitler had been beaten, and now the Third Army was basically mopping up, moving like a huge cotton swab across the scar of France. What made it dangerous was not the Nazis but what they had left behind. One day one of his closest friends in the platoon tripped over a shoe mine, a dreadful little explosive with which the Germans had studded the meadows of France. As Ed Koch cradled him in his arms, the man looked up and said, "My leg . . . I can't feel it . . ." "It's going to be fine," said Koch, fighting to hide his own horror. When the medics arrived they instantly amputated the man's leg, which had been hanging by a gelatinous thread. That was the lie Ed Koch didn't regret. What was wrong with filling those horrible moments with a little comfort?

The lie he would always regret, and that in fact had made the truth his religion, had to do with his mother. When the family found out she was dying of stomach cancer, no one told her. They barely believed it themselves, choosing instead to believe the fatuous optimism of the doctor. But Ed Koch knew better, knew that death was near for this woman who had denied herself almost everything to enhance the possibilities of little Eddie Koch, she had taught herself English phonetically by candlelight, for no other reason than to be able to pass along the wisdom of the New World to her darling Eddie. He loved her so, and he could not bear to tell her she was dying.

If Ed Koch could have taken back one thing in his life, it would have been that. The whole point of her life had been dignity. It was what she had passed along to him. To deny it to her, to instead subject her to a circus of half-smiles and lying doctors and nervous chatter, this was the greatest insult that could have been visited upon her. Surely he could have done better by the only woman he had ever truly loved.

He left the health club and stepped into his limousine. When he got to City Hall he would find out what the hell had gone wrong with POMP. Of course, POMP itself was a bit of a lie and a compromise. Why should buildings be given away to anyone? But if the advocates would not take a compromise, then fuck them, they would get both barrels right in the face. He was tired of half-truths. There had been too many of them lately.

Five

By the time little Eddie Koch was born, the Bronx of Albert Brackman had changed. Years earlier, Brackman had been assured by his friends in Tammany Hall that the astonishing new underground trains would burrow through the Manhattan schist to the Bronx. In 1911, the Lexington Avenue line found its way far closer to 850 Longwood Avenue than Albert Brackman dreamed it would, far closer in fact than he wanted it to. Emerging from the tunnel under the Harlem River, it ran on a trestle for many miles above Westchester Avenue, right past the longest side of Brackman's triangular six-story masterpiece. The limestone fire escape on which Martin Zulutoff's teenage daughter sunned herself was suddenly in the shade of the elevated tracks. Not only that, it actually trembled every time the train roared by towards Gun Hill Road. A fine mist of soot shook loose, and Rose Zulutoff soon learned not to wear her white sabbath dress on the balcony.

The families on the side of the building facing Longwood Avenue were able to endure the monstrous sound, so solid was Albert Brackman's structure. But for the families on the Westchester Avenue side, it was too much. Many of them began to look for another place to live.

It wasn't hard to find. Once the subway came, you were more likely to trip over a measuring tape than a vine. Sewer lines and utility lines were being laid out everywhere. With stunning speed, the little village of Springhust was paved over and built up. With

World War One came the end of the roving singing societies, so intense was the distaste for anything German. The meadows they had once tromped across were now rows of houses built by far less artistic and ambitious people than Albert Brackman and James Meehan.

When everything finally shook out at 850 Longwood Avenue, the very wealthiest were gone, along with their retinues of servants. Many of them settled well to the east along the waterfront in exclusive Throg's Neck. A few went west to the new boulevard known as the Grand Concourse—pre-billed as the Park Avenue of the Bronx, where, developers promised, there would never be an elevated train.

What remained at 850 Longwood was a slightly different class of people. Rather than the head of a business in the garment district, there might now be found his chief milliner or chief clerk. The building was still stable, and Passover and Yom Kippur were still celebrated with passion and solemnity. But it was no longer the country. And the topic of conversation was no longer the quality of the servants, but rather the strength of the unions to which everyone belonged. To Albert Brackman, however, all the monumental changes were insignificant. He still had his rent rolls filled and still had the feeling, seeing the lights lit at night, that he had done something wonderful.

It was into this Bronx, the Bronx of 1924, that young Eddie Koch was born. His father Louis had immigrated at the age of fourteen, as had the bride he would eventually take, a Polish beauty named Yetta Silpe. When the two eventually married, they moved into a new building on Crotona Park East, just a few blocks away from 850 Longwood Avenue. Now that the green Bronx was rapidly disappearing, attempts were being made to save some of it, and Crotona Park was one of the happiest examples. It was a thousand acres of wonderfulness, the jewel in its crown being Indian Lake, on which the Kochs boated in summer and skated in winter.

Louis never learned to write English, almost on principle, but this was more than compensated for by his wife, who was bright, loquacious, and very ambitious for her son. She was always initiating family outings, and one of the most glorious of these took place early in Eddie Koch's fifth year. Yetta Koch dressed him in the short pants and ruffled shirt he so detested, and the young family strode down the hill to the IRT subway station. They were going to the Bronx Zoo.

At the very idea, young Eddie brightened up. They were going to see zebras and elephants and camels!! Perhaps they were, but Mamma Yetta was more interested in the animal she had just read about in the Sunday Supplement of the *Daily Mirror*. They had *buffalos* at the Bronx Zoo. These beasts were the very symbol of America . . . an America lost and gone forever, granted, but American history was something her son should know about, if he was ever going to amount to anything.

Louis Koch lagged behind, trying to get his pipe lit. Louis didn't see the point of the trip, but most of all, he hated going to the neighborhood of the Prospect Avenue train stop. He might have been more amenable to the whole thing if they'd taken a horse-drawn trolley on the Boston Post Road.

The area down by the subway was known to be inhabited by trade unionists, and Louis Koch ran a non-union fur shop. The whole neighborhood was an "infestation" of radicalism, Louis groused to his friends. The whole garment industry was being infiltrated by Jews trying to undermine other Jews by driving businesses into the ground. It was rumored that Trotsky himself had lived in the neighborhood during the last years of World War One.

And of course, the trade unionists who lived around the Prospect Avenue train stop knew Louis Koch. He was a man who ran his own non-shop business, which meant he was an imperialist one step removed from the Czar himself.

But young Eddie Koch sensed none of this darkness, especially on his way to the zoo. As the family swept around the curve above Kelly Street, the hub of the Prospect Avenue train station came into view. Dominating it was 850 Longwood Avenue. Louis Koch himself had to concede it was something to see. Even partially obscured by the elevated train tracks, the limestone balconies of 850 Longwood stood in dramatic contrast to the drab fire escapes of the surrounding buildings. Yes, 850 was somewhat sooty, but it breathed life. On the street level was a cigar store where a thousand conversations and convocations were going on at once. True, some of it was political rabble-rousing. But another little knot of people were race track habitués, trying to figure out the card at Jamaica. Still another was a trio of actors from the nearby Yiddish theatre at McKinney Square, rehearsing their lines and having a heated argument about the nature of art. Even as a toddler being swept up the stairs to the train, Eddie Koch could feel the heat.

―――

No one knew where the sun had gone, or when it would be back. For two days the rain pelted Kochville. Occasionally someone would say the sky was brightening, but such remarks only seemed to encourage the awful torrents to begin again.

For most of each day a green garbage truck sat idling nearby, rain splattering off the hood. Hidden in the rear was Big Mouth, gaping and yawning, a green beast waiting to pounce. All that restrained it was the weather. To wipe out the homeless in the middle of a thunderstorm would appear heartless, and the public relations people in City Hall could afford no more blunders.

But no one doubted that the ax would soon fall. The mayor had been in a perpetual rage since learning that the homeless had sabotaged the POMP hearings. Now he wanted the problem solved, swiftly and permanently. When the rain ended, so would Kochville.

Even the imminence of its own destruction was of secondary importance to the little settlement. The homeless lived in the moment, and the problem of the moment was moisture. Nothing could be stored without breeding masses of maggots. White and swarming, they infested not just the food but the clothing. The only thing good to be said about the rain was that it kept the rats away. But at a certain point, ten rats were preferable to ten thousand swarming maggots. At least they were big and could be seen and therefore killed.

To avoid the unpleasantness of all this, the group spent many hours dozing through meetings in City Hall, leaving only a solitary figure to watch the community property. This was invariably Art, the Vietnam vet, who was uncomfortable in any building larger than a kubi hut.

But when the meetings stopped, everyone had to come out and face the rain, now so unrelenting that the shelter system, that gallery of horrors, began to look like a blazing hearth. When Big Mouth finally rolled, some began to think, it would be putting them out of their misery.

The only distraction was the arrival of a white man named Matthew. Instantly he intrigued Duke. For one thing, he was brilliant. Had he chosen to, thought Duke, Matthew could have been running City Hall himself. Or he could have been making millions, or curing AIDS, or achieving world peace. But Matthew had chosen to do none of these things. No doubt this had to do with his upbringing, of which he only slightly, but darkly, hinted. There were tales of drunken brooding Irish relatives, of beatings, even of the killing of a child. The end result was that Matthew's genius had been twisted. Every fiber of his intelligence had been bent towards getting over without ever working, at least in the conventional sense.

What Matthew had done was master the American Medicaid system. He had studied every pamphlet ever issued on the subject. He knew what benefits could still be collected for a knee injury on a city bus eight years ago. He knew how to get the signature of the head of the Cornell Medical Center on a standard requisition form and use it for endless chicanery. He understood the American pharmaceutical industry better than the head of the FDA. As a result of all this, Matthew was able to obtain prescription drugs almost at will. He then turned around and sold them at market prices and invested the profits in his own drug of choice, which was not available at Walgreen's—namely, heroin.

In short, Matthew was a junkie. Nor was he a bashful one. Matthew spent much of the afternoon talking about his scams, even drawing admiring whistles from other masters of petty crime in the camp, of which there were several. For a few hours, he was the biggest star on lower Broadway and made everyone forget the rain.

Late on the afternoon of his second day, Matthew was in the middle of a tale about posing as the chief resident of the Mayo Clinic and finding himself alone at midnight in the largest pharmaceutical warehouse in the Midwest. But even as his story built towards a climax, Matthew sensed he was losing his audience. People were looking not at him but at the sky. For the first time in recent memory, it was not gray or black. A clear dusk was breaking over City Hall Park.

The faces, which ordinarily would have basked in the return of the sun, were instead panicked. The orange light was glinting off Big Mouth. At any moment, they knew, it would roll out and finish them. Quiet good-byes were made in the camp, and since neither phone numbers nor addresses are exchanged among the homeless, names were spelled carefully and hopefully remembered.

Just as the last light was dying, a small, stocky man emerged from City Hall and strode towards the settlement. This figured to be a city official with the white-flag proposal: go peaceably, and spare us the unpleasantness of obliterating you. Marc Greenberg girded himself for the confrontation. All day he had struggled anew with the bowel-twisting question—resist and defy, putting everyone at risk, or give up gracefully and savor the small prizes already won?

Now the official was almost upon the camp, and Greenberg thought he recognized the face. He was not one of the Koch deputy mayors, nor was he a higher-up in the Parks Department, but he was somehow prominent in urban affairs. It seemed to Greenberg that the man had been on the news only recently; something about the eviction of a three-hundred-pound woman from an apartment in Queens.

Then, when the man was very close, Greenberg felt a jolt. Yes, this man had indeed been involved in the Queens eviction. But he was not the one doing the evicting; instead, he was defending the three-hundred-pound woman! His name was Norman Siegel, and he was the head of the New York Civil Liberties Union.

No greater happiness could have been felt by the people inside the Alamo had Sam Houston ever shown up. Norman Siegel! He seemed to appear at the most hopeless times to defend the most hapless people. A middle-aged Jew from Brooklyn, Siegel had worked in the southern civil rights movement alongside Ed Koch and Henry Stern. But that was where the résumés diverged. Siegel had never taken that inexplicable turn to the right, nor had he stabilized into an easy liberal complacency. Instead, middle age had only deepened his rage. He was a potent combination: a sharp legal mind, a ball-breaking persistence, and an uncanny knack for television coverage.

This time, Siegel felt he had ferreted out something very big indeed. He had seen the original story on the *Eleven O'Clock News*, and after hearing about Duke York's appearance at the POMP hearing, he had paid a visit to Henry Stern. As all of Kochville craned an ear, Siegel described the meeting.

"Hello, Henry."

"Hello, Norman."

"I wanted to talk to you about the people in the park."

"I know about them, Norman. They were in here yesterday."

"What did you tell them?"

"What do you think I told them? I told them they couldn't live in the park. It's against the law."

"They're not living there, they're holding a political demonstration."

"Really? What about all those huge bags of junk they haul around with them?"

"Aren't bags allowed?"

"Come on, Norman . . ."

"What about the sandwiches the office workers eat at lunchtime. Aren't they in bags?"

"I'm talking about *big* bags," said Henry Stern with some exasperation.

"But there are little sandwiches and big sandwiches. Would someone with a hero sandwich be barred from the park?"

"Stop it, Norman. I don't want to get into this game with you. I'm talking about foul-smelling vagrants carrying huge shopping bags!"

"So shopping bags are illegal?"

"In each hand, with all their earthly belongings in them? YES!!"

"So one hand must be free? A woman crossing Central Park with two shopping bags from Bloomingdale's is in violation of the law?"

ALL RIGHT. STOP IT!! MUZZLE THAT BULLDOG!! Stern could feel the teeth locked on his ankle. Siegel was going to take this as far as it would go. If it got into court, the case could drag on for months and kick up a disastrous dust storm of publicity. The wiser choice might be to let these derelicts stay where they were until the budget hearings were over. At least they would be more or less invisible in all the other hubbub around City Hall. And afterwards, there could be no possible justification for calling them lobbyists.

"Until July 1, Norman. Period."

"My word of honor," said Norman Siegel. And that was it.

Stern watched him amble off, doubtless no longer amused even by his own ducks.

Siegel's story astonished Kochville. A meeting between white men had actually been resolved in their favor. And the larger reality was unbelievable. July 1? That was like a date on a *lease*, for God's sake. Like a house! With a roof!! And it was three weeks away. Three solid, succulent, leisurely, summery weeks!!

Siegel prepared to leave, wishing the men luck and accepting all sorts of slovenly, profuse thanks. "That's fine, guys, glad to do it. Who should I contact if I need to?"

No one spoke.

"I mean, who's in charge?" said Siegel.

The question hung in the air, and Siegel finally realized it wasn't going to be answered. "Just call me if you need me," he said, and with that he was gone, another notch in his attaché case.

Everyone stood around looking at each other. A large question had been raised.

"What do you think?" said Duke York finally to Marc Greenberg.

"Who gives a shit what he thinks?" said an unfamiliar voice from the back. It was a strident new tone—an inappropriate one for this moment of celebration, thought Greenberg. Nevertheless, he acknowledged it. "The man's right," said Marc Greenberg. "It's none of my business."

"Well, how you think we ought to set it up, then?" said Duke York to Greenberg.

"Nigger, what is your problem?" said the hostile man from the back. Now all eyes turned to take him in more completely. The reality of the camp was that every few hours people left and new people came. Few asserted themselves this immediately. Greenberg measured him. He didn't look homeless. He was a portly middle-aged black man, and he didn't have that grimy, beaten-down aspect. He looked almost a little prosperous. But he seemed to have the bad, hot blood of a man half his age. "Finally get something from the white man," he said, "and you tryin' to give it right back. Stupid-ass fool."

Now Greenberg was feeling protective of Duke. "I don't think it's a stupid question," he said. "I think you should have a leader, or you'll never get anywhere."

There was a silence, and Greenberg sensed it would be an opportune time for him to leave. He had arranged a radio interview for Princess on WBAI, a prominent leftist station, and they were already late. Far more important than that, he felt it was time to allow these men to take a step on their own.

The young Jew and the pregnant woman disappeared, and silence continued to hang over the camp. For a long time no one moved. Then heads slowly began to raise and turn toward the direction of the shadow under a giant elm. First one face, then a couple more, then a group of five, like compass points swinging to the north. Finally every face was looking at the man named Lock.

The reclusive half-Indian, half-black man was sitting under the tree that had become his home. Until now he had more or less ignored the melodrama, as if his thoughts were on some higher plane. As he began to understand what was being asked of him, he surveyed the men with hooded, tired eyes. Finally he stared at Duke and seemed to say, "Why me?"

Duke understood the question. He himself would have been a more obvious choice for a leader. He was the most eloquent, the most at ease in front of people. Little Art had the most powerful command qualities. He had taken charge the first night like the combat veteran he was. Even the new arrival Matthew, were he not white, would have been a more likely candidate than the reticent, almost sullen Lock. But there was something about Lock that demanded attention. He drew you into him. You believed him. You wanted to follow him places.

Though there were thirty pairs of eyes on him, Lock resisted the pressure and thought slowly. He had been taught by Charles Locke, his father, always to take whatever time he needed.

Yes, Locke was the name. The *E* on his army fatigue jacket had fallen off. It was a rare name in the Northeast, but a well-known one in North Carolina, where he was born. Larry Locke, which was his real name, came from Locke's Creek, an area beside a bubbling little tributary of the Cape Fear River. Both the creek and the man were named after the British family Locke, who once owned the land and the several hundred slaves that worked it. The slaves had taken the family's last name during Reconstruction, and now there were far many more black Lockes than white Lockes along the banks of the Cape Fear.

"The owners were drinkers and whoremongers," remembers the editor of the local newspaper, "and the slaves were hard workers. So one race died out and the other survived."

During Reconstruction the land was divided up among the slaves, and the piece that Larry Locke's great-great-grandfather got was a piece of good luck. Anything could grow on it, and over a couple of hundred years, just about everything did. First had come cotton, during slavery. Then the blacks put in tobacco as their first cash crop. Tobacco will ultimately ruin a piece of land, as it will a lung. The land gets chunked up somehow, and blanched of all its minerals. But this little twenty-acre piece was so resilient that it was reincarnated, miraculously soon, as a cherry orchard. The first tree that young Larry Locke remembered seeing out his window was a cherry tree, and his crib was fashioned by his father from a gorgeous hunk of cherry wood.

But that was to be Charles Locke's only presence in his son's early life—the cradle that rocked him. Otherwise, the father was absent, and the boy grew up among women, his grandmother and one of Charles's sisters. Rarely did his father visit, and when he did, he was preoccupied. The women spoke quietly of the bad feelings between Larry's parents, of dreadful fights, of spilled blood. This they attributed to the Indian heritage of Locke's mother. It was rumored that *her* mother, a full-blooded Cherokee, had killed her husband with an ax.

It was with some dismay, then, that the four-year-old Larry Locke learned that he was being sent to live with his mother. He was taken away from Locke's Creek, with its cherry trees and its rushing water, and brought to a sterile subdivision closer to town. His reaction was intense and visceral. The change seemed to damage him physically. Soon he was known as the frail little boy who could not even walk the half-mile to school without stopping several times to get some air into his feeble lungs.

Ever since, whenever he had to reach deeply for a decision, it was the clear voice of his father that he heard and the shrill voice of his mother that he rejected. Now, with the offer of leadership in front of him, he closed his eyes and addressed it as his father would have sized up a farm chore: large task or small, you always did what you could. That was your duty, particularly to yourself. And so Larry Locke wrestled on the cloak of leadership, to see if it fit.

In his mind's eye he saw the panel of the Board of Estimates behind a horseshoe-shaped desk in front of a few dozen spectator's benches. This had never seemed right to Larry Locke. The board members sat whispering and chuckling to themselves at a great distance from the people they were supposed to be serving.

That very morning, to avoid a particularly intense early shower, everyone had sat in on a meeting of the City Council. In the council chambers, the gallery was a horseshoe on a mezzanine floor, and all the council members were down below, as if in a pit. Their individual desks faced the front of the room, away from the gallery. This also struck Larry Locke as a bit remote. What he liked about it, though, was the procedures. If members had something to say, they stood up at their desk and talked. They could talk to the headman at the front, they could pivot and talk to another council member, they could even look up and address the gallery. Locke was struck with the good will of it all. The person who was standing was allowed to finish. Sometimes someone would try to hoot him or her down, but then the headman would intervene and protect the rights of the speaker. You could say your piece, and when you were finished, you sat down. That struck Larry Locke as pretty sound.

"Let's pull these around," he said suddenly, indicating the green park benches.

The men began to wrestle with the benches, some of which had been chained together just to prevent them from being moved. Eventually, half a dozen were manipulated into a circle. Larry Locke walked into the middle of it. "Everyone sit, please," he said. Everyone did so.

"I never did this before . . ."

"Can't hear you," said a voice.

Larry Locke turned to the voice and repeated himself, but now the people behind him couldn't hear. So this was the first problem. In a circle, especially outdoors, you had to keep rotating to take everyone in. And you had to be loud. But after a couple of more sentences, that felt fine to Larry Locke. Because to say something loud you had to mean it, and that was the point.

"I never did this kind of thing before, but I think we should do it like this. Anybody that's got something to say, stand up and say it."

These last couple of words seem to hang in the air long after they were spoken. It was a while before his thoughts churned out another sentence. Larry Locke, as it turned out, was not a man of words. But by the time he sat down, people felt as if the first rule of Kochville had been drawn up. Anybody who had anything to say stood up and said it. There was nothing more to it.

It wasn't necessarily simple, however. The next man who stood to talk was little Art, who requested that people stow their gear by the railing, where it would be easier to keep an eye on it. To this someone immediately objected, suggesting that the concrete area by the benches was less muddy. But Art had been interrupted, which was not allowed. All eyes turned to Larry Locke for a ruling. "Let the man speak," said Larry, and so little Art finished his remarks before the man with the opposite point of view was allowed to rise.

Then the man who had been so hostile to Marc Greenberg rose to speak. He identified himself as Horace and said he had been an activist when the rest of them were in their cradles. He proceeded to dump a load of invective on everyone involved, from Greenberg to Art to Locke to Duke. The insultees, however, were constrained by the rule to be silent, at least until their turn came. All instincts to shout down the irritating, belligerent man had to be repressed.

Then a gangling, light-skinned man rose whom no one recognized. His name, as he spoke it from the circle, was hard to catch. It sounded like Mr. Cooper, but the man seemed to be Indian, as in Bombay, so perhaps the name was Koo-pah, or Cupta, or something like it. In any case, Mr. Cooper was not in his right mind. Not long after he began, it became clear to everyone that the issue he was addressing was unique to him. He was complaining about the array of multicolored laser lights being shot through his brain by the federal government.

All eyes swivelled to Larry Locke. Larry struggled for a moment with the extenuating circumstances, but decided that the basic principle was important to uphold. "Let the man speak," he said.

And speak he did. Mr. Cooper touched for a while on the subject of microbes from the planet Venus. He spoke of giant vaginas the size of the Grand Canyon, steaming and hissing poisonous gasses. At one point Mr. Cooper said the word *purple* a hundred times in rapid succession and shortly afterward repeated the word *flagellation* roughly the same number of times. By the time he was winding down, about an hour later, Mr. Cooper was drenched with sweat. Upon concluding, he took off into the night on the dead run.

After a considerable silence, Larry Locke rose. "I think we ought to call it a night," he said, and the group split off into various small clusters, unrolling their blankets and considering the problems of democracy.

Sometime later, everyone who was still awake gathered around a small transistor radio tuned to WBAI, which was now broadcasting the interview with Marc Greenberg and Princess. In a sense, she was everyone's bride, especially for the men who had left children behind somewhere. They felt a stake in her pregnancy and tried to coddle her and baby her, while at the same time rejecting her sexual advances.

The radio crackled to life and there she was, answering questions in that voice of hers that was itself so like a baby's. She revealed on the airwaves what she had until now not shared with anyone in Kochville. Who was the father of her child? She wasn't sure, she said, because she had been raped several different times one night in the tunnels below Grand Central Station. It might have been any of a number of terrifying men. Squatting over the radio in the darkness of City Hall Park, Kochville felt a deep sadness and indignation, not just for her, or for themselves, but for all the world.

<hr />

Nothing set the mayor off like the sight of Norman Siegel.

That was under ordinary circumstances. But on the night of June 5, the outline of Siegel's figure moving across the plaza of City Hall made the mayor's bile absolutely percolate. The word had reached him about Siegel's deal with Henry Stern; what it meant for Ed Koch was another three weeks of public humiliation.

What the hell had Stern been thinking of? Who the hell empowered him to make this deal anyway?! The mayor's last memo to Stern had said that the matter had to be handled sensitively. That didn't mean give away the whole store! It meant find a middle ground between coddling these people and grinding them up with a garbage truck in front of a dozen goddamn reporters!

But Henry Stern was not in his office, so Ed Koch had no choice but to focus his anger on the only available target: the dim silhouette of Norman Siegel. As Siegel leaned against a pillar and riffled through the contents of his attaché case, the mayor imagined what was in there—legal briefs on behalf of every scumbag in New York. No, that wasn't quite fair. Ed Koch was still enough of a lawyer to admire the spirit of the public defender. And in a sense Siegel, as the head of the New York Civil Liberties Union, was the public defender of mankind. Koch understood the need to defend the most unpopular cases, even if it made one's blood boil. In fact, he had always been rather proud of his own position on the rights of the Nazi Party to march through the Jewish suburb of Skokie, Illinois. Talk about having to bite a bullet!! Koch was a fiercely proud Jew with several personal ties to the Holocaust, and yet he understood the constitutional importance of allowing these morons to stage their parade.

So in principle, Norman Siegel did what had to be done. What made him so despicable, thought the mayor, was that he didn't really give a damn about his clients. He was willing to put them through just about anything to make a splash or a legal point. The most irritating example was the last time Siegel and the mayor had clashed directly, in a case that captured the attention of all eight million New Yorkers. Just thinking about the Billie Boggs case so distressed the mayor that he reached into his drawer for his new tranquilizer of choice—white mushrooms. When the mayor had stress he ate, and so his doctors had told him "eat these. At least they're healthy."

As it happens, the Billie Boggs case was also about homelessness. But even more to the point, thought Ed Koch, it was about mental illness. Billie Boggs was a middle-aged black woman who had lived on the street in midtown Manhattan. Even among bag women she stood out as particularly disturbing. She urinated and defecated on herself, and those were her most endearing acts. When people gave her money she tore it up, and when clothes were given to her she ran into traffic and flung them away. She physically attacked black men on the street, with whom she clearly had deep issues; when social workers approached her, she chased them away, screaming "Suck my big black dick!!" And then, as a final garnish on her dish of insanity, there was the matter of her umbrella. She had a huge, shabby black umbrella that she held over her head every moment of every day . . . except when it rained.

Surely this woman was as mad as a hatter and the perfect test case for the mayor's Project Help, which was designed to get crazy people off the streets—involuntarily—and into hospitals. Predictably, the Norman Siegels of the world objected, invoking the claptrap of the sixties' intellectuals who the mayor felt were responsible for the whole problem to begin with.

In the sixties, budget cuts and wonder drugs like Thorazine caused many state mental hospitals to close. Bravo, cried people like Ken Kesey, Tomas Szasz, and R. D. Laing. The former, with his novel *One Flew Over the Cuckoo's Nest*, had convinced everyone that mental institutions were merely places of political repression. The latter pair declared that "in an insane world, insanity is the only appropriate response." The legacy of all this, in Ed Koch's opinion, was the army of madmen roaming the streets of New York . . . defended in their right to do so by Norman Siegel.

Of course, Siegel would justify himself on constitutional grounds. To incarcerate the harmless mentally ill, he would say, was like putting people in jail because they were ugly. He would go on to recite the abuses of the psychiatric profession: the lobotomies, the shock treatments . . . things that had no medical justification whatsoever, other than that because the patients were so screwed up it couldn't hurt.

Fine. The mayor accepted all that. What he could not accept was dangerous madmen on the loose. Shortly after his second inauguration, a man prematurely released from a mental ward boarded the Staten Island Ferry and killed two people with a saber. So the primary question, legally, had come down to this: how dangerous were they, to themselves or to others?

For Koch, the Billie Boggs case had been airtight. Could anybody seriously suggest that this woman was *not* harmful to herself? How could Siegel even take the case with a straight face?

But take it he did, and for every one of the city lawyer's points, Siegel had an irritating parry.

She darted into traffic? . . . What New Yorker in a hurry didn't?

She tore up money? . . . She was insulted by it, by the unspoken implication that all black women could be bought.

She urinated and defecated on herself? . . . Hey, what New Yorker had not experienced the difficulty of finding a rest room in midtown?

She chased social workers away, screaming obscenities? . . . Well, her experiences with authority had not been good. The last time someone from the city had come to talk to her, she had found herself handcuffed to a radiator for six hours.

All of it was semantics and legal rapier play. What it would hinge on, ultimately, was the testimony of Billie Boggs. The day she took the witness stand, the fox Siegel had her dressed in a modest shift. She had a bit of the actress in her, and she seemed to delight in taking on the persona of a reasonable human being. In an even, crisp tone she recounted her employment history: she had worked for a while for a human rights agency, and briefly with Bell Laboratories. She expressed her joys and regrets with modesty and self-deprecating humor. She was someone you wanted to go out with for coffee.

Mad with frustration, the city's lawyer tried to rattle her but only succeeded in making himself look like a petulant bully. As a last, desperate measure he played the prosecution's trump card. What about the umbrella? What human being in her right mind holds an umbrella over her head all day long EXCEPT WHEN IT'S RAINING??!!

Well, replied Billie Boggs, she supposed it was something she had picked up as a child in the South. The gracious southern white ladies carried around petite umbrellas on lots of sunny days. They called them . . . (and here Ms. Boggs fluttered her eyes a bit before saying the word) . . . *parasols.*

Barely able to contain his own infatuation with Billie Boggs, the judge ordered her instant release. Within twenty-four hours, she was back on the corner of Fifty-Third Street and Third Avenue, urinating and defecating on herself and screaming to passersby "Suck my big black dick!!"

Ed Koch watched Norman Siegel disappear into a New York City taxicab. Then he grabbed a fistful of white mushrooms, stuffed them into his cheeks, and tried Henry Stern's office one more time.

<hr>

Spring proceeds in old City Hall Park like the ripening of a fruit. At first there is a rawness and a harshness. Then come the first messengers of summer: the magnolia and the apple blossoms. Then, as these fall away, man-made beauty arrives: beds of tulips and other groomed patches of color. But as June deepens towards July, even the planned gardens give up and are overwhelmed by the lushness of summer. Were you to edit out everything else— the buildings and machinery of the largest municipal government on earth—you would be left with a rioting overgrown meadow. Bees and flies buzz lazily around. Even though the employees of the Parks Department are very much in evidence— cleaning, tending, digging—it is as if a giant sign hung over the place saying GONE FISHING.

Thomas Sligh, the custodian in charge of City Hall Park, was a black man of about fifty. He had many gifts, not the least of which was the joy he took in his work. You would have thought him an English Lord tending his personal hydrangeas. Above him in the byzantine hierarchy of the Parks Department, anxious memos caromed about concerning the thirty homeless people in the park. But Sligh had already reached a practical understanding with them. Like many of them, he was a black veteran of the United States Armed Forces. There was a social bond among black vets, and it had to do with dignity. You were putting your ass on the line for a society that basically despised you, so you did your work as well as you could, for its own sake. If you were doing it for approval from above, you were barking up the wrong tree. That approval, no matter what you did, would ultimately be withheld.

Thomas Sligh cultivated the gardens of City Hall Park not to impress Henry Stern but to please himself. The homeless vets of Kochville were bivouacking to perfection, cleaning up not only after themselves but after the slovenly lunch hour office workers. Sligh had absolutely no problem with them. All the tools of his trade—the rakes, the stiff metal brooms, the trowels—all of it was at the disposal of Kochville. Horticulturally, they were the platoon and he was the sergeant.

For the men and women of Kochville, however, the semi-permanence of June brought greater challenges than gardening. It soon became clear that a method of food gathering had to be found beyond arbitrary begging or depending on socialites for hors d'oeuvres. It was a long way to any soup kitchens. At one point the Hare Krishna people passed through and set up for a while, but good luck trying to find anything substantial in their gruel. Lonnie from Tennessee jammed his arms in up to the elbows, looking for a piece of meat or even a carrot. The horrified young Krishnas withdrew and did not return.

It was time for a display of leadership from Larry Locke.

There was a prosperous delicatessen across Park Row, and one morning Larry strode in to see the owner, a slight, frazzled Greek. Larry explained that there were thirty people across the street in the park, they were part of an important social movement, and they needed coffee.

Usually there was no love lost between black men and immigrant New Yorkers. The prevailing attitude was "Get the hell out of here, nobody ever gave *me* anything!!" But Larry Locke was not begging. His ragged appearance notwithstanding, he presented himself with a curious mixture of dignity and pragmatism. He made the request in the same spirit with which he once might have said, when he was a sergeant in the United States Army, "Yo, I need coffee for thirty men!" The Greek was impressed. Social movements were important. Coffee was important. When he needed help from his uncle Stavros to start a business, he got it. Locke walked back across Park Row with thirty cups of coffee.

This was the model from which they would work. There were restaurants all over the City Hall area that threw out tons of food at the end of every business day. A food committee was assembled consisting of Duke, Matthew, and Lonnie, the most silver-tongued manipulators. Larry was wary of this last appointment, because Lonnie continued to give off the scent of danger. But there could be no quarrelling with his results. The man from Tennessee could talk a beaver out of his teeth, as he put it.

What more cunning trio ever set out on a mission! Soon Matthew the devious junkie had gotten a Pizza Hut to agree to donate the day's remnants. Duke scored with a Taco Bell and wrung a few tears and a daily box of stale donuts out of a bakery. Lonnie, oozing treacly southern charm, convinced a chubby teenage countergirl at Au Bon Pain to part with her leftover croissants. Nutritionally it was all a mess, but nutrition is the last concern of the homeless.

Once the food problem was under control, the security system was established. Each man would pull a two-hour watch duty throughout the night on a rotating basis. You never went to sleep until you knew your replacement was awake and erect. In the wee small hours, part of your duty was to bring him a cup of coffee from the Greek place across the street.

Art was in charge of this operation, and he and Duke became Larry's undisputed lieutenants. Directly below them in the hierarchy was Matthew. Larry tended to trust the white man with certain matters because of his enormous intelligence and because it was important, politically, to have a white man on the ruling council.

"Don't seem fair to me," said Lonnie. "I been here longer. Ought to be me." But the appointment stood, and Lonnie's contentiousness became a part of the daily life.

Horace was a far greater problem. His roly-poly looks belied a vicious, devouring intellect. He found fault with everything and tried to undermine the Locke government at every turn. He never tired of reminding everyone how pathetic Kochville was within the larger scheme of black politics . . . but he never left.

The dissent of Horace and Lonnie, however, remained impotent. First of all, they hated each other and could offer no unified opposition. Far more important, there was nothing to complain about. Incumbents win elections when the economy is good and the country is at peace. Revolutions in homeless camps rarely succeed when food is plentiful and the trees are blossoming.

The camp fell into a sublime rhythm. Before first light, Locke made his trip across the street to get the coffee. The men would be lured out of their blankets by the smell, and as dawn washed through the glen they rose, sipping, conversing, philosophizing, greeting the new day. When the rush hour seemed imminent, the bivouac began. Deploying Thomas Sligh's brooms and rakes, they cleaned up City Hall Park. By the time the office workers began crisscrossing the park on their way to work, it was as prim as a formal garden. Then, after the workers were safely in their offices, Kochville addressed its personal needs. There was a bathroom in the emergency room of nearby Beekman Hospital, and Duke had talked the officials into making it available for the homeless.

When they returned, teeth brushed and bladders empty, clothes were washed in the charming old Delacorte Fountain and dried on railings. At first this seemed brazen, but finally quite consistent with Siegel's arrangement with the city. They had a lease through June, and so they moved in.

Then, in the afternoon, they went inside the big building. Their political sophistication had grown considerably. No longer did they merely doze in the splendid air-conditioning. Now they were beginning to understand what was going on and how they could influence it. They were learning the ways of the enemy. Once, at a Rent Guidelines hearing, landlords arrived bearing signs with hammers and sickles . . . implying that anyone who wanted to keep rents low was a communist. The strategy worked, and the landlords got their rent increases.

The lesson was not lost on Kochville. Soon they had acquired posterboard and magic markers from sympathetic stationery stores. After that the camp's artistic talent had an outlet, and they rarely attended a city council meeting without a visual aid. Sometimes the signs had little to do with the issue on the floor of the council . . . like the florid, hallucinogenic drawings that seemed to be Duke's specialty. At other times the drawings cut right to the essence of something, like the time Princess held a picture of a single teardrop over her head.

And so the time passed. One day a young girl named Patricia arrived and seemed to round out the camp in some rich, fulsome way, like a cherry on top. She was no more than eleven but had already endured unspeakable abuse from her so-called family and now preferred the street to home. And so a tribal feeling grew. Generations cared for generations, and there were elders and wise chiefs of the tribe, and maidens, and foolish young braves.

Six

Shortly before young Eddie Koch's family left the Bronx in 1929, Loew's Paradise went up on the Grand Concourse. For the people on Crotona Park, for the residents of 850 Longwood Avenue, and even for the now elderly Albert Brackman, the sumptuous movie palace was the miracle of the age. It cost four million dollars to build, which would have supplied much of the armaments of World War One. The theatre had four thousand seats, and its vast domed ceiling was designed to look like the night sky, studded with a thousand light bulbs for stars. And across this firmament every night, diaphanous cottony clouds were blown by machine.

In the ensuing Depression, of course, the opulence of the Paradise seemed a cruel joke. But as the economy regained its health, the ornate theatre became the symbol of recovery. On a practical level it pumped huge amounts of money into the Bronx . . . or at least kept it there. Why journey to Radio City Music Hall in Manhattan when you had something even grander a few blocks away?

The residents of 850 Longwood Avenue went a step further. Why schlep all the way to the Grand Concourse when you had the RKO Franklin across the street? The Franklin was to the Paradise what a park is to a forest. A little jewel box, it had started life as a vaudeville house not long after the mason named McGraw laid the cornerstone of the synagogue on Prospect Avenue. Now it had made the transition to the movies.

On a summer night in 1940, the former Rose Zulutoff awaited

the arrival of the young man who was courting her daughter. No longer the girl in white worried about the soot from the new subway trains but instead a portly matron, Rose sat tonight on the same limestone fire escape where she had once posed languidly, hoping to attract the attention of that promising young furrier, Maurice Rifkin.

The Number 2 train roared past and Rose cursed it silently, as she had a thousand times before. But when the street, the trestle, the very universe stopped quaking, Rose surveyed the vista with satisfaction. She could plan the young people's evening from where she sat. Dinner would be taken care of right downstairs, in the Blue Danube restaurant. The owners were Austrian Jews who had gotten out just ahead of Hitler. The food was OK as long as the stupid daughter-in-law didn't undercook the veal. For the main event of the night, of course, they need go no further than the RKO Franklin. Rose could see the marquee very clearly: an Errol Flynn movie, and *Footlight Parade*, a musical. Nice. They wanted to go somewhere afterwards? What was wrong with—indeed what could be better than—Shapiro's Ice Cream Parlor, right next to the Franklin? They could be home by midnight, never having left the purview of Rose Zulutoff Rifkin.

Unfortunately, young Richard Silverblatt had other designs. He arrived breathless from work (an accounting firm in Manhattan, of which Rose approved) bearing two tickets to the ball game at Yankee Stadium. Of this Rose didn't approve. At this point she had to concede that the ballpark on River Avenue, now sixteen years old, was probably here to stay. But why leave the neighborhood when there was so much to do right here?

Because, explained young Silverblatt, the Yankees had a hot new player, an Italian kid from San Francisco named DiMaggio who was tearing up the league. He was supposed to be a Ruth with speed, a Honus Wagner with power.

We'll see about that, thought Rose, watching them go. But how mad could she be? It wasn't like he was taking her to the

Latin Quarter to see naked girls. He was a good kid, and despite the long shadows of the events in Europe, the Bronx life was a good life.

Through the Second World War, 850 Longwood kept its head up and kept the home fires burning. Many windows, including the Zulutoff's curved oval window on the top floor, displayed flags bearing various numbers of stars. Each star indicated a kid fighting overseas, and someone counted thirty–five stars in all in the windows of 850 Longwood. And every so often an unfamiliar young officer arrived, and stared down at his polished shoes as he rang a doorbell with one of those awful telegrams.

But most of the young men of the Bronx survived and came home to a different world. Shortly after VJ day, a curious new store appeared at 850 Longwood Avenue. Rose Zulutoff Rifkin was known to spend an hour at the bus stop, letting two or three busses go by as she watched the new walls and counters going up. The new owner fascinated her. She was a beautiful, lithe, olive-skinned woman who supervised the construction with grace and authority. Many in the building assumed she was some sort of Sephardic Jew, perhaps from Turkey or Eastern Russia, but others had more exotic speculations. Could she be a gypsy? Was this to be a Romanian fortune-telling parlor?

The truth was more exotic than the rumor. Her name was Victoria Hernandez, and she was establishing the first Spanish music store in the Bronx. She had started Casa Hernandez in the twenties, on upper Madison Avenue in Manhattan, several miles to the south. The enterprise had seemed as eccentric then as it did now. In the twenties there were only a smattering of Spanish-speaking people in New York, hardly enough to support a music store. Slowly, however, refugees from the dreadful poverty of the Caribbean were arriving. Here in *Nueva York*, they would not have to walk barefoot over rocky, scorpion-infested roads, not have to subsist on rice and green bananas.

Then came the Harlem riots of 1943, shredding the fabric of a stable, fashionable neighborhood, and forcing Victoria Hernandez to relocate. To her later chagrin, the great waves of Puerto Rican immigration would arrive at the very spot she was vacating, a neighborhood that would become known as El Barrio, or Spanish Harlem.

But the business would eventually come to her, she was confident, even in the Bronx. The reputation of Casa Hernandez was assured: she was the sister of Rafael Hernandez, the great troubadour-composer, arguably the greatest in the Latin culture. Rafael opened his mouth, and even the orchids swooned.

Not only that, she felt at home among the Jews. Albert Brackman, the old man with whom she negotiated the lease, was a gentleman, unmistakable in any language. She felt equally welcomed by her neighbors, for whom she was an exotic spice on a wholesome meal. Her presence was not something to be overlooked but embraced. The old trade unionists' philosophy was pure and clear on this point: the brotherhood of man was inviolable. The elderly Albert Brackman, especially, beamed. Hadn't it been a forbidden friendship between himself and the architect James Meehan that had created the building?

It would have taken a truly dark cloud, at this point, to mitigate old Brackman's joy in the thing he had wrought. Every space rented, even the stores . . . because of Brackman's insistence on the bay windows that Meehan had tried to talk him out of. Shopkeepers could display their wares panoramically, and 850 was the most desirable retail space in the neighborhood.

But this old man's joy sprang from an even deeper well. This was his creation. He was not an artistic man. His skill with a drawn line or a note of music or a piece of doggerel was not even worth mentioning. He loved his only daughter, but she lived in the West now with her own family. His wife was long dead. His other buildings, while serviceable, were lackluster. But this one people noticed. They remarked on the deep cornices, on the limestone balconies (to the day he died he would insist on calling

III

them that, never fire escapes), and on the miraculous curved oval window.

Indeed, at night, when all the lights were on, it looked like six strings of jewels, something a countess would wear. And behind every light, Albert Brackman knew, there was life. People were arguing, cooking dinner, making love, making monumental plans, making trivial ones. And he had set it all in motion, like Chekhov, the great writer of Russian plays to whom he was said to be distantly related. Albert Brackman did not write his characters' lines, but he had made the great marble and brick stage on which they played it all out.

≡

The month of June in City Hall Park was, for most of Kochville, a period of grace in hard, troubled lives. Things grew—on the lush lawns around them, and inside them: delicate buds of confidence and security. But for the homeless the clock is always ticking towards some inexorable doom—whether of their own creation or of the killing winter itself. This year, for thirty of them, the clock was ticking towards July 1.

Finally, after a month of clipping, trimming, adding here, taking there, robbing Peter to pay Paul, robbing Peter generally, embezzling Paul, Phil, and Polly, and all of the above, the budget for New York City, fiscal year 1989, was agreed upon. At 8 P.M. on the night of July 1, it was scheduled to come to a vote. Kochville filed into the gallery of the City Council chambers like the condemned to their execution. Some of them had hoped the budget talks might never end. It only seemed that way, cracked the City Hall pundits.

Had they been less naive, the homeless would have known that even tonight's vote was a foregone conclusion. Once presented to the City Council, the budget was a fait accompli. Not only was it never outvoted, no one ever voted against it. Unanimity was a way the council members had of saying to each other "We had our little squabbles, but screw it, it's summer, let's put this thing to bed and go to the beach!!"

In a sense, this was literally true. The next day was the City Council picnic, a time for reconciliation and beer and potato salad and the beginning of the light summer workload.

But tonight the old hall was about to experience something new. Abe Gerges had asked to address the entire body before the vote. Gerges was the lanky, quiet council member who along with Ruth Messinger had received Duke and Greenberg and the original vigil keepers on the very first day. As he rose to speak, an ominous feeling ran along the row of *fin-de-siècle* desks. Gerges had a serious look on his face. Clearly, he was not rising to say "Surf's up."

As far as the council leadership was concerned, Gerges had always been a handful. It was predictable. As a young lawyer with long hair, Gerges had defended several Black Panthers. After his election to the council, he served briefly on the Committee on Economic Development, but when it became clear that his mission was to obstruct construction and to insult the city's real estate kings, he was thrown off. Then they tried to mollify him by giving him his own committee, the Homeless Committee.

But did he have to take it so goddamn seriously?! It was meant to be an area of interest, a sort of hobby, not a crusade, for God's sake! Every day Gerges was in a different shelter, testing the air for tuberculosis, checking the kitchen for cockroaches, measuring the space between beds.

It was vexing to the leadership because there was always the other Abe Gerges; affable Abe, the son of Sol Gerges, the garment center presser and his gorgeous wife Bella. Abe Gerges, president of his local B'nai B'rith lodge. Abe Gerges, who as a kid out of college got a job as a waiter in the borscht belt and sang in the variety shows and danced with the single women. Good neighbor Abe, who just last week closed in *The Music Man* at the community theatre around the corner from his house in Brooklyn.

So the council leadership held its breath: which Abe Gerges was going to show up tonight? The William Kunstler clone who was going to hold your feet to the fire, or some lightweight who was going to sing "Seventy-Six Trombones"?

After Gerges had spoken for about a minute, they had their answer. Clearly he was not making a symbolic protest or going on record with a respectful minority position. He was breaking balls. He did not consider his Homeless Committee a "hobby," he told the council. He considered homelessness a deep embarrassment to himself and to the prosperous New York he had grown up in. He found the budget insensitive to these issues, and he was voting against it, and he wanted everyone else to do the same.

The reactions on the floor ran from mortification to rage. Voting against the budget was the ultimate foul, a terminal act of bad sportsmanship. Was he also hoping the potato salad at tomorrow's picnic would be rancid?

Even his allies felt he'd gone over an invisible line. Miriam Friedlander, the brilliant councilwoman from Manhattan, knew that everything Gerges was saying was true, but twisted away in embarrassment. The fiery Ruth Messinger, who understood even better than Gerges how profoundly the poor got screwed, was trying to broaden her base for a run at citywide office. She was not about to make a roomful of enemies by supporting this pointless display of bad manners.

But with everyone wishing he'd either drop dead or stop talking, Gerges went on like some Mr. Smith-Gone-to-Washington run amuck. For the thirty homeless people in the gallery, it was a thrilling, heroic act. They cheered his every point, even as he became hoarse and ragged, even as he destroyed relationships he would never mend, even as he dissipated into incoherence and rage.

When he finally sat down, throat muscles engorged, the citizenry of Kochville stood and roared for him. A white man had gone to the wall for them. As soon as the ruckus subsided, the same expressionless clerk who seemed to be at all meetings everywhere since the beginning of time stood and asked for the vote. The budget passed, 50 to 1.

⚏

About a half-hour later, Duke, Larry Locke, little Art, and Matthew sat across the street at the Greek delicatessen saying nothing. Midnight had come for Cinderella. They felt as if they'd been kicked in the head.

"Let's call up Greenberg."

"I think he's sleeping."

"So wake the motherfucker up. He got us into this."

Then they abandoned that idea and silently stirred their coffee. Greenberg's presence had been minimal the last couple of weeks—purposely so, it seemed—and there was nothing he could tell them that they didn't already know. At dawn the garbage crushers would roll, and Big Mouth would eat. So if there was to be a solution, a moment of clear thought, it would have to come now. From them.

For these four in particular, the end of Kochville would be a bitter pill. For a month they had enjoyed a certain untouchable status within City Hall. They were treated gingerly and even respectfully, a rare sensation. And in the satellite system of city council offices in, under, and around City Hall, they were welcomed like royalty. Because their very existence embarrassed the mayor, it delighted his opponents.

Hello, boys! Need to use the Xerox machine to run off some ugly caricatures of Ed Koch, exaggerating his ears and nose? Fine, step right in. Need to take a nap on a desk? Fine, let me just clear some things away.

Couldn't this continue somehow? wondered Matthew. Couldn't this fat cow be milked a little drier? Couldn't a few of them keep this going someplace nearby? What about an abandoned building? People were squatting all over the place these days. There were thousands of empty buildings, for God's sake! Why not just move in?

"I don't think we have the personnel for a squat," said Larry Locke.

He was right, of course. There were a handful of competent people in the camp, but the rest were too feebleminded or dependent to carry off a mission of any real danger or complexity. Squatting required not just guerrilla construction skills but nerves of steel. The confrontations would be intense and frequent.

"All right," said Art, "what about this?" He started to draw up a list of the fittest warriors. With ten or fifteen good men, he felt, they could manage it.

Art began to call out names, and Duke and Matthew gave thumbs up or thumbs down. But it wasn't sitting right with Larry. He was still feeling his way along and knew little of the ethics of leadership, except for children's books about Abe Lincoln and say, Moses or Jesus. But those people would not be making up lists. You didn't cut loose the misfits when times got rough. You tried to bring them along somehow. Hell, in this situation all you *had* were misfits. Besides, the decision about what to do now ought not be made behind closed doors. It should be put to all thirty of them, at a meeting of the park benches in a circle, in the grand, three-week-old tradition of Kochville. And since most everyone was now asleep, the meeting should be tomorrow, hopefully before the garbage crusher rolled.

Locke made this pronouncement. The list-making stopped. Duke and little Art, wishing they weren't being made to behave with such nobility, nonetheless agreed. Matthew was outraged. Sometimes Negroes were so incredibly docile! Especially the ones who had spent a lot of time in church. The four of them had been in a very sweet position for a couple of weeks, and the very first consideration was to find a way to perpetuate that. The *first* consideration, for God's sake! Then there might be time to think about "Doing unto others" and the rest of that bullshit. Maybe the four of them could get gigs as some councilman's assistant. Maybe they could get placed in apartments as model homeless people. *Something.* I mean, WAKE UP, BLACK PEOPLE!!, Matthew wanted to scream. How much shit did they have to take before they discovered there was no hereafter, only here?

Larry Locke was becoming cloyingly self-righteous. The only consolation, thought Matthew as they left the coffee shop, was that he was vulnerable. There was a look to Larry that Matthew had seen before. It was subtle—a sort of flutter of the eye, a shadow moving behind a window—but it spoke to Matthew, who had travelled so widely in the realms of human weakness. It told him that under the slow, stolid, steady pace of Larry Locke there was a nervousness, a stutter-step that could do him in. Possibly, at times in the past, it already had.

≡

The garbage crushers didn't even wait for dawn. Big Mouth wanted an early breakfast. By the time Larry Locke was crossing the street at 5 A.M. with his thirty cups of coffee, three big green trucks were already in the camp, and the sanitation men were rolling up their sleeves. Obviously, Henry Stern wanted this cleared up before the morning rush hour. Anyone who doubted that had only to look closely. There was the commissioner himself, supervising the demolition in a thick corduroy jacket. He had the look of a country gentleman just in from field and stream.

"The party's over, I'm afraid," Locke heard him saying to Duke, who had apparently been trying to stop things, without success. When Larry Locke got there, his one-eyed lieutenant was seething with frustration, almost to the point of doing something dangerous.

"Relax," said Locke to Duke York. Then he turned to Henry Stern. "What's the problem here?"

"There's no problem at all," replied Stern. "We're just enforcing your agreement with the city. The budget hearings are over, and now you have to leave."

"Understood," said Locke. "We thought maybe you'd give us a day, like a grace period, so we could figure it out and make some plans. Much easier on us that way."

Stern fumed silently. A grace period? What the hell would you call the last *month*?

"Or maybe you just want to wipe us out now, and we'll get the reporters down here to watch it," said Duke York.

Stern grimaced. This odious kind of blackmail wasn't going to work anymore. He was steaming. It had gotten to the point where the whole thing was giving him physical pain. But after breathing deeply several times, he began to think it through. If they really were going to leave voluntarily later on, in a matter of a few hours, perhaps there was no need to incur any bad publicity by doing something unpleasant now.

"This afternoon," said Stern slowly, "is the absolute limit."

"This afternoon, without fail," said Locke, and Big Mouth backed away, teased, ravenous.

Larry set down the morning coffee, and the thirty men and women of Kochville drank it in silence. "We'll have a meeting," said the headman, "after the rush hour."

The rush hour came, and for a while Kochville was a swarm of bureaucratic New York. There were secretaries from Brooklyn packed into summer dresses, trying to make somebody want them. There was bejowled upper level management. There were sweet-smelling Latinos, *perfumados* from the mail room. There were lawyers, male and female, fresh from morning jogs, minds sharp as pins. When the last wisps of them had eddied away and Kochville was once again a sleepy little village, Locke said "Let's do it," and the benches were drawn in a circle.

Little Art was the first to speak.

"I say what we do is, we tell them we want them to put us in a building. We tell them we can fix it up. One of them old boarded-up buildings."

"Nigger, ain't nobody givin' you a building," said Horace.

"You're out of order," said someone.

"According to what? White man's rules? Man, you suckers on your way out of here, and you ain't gonna have nothin' to show for it except a thousand mosquito bites. Serve you the fuck right."

Nobody had the energy to challenge Horace, either for being out of order or for what he was saying. So he went on.

"Out here all day all night gettin' rained on, because some Jew come along and tell you you gonna do some good. For who? For him, that's who. How you think he make a livin'? He get money to work with the poor. So if there was no poor, he be out of a fuckin' job. So he don't even want you to get nowhere. And meanwhile you out here in the goddamn rain singin' folk songs. Man, you the sorriest bunch of niggers I ever seen."

Again there was silence. They lowered their heads, absorbing the tongue lashing.

"Excuse me . . ."

A stranger was standing there, an elderly black woman. She looked like she was dressed for Easter, with a bright purple dress, straw bonnet, and white shoes. She was no doubt a well-wisher, of whom the camp greeted several every day. But this was not the moment to entertain her. Duke stood up and guided her to a spot several yards away,

"I'm sorry, ma'am, but we can't really talk to you now. We're havin' a meeting."

"I just want to leave somethin' off for you," she said.

"That's fine," said Duke. Frequently people brought little things. Pies, toothbrushes, whatever. "You can put it anywhere."

The old woman turned and motioned to a man standing several yards away in the plaza. "Just bring it right on in here," she said. Duke rejoined the meeting, which was still stalled in silence.

Within a minute, two men appeared on the concrete walkway

carrying something huge, wrapped in brown paper. All eyes were on them. They set it down and took off the paper to reveal a large bureau of drawers. It was sky blue, and the knobs on the drawers were cream colored.

"This here was from our bedroom, my husband and me," said the old woman. "He died last year and I don't have no more use for it."

Some of the men couldn't help smiling. What would Henry Stern think about a *bedroom set* in the park?

"Ma'am, I'm not sure we'd know what to do with this," said Duke.

"Well, *I* sure as hell don't know what to do with it," she said. This provoked some laughter from Kochville, which she took as an icebreaker. She then introduced herself as Mrs. Ralph Williams, and said she had lived on 127th Street for forty-five years. Now, as a widow, she was moving into a planned residence. With the help of a brother and a nephew, she was straightening out her effects. "Heard about you on the news, and figured you need a place to fold up your clothes, so you can present yourselves well. That's very important, to present yourself well." Mrs. Williams then went on a bit and told stories of having been courted, briefly, by Bojangles Bill Robinson, the great dancer, and of losing a son in the war. She didn't say which one. Finally, with the heat of the morning beginning to bother her, she excused herself, and with her brother and nephew, who had been waiting under a tree, she left.

The men sat around absorbing it all. In the black culture, mother figures, even frail and dotty, are powerful symbols. They are never disobeyed.

After more silence, Duke stood and moved into the center of the circle. Huge emotions roiled within him, and he said nothing until they had sorted themselves out and formed a clear thought.

Where in their lives, he asked them finally, had they ever or would they ever stand in front of each other like this, underneath a big sky, and speak their hearts? When had they ever or would they ever step inside a door as ornate as City Hall's without some-body saying 'You delivering the sandwiches, son?'

"So what's the point?" snapped Horace.

"How many of you know how to frame a window or wire a wall?"

No hands went up.

"So I guess the thirty of us ain't gonna crawl into no burnt-out building without a roof."

"So?"

"And I guess you don't want to split up and go back into the shelters, either."

A shudder ran through them at the contemplation of it.

"So then where you wanna go?" he asked them.

There was no reply.

"So why should we go anywhere?" Duke York said finally.

Even little Art, the veteran of foreign wars was unnerved by this. "You sayin' we should stay here!?"

"Why not?" said Duke York.

"Because they gonna mutilate us," said Art. "They gonna swallow up every goddamn thing we own, and then they gonna swallow *us* up."

"So I guess it's the shelters, then," said Duke, staring him down.

There was another universal silence. Even Horace could not condemn the idea of defying the world and going down in flames.

The silence continued as everyone absorbed the implications. If they stayed, they would no longer be playing by the white man's rules . . . of living up to agreements with the city, of pretending to be lobbying for the public good, any of that. They would be making liars of the Great White Fathers who had so far protected them. They would be riding wild and free, towards what kind of end? Even if nothing more dramatic happened than the old earth turned winter would come? Death by fire, death by ice, what was the difference?

"So we just gonna hope somebody takes pity on us?" someone said finally.

"Ain't nobody gonna do that," said Horace.

There was more silence, just the hum of the city noise.

Then an old man named James spoke up. He had lived in the park long before Kochville, a skinny old man that the men had adopted almost as a mascot. "Rather die out here next week," he said, "than pick through garbage whatever time I got left."

Everyone thought about that a while.

"Rather die out here than go back into some shelter," said Larry Locke. This remark, too, resonated in silence—the longest silence yet.

In the month-long protocol of Kochville, silence had meaning. If it went on long enough, it was louder than a banging gavel. It meant that a matter had been thought through, and that there were no further objections. In this case, it meant that if the question was "Where are we going?" the answer was "Nowhere."

For a long while the men absorbed the enormity of the decision, then slowly moved off to digest the idea alone. After a time only the leaders remained in the circle. They looked at each other intensely, then moved on to a smaller matter. How would they transmit this information to the world? To a group of people as newly sophisticated as Kochville, there was only one answer to this question too. They would call a press conference.

Within a few minutes Duke was in Room 9 of City Hall, where from time immemorial, from the days of *The Front Page* and ten New York dailies, the press has lounged and observed the circus of politics. "We're gonna have a press conference at four o'clock," he said, "to let the world know what we're gonna do next."

The reporters consulted their daily calendars with wry smiles. By now they had learned to enjoy Duke's boisterous presence in the stale old room. What were the conflicts? Well, at four o'clock there was also a meeting of the city regulatory agency that mea-

sured the amount of microbes in various sewage systems around
northern Queens.

No contest.

<hr>

Ruth Messinger sat in Ellen's Café over a cup of coffee. It was a
rare moment of stillness for the frenetic councilwoman, but she
had time to kill, and she liked the place. It was an old haunt of
cigar-chewing City Hall pols, whom as a reformer she theoretically detested. But places with real texture and odor were rapidly
vanishing in lower Manhattan, and Ellen's was one of them.

Mainly, she loved to look at the pictures on the wall: old
posters of Miss Subways. These had been everywhere in the New
York subways of the fifties and sixties, monthly pinups of a pretty
girl to distract the commuters. Oh, no cheesecake, or anything;
just a headshot, and a little spiel about the lovely creature's ambi-
tions. Ellen, the proprietress, had herself been a Miss Subways,
and so she had lined the walls with pictures of her fellow hon-
orees. As a feminist, Messinger knew she ought to have detested
all this too, but she couldn't help herself. She liked to imagine
where the girls were now. "Karen Patterson, June 1951," read one.
"Karen dreams of being a model, or possibly a foreign correspon-
dent." Somehow, gazing at the photo of the simple, round-faced
girl, Messinger doubted that either ambition had come true. She
had spent most of her life in New York City politics and had few
illusions.

The whole subject of naiveté reminded her of her next appointment: the farewell press conference of the homeless group
in the park. For Messinger, this was a vindication. She had been
right to prod them to stay put during the budget hearings. Not
only had they embarrassed the mayor, but they had also empowered themselves to the point where they were calling press conferences. Wherever their individual paths led, they could only be
richer for the experience.

Arriving at the City Hall steps, she spotted Parks Commissioner Henry Stern, whom she greeted with an even civility. Once an ally, Stern had become an enemy. There had been a war for his political soul, and Ed Koch had won. That was a pity, because Stern had a quixotic integrity that Messinger still admired. Recently the commissioner had interrupted one of his own press conferences so he could rescue a woodpecker that had fallen from a tree. On another occasion, leading reporters on a tour of the Central Park Zoo's brand-new reptile house, Stern suddenly began crawling around on all fours, urging the reporters to do the same. It would make the creatures feel more at home, he said. Messinger liked his style.

Today, though, he was looking rather tightly wound, which surprised Ruth Messinger. Presumably, he was about to get a big weight off his neck. Had she been able to see into the commissioner's head, she would have perceived that the problem had to do with violated dignity. Henry Stern couldn't believe he was waiting here to be *told* about the next move of the vagrants in City Hall Park. Trying to stand still, he was almost quivering with rage.

Standing near Stern were many people she didn't recognize, most of them black. The rest were reporters or photographers, with the exception of Marc Greenberg, who took the microphone and began the proceedings.

"Ladies and gentlemen, you're about to hear from a remarkable group of people whom I've had the privilege of coming to know very well," he said. "I've just gotten here myself, and I have no idea what they're going to tell you, but I assure you it will be worth listening to." Greenberg was speaking with great candor. He had arrived five minutes ago, and was as in the dark as everyone else.

With that, Larry Locke took the microphone and began to speak. "I'm here, we're here, to tell you that we've been here . . . that since we . . . that we . . . that why we're here . . ." He felt the eyes on him, and it was making him dry up. In the circle of benches he never had this problem, but something about standing in front of these so-called important white people was throwing him. Not that he was scared of them. Far from it. He just couldn't get his thoughts together. Greenberg felt for him. It was much like his own agony the first night he addressed Kochville.

Luckily, the loquacious Duke was there to grab the mike. As he opened his mouth to talk, everything went into slow motion for him. With this highly public act, Duke York was saying to the world and to himself that he was not merely vacationing on a park bench. He wasn't here because his house was being painted. He was a homeless man. He had no place to go on this earth, despite having been married and having fathered two of the most beautiful little girls God ever made. But he had blown it somehow, had failed to figure out something critical, and as a result, he was adrift.

So whatever else he said, he was saying that.

When he felt the eyes on him, he began. "We been out here for a month. Some of us are out here because we screwed up . . . but nobody's perfect, it could happen to anybody. You lose your car keys, you lose your wallet, you lose your wife, you lose your job— you lose enough things, couldn't *nobody* keep himself together.

"Now I'm not sayin' it ain't our fault, but even if it is, ain't you supposed to get another chance? Even sinners is supposed to get another chance. And if you don't think so, what you think about the sinners in the building right behind me? They sittin' in there right now, champagne on ice, plannin' who they gonna sell all these empty buildings around here to. Meanwhile you got grandmothers sleepin' in the gutter. You got babies bein' born on subway trains. So you tell me who's the sinner."

He was rolling.

"So all of you who come to find out where we're goin', answer is, *no* damn where. Just gonna sit right here, till something changes."

Then he set the microphone down and stepped away.

Everyone waited for more, but that was it.

To a young reporter new to the beat, it seemed like no news at all, a nonevent. But to the veterans who understood the psychological circus of City Hall, it was delicious. They could feel the mayor's blood pressure in their own arteries. The drama, and the feature stories, would continue.

Henry Stern had never felt more deeply betrayed. Both his agreement with Norman Siegel granting a month's stay and his agreement of this morning granting a day's grace had been violated. He was not a vindictive man, but he felt a dark and potentially brutal anger overtake him.

As the crowd buzzed, Greenberg took the microphone and tried to fill everyone in on the group's history. But even as he remained the affable host, Greenberg's face betrayed a mild state of shock. He knew that a line had been crossed and that even Norman Siegel would no longer be an ally; a lawyer's deals are his currency, and Siegel had just been made a liar.

Ruth Messinger was full of the greatest foreboding of all. Guilt was a rare emotion for the councilwoman: she considered it unproductive. At the moment, though, she was getting a strong dose of it.

A lifetime of activism had taught her something about demonstrations. You had to have a goal. You had to be out there saying "We want this in particular." That had been the success of Martin Luther King's work in the South; on a given day, he wanted to integrate the very lunch counter at which he was sitting. It was that specific.

But these people were just . . . out there. If Messinger were honest with herself, their purpose had been disturbingly vague even during the budget hearings. Did they want money for new housing? Money to rehabilitate old housing? Programs to help the homeless? What kind? Did they want a building for themselves? It had all been unclear, but at least they had had a target: the budget hearings going on inside City Hall. Now they didn't even have that. Now they were merely floating on a dangerous sea with no compass.

How dangerous a sea, no one knew better than Ruth Messinger. She knew Ed Koch. The latest polls had been released, and the homeless issue was killing him. He could no longer tolerate these people on his doorstep. They were now more than an embarrassment; they threatened his right to rule.

Ruth Messinger understood how the mayor punished his enemies, because she was one of them. Ms. Messinger knew a bit of German, and there was a word in that language called schadenfreude. Loosely translated, it meant "the joy of hating." In Ed Koch's case, when the object of hatred was universal, his fellow New Yorkers dove joyously into schadenfreude right along with him. When child molester Joel Steinberg was convicted of abusing his own daughter, the mayor suggested the punishment. "He should be dipped in hot oil many, many times," said the mayor, and New York cried "Amen!"

But sometimes the mayor was so vindictive it was impossible to do anything but back away in dismay. Recently, he had suggested turning wolves loose in the subway yards at night as a way of discouraging graffiti artists. But even that did not trouble Messinger as much as a subtler incident. Last year, in a fit of rage, the mayor compared Comptroller Jay Goldin to Joseph Goebbels. The sprightly, Jewish Goldin was wounded deeply, and friends said the light went out of his eyes for six months.

For Messinger, that kind of thing was profoundly disturbing. Politics pushed enough buttons as it was. When it got personal, it got intolerable. But for Ed Koch, the personal moments seemed to be when his greatest passions engaged. He was a man without an intimate relationship, and this meant no confidante, no outlet for his large and small hurts. He was isolated, and that isolation had grown toxic, in Messinger's opinion. And when it was brought fully to bear on someone, backed up by the power of the mayoralty, it could be brutal to the point of savagery.

The thirty simple souls in the park did not appear to be particularly well-suited to absorb the complex rage of this man. Whatever she had thought to accomplish by urging them on, be it the defeat of Ed Koch or a cure for cancer or peace on earth, now hardly seemed worth it.

Seven

Though he did not know it at the time, the lease for Casa Hernandez, the record shop of the beautiful Victoria Hernandez, was the last one Albert Brackman would ever write. He was in the process of selling the building.

It was 1946, Brackman was now in his eighties, and apart from his daughter and a few grandchildren and a legion of great-grandchildren who lived in distant places, he was alone in the world. The postwar era had brought developments in real estate he didn't understand. There were now controls on rent, which meant that he didn't have the right to raise them beyond a certain point, no matter how much greater his own costs became. The only alternative, as he saw it, was to diminish the quality of the services he provided—the heat and maintenance in particular. This he did not have the heart to do, either to his beloved building or to his tenants. He was too exhausted for this new world.

The man to whom he was selling seemed like a good choice. He was a Jew, and he had a head on his shoulders. The only thing he seemed to lack was heart. Old Brackman could not engage young Emmanuel Margulies in a conversation about the building's history. The new young owner did not care that it had been the first elevator building in the Bronx, did not care about the meadowlarks that had once flitted past the windows, did not care about the Flemish oak that framed those windows. Margulies was interested in dollars and cents.

Once Brackman had made the deal, he moved out of the neighborhood rather than endure anyone else's stewardship. His final home was a small rental apartment on the Upper West Side of Manhattan, not far from the George Washington Bridge. There, on clear days, the Hudson sparkled blue as the Bronx River had in his youth, when he took his wife and little girl down the hill to angle for their dinner among squadrons of silver fish.

In letters to his daughter, now a portly matron in the West, Brackman wrote that his dreams were vivid. Images of 850 Longwood Avenue danced in his head. The long, dramatic cornice was studded with gold. The oval window on the top floor was a mystical passageway to an Alice-like netherworld. Sometimes he would see himself on a limestone balcony, and below him, the endless fields and streams of his native Ukraine. On a night in December of 1946, possibly in the middle of dreams like these, Albert Brackman passed away.

The death listing in the newspapers was noticed by only a few. One of them was James Meehan, living out his retirement in the Bronx. A long career in architecture capped by a term as Tenement Commissioner of New York had brought him into contact with many builders, but few with the integrity and sheer wide-eyed joy of Albert Brackman. The night he learned of Brackman's death, he stood alone on his porch facing the woods of Pelham Bay Park and drank a toast to the memory of the man who had pushed him to the limits of his talent.

Many of the older tenants at 850 Longwood Avenue also noted the passing with sadness. One of the Lubinskies, who for three generations had occupied the third-floor rear, laid a wreath in the marble lobby. Someone remarked on the ironic timing of it all. About a mile to the north, the world of Albert Brackman was being finally, brutally obliterated.

There was new thinking in urban planning. No longer were subways the marvel of the age. In the mind of Robert Moses, who had for years presided over the great urban constructions of New

York, they were a decaying, limited system of transport. Since the future lay in the sprawling suburbs, the future belonged to the car. New highways were being built, in many cases wiping out the neighborhoods through which they ran. That was regrettable, but necessary. Congested neighborhoods of low buildings were obsolete anyway, in Moses's opinion.

Rose Zulutoff's sister Sarah, who lived just north of Crotona Park, was informed that her building lay in the path of Moses's newest road, the Cross Bronx Expressway. Citizen's groups formed to protest the outrage, but Moses, who wielded enormous, intimidating influence, prevailed. Sarah Zulutoff was welcome to remain in her apartment even as construction began, but she had better be prepared for wrecking balls flying all around her, and explosives punctuating her every thought.

A neighborhood was shredding. Many of the old Jews on Crotona Park had known no other home since fleeing Eastern Europe as children. The entire fabric of their social lives stretched between East Tremont Avenue and the northern edge of the park. The pickle man on Charlotte Street, the greengrocer on the Post Road, the fat Feinstein brothers who doled out the herring in sour cream, all of them were part of a fragile, contained universe. Leaving the Bronx would be no less violent an upheaval than fleeing Russia before the Czar's cossacks. But all Jews understood at some level the meaning of exodus. One by one, family by family, they began to move out.

Many of the proud old buildings were demolished, and many that remained were filled by newcomers. The Puerto Ricans did indeed follow Victoria Hernandez to the Bronx. Popularly called Marine Tigers after the retired troop transport ship that brought many of them north, they settled first in Manhattan. But they were not warmly welcomed. Puerto Rican children would get beaten up walking a block to school, much as Albert Brackman's daughter had been harassed by Irish kids fifty years earlier. The Puerto Rican parents saw no reason to endure it. Real estate was opening up in the Bronx. First it was a trickle, as buildings that no longer used coal suddenly had rentable space in the basements. Then there were the thousands of vacancies left by the first wave of Jews to flee Moses's bulldozers.

But the Marine Tigers were not welcomed in the Bronx, either. The Jews who remained were not the great liberal thinkers who had embraced Victoria Hernandez a few years earlier. The Holocaust had made a sea change.

There were a few who felt that the horrors in Europe were a reason to clasp these newly arrived, disoriented Americans to their bosom. This was the compassion implicit in the Talmud. But for other Jews, the Holocaust was something to forget. Victims no more, they felt at last entitled to indulge themselves in a little selfishness. Now, in the fifties, the sun had finally come out. So forget suffering, ours or anyone else's. To make matters worse, jobs in the garment district were drying up. Worse still, the Puerto Ricans and the blacks were competing for the few that were left.

Finally, a single incident tipped the scales. One day a pretty Jewish schoolteacher took her class to Crotona Park, still a sylvan paradise, the proximity of Moses's bulldozers notwithstanding. There, in the very glen where Weckquasgeek Indians had once held their sacred ceremonies, the teacher was pulled into a bush and raped. The horrified schoolchildren did not see her attacker, nor, in her terror, did the victim. But the rumors spread instantly: it was "the element," the euphemism for the newly arrived people of color.

Now the exodus was rapid. Not just Crotona Park North, but even the once grand Grand Concourse began to empty out. Everyone was looking for a spot north of the "Great Wall of China," as the path of the Cross Bronx Expressway was now called. For some Jews, the irresistible magnet was Co-op City, a vast development on the site of Freedomland, a failed amusement park. The same breed of clever realtors that had once seduced them to the Grand

Concourse now seduced them away from it. Co-op City!! Water views, clean air, and of greatest importance, Security—a code word for "no coloreds."

One day Rose Zulutoff Rifkin, now a widow still occupying rooms beside the oval window of 850 Longwood Avenue, heard a knock on the door. Her son-in-law had come to inform her that he was moving the whole family, including her and her sister Sarah, to a house in New Jersey. Yes, it seemed remote, but within a few years it would be within easy reach of New York, thanks largely to the new Cross Bronx Expressway.

So old Rose Zulutoff left the building into which she had been carried like a princess at the age of five. Waving good-bye from the door of her record store was Victoria Hernandez, who had taken a liking to the old woman and was sad to see her go.

For Emmanuel Margulies, the departure of the Jews created mixed feelings. Yes, they were stable, reliable rent payers, probably far more so than the Negroes and the Puerto Ricans would be. But Margulies now had the option of subdividing. Who needed the "libraries" and "parlors" that Albert Brackman and James Meehan had so extravagantly stitched into the design of the building? Instead, the spaces could now be carved up into two and sometimes three small apartments. And that made for a more abundant bottom line.

≡

Great politicians, like great actors, surprise. That's what keeps you watching them. Edwin Booth is said to have played Hamlet's dying speech in a gale of laughter.

So it was with Ed Koch. Just when everyone assumed the hammer was coming down hard after Kochville's defiant press conference, it came down not at all. A fleet of Big Mouths from the Sanitation Department did not storm the park. Instead, a little old man arrived with a bucket of paint. With everyone watching in puzzlement, he gave the benches a new coat of green.

At first, Kochville saw treachery even in this. "The son of a bitch don't even want us sitting down here no more. This is the first step. You watch. While we're gone somewhere waiting for the motherfuckers to dry, he'll come and wipe us out." But as the little old man explained when he left, the paint was quick drying, so as to minimize the inconvenience.

Marc Greenberg, however, had deep suspicions. An hour later they were confirmed. Without warning, Ed Koch strode into the park, hauling in his wake a couple of city officials, a few dazed reporters, and a camera crew. The first thing he said was "How do you like the paint job?" As the citizens of Kochville groped for an answer, he went on to explain that other cities experimented with fancy colors, but for his money there had never been an improvement on the Parks Department's forest green.

Both Duke York and Larry Locke were in shock. They found themselves drawn into conversation, a rather pleasant one, with a man they deeply feared. There was almost a sweetness about him. Though he was large, larger by far than photographs suggested, he had a sort of stoop to him that implied he was uncomfortable towering over people and just wanted to come down out of the clouds.

Soon the disarming man had created a picnic–like congeniality on the lawn. Then he suddenly got to his point. "I am here," he said after ascertaining that the cameras were rolling, "to offer jobs to every one of you. This lady to my left is the head of the City Employment Commission. Now, how many want a job? Raise your hands."

The offer was made so abruptly that the men barely had time to digest it. The ones with legal problems had to think twice about drawing the scrutiny of a camera. Only one hand shot up in the air in time to be included in the mayor's sudden tally. "One," said Ed Koch. "One out of thirty. Need I say more?" And with a final warm smile to the television cameras, the mayor turned on his heels and went back inside City Hall. The press followed immediately behind, like dogs that had just been offered a better brand of dog food. Only one person remained, the beleaguered lady who was in charge of handing out the jobs. She gave an address to Mickey, the man who had raised his hand, and said "Be there tomorrow morning and they'll take care of you." Then she too left. Only Marc Greenberg grasped what had happened. The amateurs had just been given a lesson by a public relations professional.

The evening news confirmed this, as did the morning papers. "First he painted the benches for them," wrote a columnist normally hostile to the mayor. "Then he offered them all jobs, which virtually none of them wanted. Apparently, they just want to lie around on the lawn all day." Once the reporters grew bored or antagonistic, that was the end. Everyone understood this, and an air of doom settled in. The men padded about sluggishly, muttering farewells. Then Mickey returned from his job interview.

Until now, the tall, light-skinned man had been a source of trouble in the camp. He had arrived the week before in a ragged Chanel dress and full makeup, an unabashed transvestite. This struck a deep, uncomfortable chord in the other men. There had been arguments about whether to throw him out, and only at Larry's insistence, based on the principles of an open democracy, had he been allowed to stay. But he was paying a price: threats of violence and insulting whispers filled his ears every time he sashayed past.

The gay issue had been a sensitive one even before his arrival. The ACT UP group had been loudly, dramatically petitioning City Hall all month. Several times they had approached the camp on the grounds that "we're all in this together." That argument did not wash with the proud black men of Kochville. They wanted nothing to do with ACT UP, or with gay people of any kind . . . particularly those in designer dresses.

So Mickey was an outcast—until this moment.

As instructed, he had gone to the office designated by the

mayor's employment commissioner. He had been given a form to fill out that included a space for "address," which he left blank. Then he was informed that no one without an address could be given a job. Mickey reminded the clerk of the mayor's very public offer the day before, but she was a dense bureaucrat who continued to shake her head no. When Mickey returned to the camp with this news, Greenberg saw a golden opportunity. Mickey was sent immediately to the press room of City Hall, where he told his story to a dozen languid reporters.

How could they be sure it was true? the reporters wanted to know. How could they be sure Mickey wasn't turned down because he was unqualified? "Unqualified?" snapped Mickey. The position was clerical, and he had won speed typing contests in high school. Prove it, said a reporter. Mickey did just that, retyping the lead story in *The New York Times*, error free, in less than a minute. And so, without knowing it, Ed Koch had been outmaneuvered again. As he sat not a hundred yards away munching a brioche with the visiting mayor of Lod, Israel, the story went into the late editions that his offer of jobs had been proven ungenuine.

Word of the reversal spread quickly around the government buildings, which were by now full of fans of this little cat-and-mouse game. So delighted was State Senator Roy Goodman, a liberal Republican and longtime enemy of the mayor, that he was moved to make an extraordinary offer. Later in the day he was holding his annual staff outing aboard a Circle Line boat on the Hudson River. How would Kochville like a boat ride?

How, indeed! Within minutes they were rummaging through their gear for tank tops and shorts. Marc Greenberg agreed to stick around to keep an eye on the plastic bags and knapsacks and U.S. Army duffel bags, as well as old Mrs. Williams's bedroom set. The entire population of Kochville then took an A-train to Forty-Second Street and set sail on the Hudson River.

It was a moment of grace. They had been delivered not just

from extinction, but from the hottest, most fetid day of the summer. They sang songs and chattered endlessly among cigarettes and coffee as they rolled up the river, enjoying the only breeze in town.

Somewhat less inclined to go hog wild, Larry Locke reclined on a lower deck and let a more modest breeze eddy across him. Not far away, Ellen McCarthy, Irish linen blouse fluttering, watched him.

Since Duke York had encountered her the very first rain-soaked night of the vigil, Ms. McCarthy had been a frequent presence in the park. No one knew much about her except Greenberg, and he knew only the barest outline. A middle-aged divorcée, she had begun to work late in life for the New York City welfare system and by now had experienced all its sadnesses and frustrations. The overnight candlelight vigil had seemed like a joyous corrective to all the drudgery, and she had come along and gotten drenched like everyone else. Then, strangely, she had returned, day after day after day, even after putting in long hours at her job at a soup kitchen. Her friends were mystified. Didn't she get enough of the homeless at work?

Ellen McCarthy herself was at a loss to explain it, but Duke York had his own theory, and it applied not just to Ellen but to many other saints who worked among the homeless, including Marc Greenberg. Most of them were in some ways homeless themselves, Duke felt. Ellen McCarthy no longer had a husband, her children were grown, and her life for many years had yielded little meaning or comfort. The circle of benches in the park was a home.

As the boat rounded the tip of Manhattan Island, she loosened the scarf that bound her salt-and-pepper hair, stretched, and let the sun hit her face. Usually this was a disaster for her fair Irish skin, but today she didn't care. She was feeling the breeze not just for herself, but for all thirty of them. As a lifelong New Yorker she had taken this ride a dozen times, but it seemed like the first time.

She continued to study the outstretched form of Larry Locke. Usually, he was tied into a knot. He did not wear the mantle of leadership lightly. But at the moment, he lay there like a decadent prince.

Sensing her, he opened an eye.

"Enjoying yourself?"

"Very much," she replied. She thought briefly of her former husband, a dour squat man, a lifelong employee of Standard Oil.

"Get you a drink?" he asked her.

"I'll get the drinks," she said. "This is your day."

"I'll get them," he said with some finality, rising. She made a mental note. Proud black males have certain rules when it comes to women. The very thought made her blush.

Leaning against the bar and waiting for two gin and tonics, Larry Locke felt a vague stirring. Romance had not been present in his life for a long time. True love had been his only once, and he winced even to think of it. Her name was Pat, and he'd met her as a teenager, shortly after his mother moved the family to Newark. Larry hated the move and cried bitterly about leaving North Carolina and his father. But Pat changed everything. The earth exploded, the sky spun. Then the hammer came down, as it always did. Both his mother and the girl's father opposed the match, for reasons the parents never explained, possibly never understood themselves. Larry felt deeply betrayed and his anger at his mother, both for this and for the wrenching move from the South, seared into him. He spent weeks weeping in his room.

But the worst consequences were yet to come. After Pat, all future romances seemed like pale compromises. Even Nancy, the mother of his children (strangers to him since infancy), was no one special. Deborah, his most recent, had turned against him in the most painful way. After that he had taken a long, long vacation from love. And now, here on a breezy summer boat deck, was an overture from a white woman. Or was it? The gin and tonics arrived, and he sipped one of them and finally drank it all down and ordered another. Inside Larry Locke a knot slipped, as sailors say, and great amounts of anger and sadness fell away into the river. He returned to the promenade deck with a clear mind and a remarkable inclination: to let the sweet afternoon pass sweetly, with liquor, flirtation, or whatever else the salt wind offered up.

⚌

"Tell them to shove it up their ass."

The young mayoral aide remained beside the big desk, shuffling his feet.

"Wasn't that clear?" asked the mayor.

"Uhh . . ."

"Then relay the message, please," said Ed Koch, and the young man scurried out of the office. The mayor studied the invitation again. The sheer gall of it!! He was being offered two seats *in the balcony* to the final night of the Democratic Convention in Atlanta. Not every night, not on the floor, but for *one night in the goddamn balcony*!! This, for the mayor of the largest city in the United States, arguably the most powerful mayor in the history of that city.

Of course, if he were utterly honest with himself, what else did he expect? Ed Koch was a political creature, and he understood that at this moment he was a liability to the party, at least to the national ticket. Not that Michael Dukakis had any chance of winning. Yes, the polls showed him ten points ahead of George Bush, but the mayor considered that meaningless. Dukakis was a stiff, a dreadfully colorless politician. Christ, he made George Bush look like Cole Porter at the piano!

But the pooh-bahs of the Democratic Party didn't want to hear that, any more than they wanted to hear what Ed Koch had to say during the primary itself. That was back in April, and the mayor had made a couple of mistakes he was still paying for. Check that. Not mistakes. Excessive remarks. Truthful, but excessive. For one thing, he had been vocal in his support of Al Gore, the handsome, laconic young senator from Tennessee. Gore was the obvious choice. He was a big backer of Israel and he could be sold to the New York Jews. And if he ever got the nomination, he might actually win. Somewhere underneath that narcoleptic Southern drawl was a personality, which was more than could be said for Dukakis.

But the real reason Ed Koch had been relegated to the balcony of the Atlanta Civic Center, he knew, had to do with Jesse Jackson, the sacred cow of the party. In Koch's opinion, Jackson was a mediocre politician who had offended every Jew in the world by referring to New York as Hymietown, and then had compounded it by refusing to disassociate himself from Louis Farrakhan, whom Koch considered the most dangerous anti–Semite since Hitler. So the mayor had said "Jews would have to be crazy to vote for Jackson." This single remark had gotten the airplay of "We have nothing to fear but fear itself," obliterating the reams of ma-terial the mayor had put out, verbally and in print, about the campaign. And it had made him look like a simple–minded racist.

No matter. The truth was the truth. Sometimes the people loved you for it, sometimes they crucified you. It just so happened the mayor had other plans for the week of the convention anyway. Plans made after the fact, granted, but plans.

The press accused him of being the petulant teenage girl pre-tending to have another date. Think what you like, he snapped. He was going to Ireland with Cardinal O'Connor of New York, the absolute lynchpin to the Irish vote. The middle-class Irish had been a critical part of the Koch coalition in every election so far, and undoubtedly would be again in '89. The mayor never missed an opportunity to don a tam o' shanter and march up Fifth Ave-nue in the St. Patrick's Day parade, or to dance a jig, or whatever else was required. And now he was virtually going to Ireland with St. Patrick himself. He and the Cardinal were close friends and were even contemplating writing a book together. And so the mayor was packing his white Aran Islands sweater and getting the hell out of the heat of July. Atlanta in the summer? Forget it!!

He threw his eau de cologne into his dop kit along with a family-size bottle of mouthwash. No doubt there would be pints of Guinness to consume, a taste and smell the mayor loathed. It made him feel like a homeless person. No sooner did the thought form that it pricked him like a pin. The bastards were still out there!

He liked to think he was a superb manipulator of personnel, but somehow he had failed with Henry Stern, who despite a sea of memos had not grasped the seriousness of the problem, much less dealt with it. The mayor felt hamstrung. Stern could not be fired. The mayor didn't *want* to fire him. He was the godfather of Stern's oldest son, for God's sake! And except for this one irritating lapse, Stern was a magnificent parks commissioner.

Probably, suspected the mayor, it had to do with the man's obstinacy. Stern was ten years younger than Koch and the relationship between the two had always been slightly out of balance. Koch was the teacher, Stern the student, the acolyte, the follower, the younger brother.

Of course the truth was that Henry Stern did not follow Ed Koch anywhere. He just happened to have followed a similar career path, slightly later. But he clearly hated the idea of appearing to be some sort of pathetic vassal, especially now, in a job to which he had been appointed by the mayor. That's what this City Hall Park thing was all about, the mayor suspected. But Stern had picked a lousy time to assert himself; the homeless issue had festered to the point of being damaging.

The mayor reached for the phone, then stopped himself. He was not going to bark at Stern to "deal with it or else," which every instinct in his body strained to do. That might only bring out a more deeply perverse streak in the man. Instead, the mayor would assume that everything was going to be resolved in his absence. He would postpone getting pissed off until he discovered that it had not.

This was the new thinking, and the lesson of last year's mild stroke. Life was to be lived, each second of it. Angst was not to be invited, certainly not anticipated.

Next stop, the wild green hills of Ireland! It had been a long time, he thought, since a trip lay in front of him with no pregnant political agenda. Perhaps, in the shank of an evening, he might wander aimlessly through a glen.

≡

The period of grace initiated by Senator Roy Goodman's boat ride lasted a long while in City Hall Park. Perhaps to mark the mayor's trip, a vale of Irish weather settled over New York, a series of cool days that made living outdoors less a hardship than a pleasure. And with the mayor's absence, the heat was off in other ways too. In the week following his departure, Big Mouth was not even glimpsed.

One perfect afternoon the men of Kochville removed their shirts, laid aside their various agendas, and played football. The event startled passersby with its sheer exuberance. Invisible were the psychic wounds. Instead muscular young torsos contorted, leaped, raced through the perfect afternoon. At nightfall everyone sat exhausted on the lawn and watched the fireflies come out, like aristocrats at a picnic.

Larry Locke was radiant. Back in North Carolina he had been an all-state linebacker in high school, and much of the sadness and confusion of his life, the endless wars between his parents, could be taken out on some hapless running back. It was his moment of greatest glory, and the rest of his life had seemed a long, inevitable slide into mediocrity and confusion. Now, for the first time since high school, people knew who he was. After the touch football game, which he dominated, he was brimming with a new potency.

All of which reminded him to clean himself up. He was due to appear at a dress-up event in an hour, a fund-raiser for David Dinkins, the black Manhattan borough president. Dinkins was contemplating a run for mayor and was beginning to raise money. A free invitation to the event was highly prized, since ordinary tickets cost five hundred dollars each.

Larry Locke was a celebrity. The New York media had embraced the David and Goliath story of the homeless vs. Ed Koch, and someone was needed to personify David. That was Larry: handsome, moderately articulate, light skinned, an army veteran. It was only of peripheral importance that he actually *was* the leader of Kochville. Duke York, even more articulate and passionate, might have been cast in the role but for his troubling glass eye and even more troubling very dark skin.

But Larry Locke was far more than a figurehead. Good looks meant little when the circle of benches were drawn close and shadows fell across the park. He was a man of great personal weight, and he was applying it to the craft of leadership. He was a country boy in charge of a bunch of hardened New Yorkers, but he had turned even that to his advantage. He often spoke to them of Locke's Creek and of his trips into nearby Fayetteville as a child. He described in low tones the Market House in the town square where slaves had once been auctioned. This made him closer to the source than most of the men, who had grown up in Brooklyn or Harlem. Almost mystical were Larry's tales of the cotton and peanut fields, of the dense fog off the Cape Fear River, of the Civil War graveyards.

Larry Locke drew his moral authority from a man who still worked those fields. Old Charles Locke was a man of few ambiguities. If a day was dry, it was a good day to gather hay; if not, it wasn't. If a thing was right, it was right; if not, then wrong.

Larry had inherited this moral compass from his father, as well as his inability to manage shades of gray. Charles Locke dealt with troubling complexities, like his failed marriage, by shutting down, by putting his back into his task and saying nothing more about it. Larry Locke was not a solitary man standing in the middle of a field, and so he had found other solutions. When things went wrong in Larry's life, his inclination was to dull the pain with drugs.

Kochville was not his first position of authority. Last winter he had found himself becoming influential at the Borden Avenue Veteran's Shelter. But he became so frustrated by the problems of leadership and the stupidity of the people around him that he stomped out and found himself on a pier of the Hudson a few hours later, smoking several bowls of crack. That had led to a month of real degradation from which he almost did not emerge. Though no one knew it, Larry Locke considered Kochville a kind of last chance.

In Kochville, the problem that wouldn't go away, that darkened Larry Locke's mood even as the fireflies danced around him, was money. It had caused fights, resignations, and accusations, and threatened to kill the spirit behind everything. It had all come to a head last week in an incident that had alienated Marc Greenberg—perhaps permanently.

As a way of dealing with his own pressures (and there must have been many, Larry often thought, spending one's days and nights among the hopeless and the foul smelling), Greenberg would pick up his beautiful old wooden flute and play it for hours on end. He and the flute had an intimate relationship, perhaps his only one.

And then somebody had stolen it. Undoubtedly, it was somebody from Kochville whom Greenberg had allowed to crash at his apartment, which he was kind enough to do from time to time. Greenberg was deeply wounded and had not been seen in the camp since. The naive Jew had been asking for it, in Larry's opinion, but the result was that Kochville had lost its best friend.

The other endless source of vexation was a huge glass jar into which sympathetic passersby dropped money. With the growing publicity of the group, these donations were frequent and generous. But what happened to this money? Who should be in charge of it? At one point a man named Marcus was appointed treasurer and shortly afterward disappeared. He was found on his back in a crack alley in Chinatown, with the jar empty. If he ever showed his face in the park again, he would probably be killed.

Now things had degenerated into a free-for-all. People dipped their hand into the jar and took whatever they needed, for whatever they needed. The silver tongued, like Lonnie, went around to stores soliciting not only food but cash donations for the valiant homeless group in the park. Then they simply pocketed the money, bought themselves a fifth of liquor, and disappeared for a few days.

Larry Locke felt it was time for some stroke of leadership, but he had no idea what that might be. Convince a bunch of chronically poor people not to take money when it's handed to them? Good luck. The problem felt insoluble. He felt like going off somewhere and getting high, which he knew in his bones would be a terminal mistake.

Duke York saw him on the lawn and sat down next to him. Ordinarily, the two men would not have been close but for the extreme circumstances of Kochville. Larry was the dour one, Duke was forever wild-eyed and passionate.

"You all right?"

"Yeh . . ." mumbled Larry, and they sat a while.

"You know this is sacred ground, right?"

"Huh?"

"See, the deal is," Duke went on, "that all the black people from like Revolutionary War times was buried here, because it was sacred ground. The Indians did all their voodoo and shit here. Goin' back like a thousand years."

"Yeh," grunted Larry. He was not a man disposed to thinking of the spiritual. Even something as ordinary as the Christian church gave him the creeps. As a child, he had dreaded the endless

Sundays: four-hour morning service, afternoon choir practice, back at night for another four hours.

"See, the thing is," said Duke, "that's why we're here. We're supposed to do somethin' here. It's like ordained. The money thing, the way I see it, don't mean nothing. Same way we keepin' clean, not takin' no drugs or nothin', we shouldn't be handling no money. We're on a spiritual mission. In church, the priests don't handle the money, right?"

Larry smiled sardonically. Duke was such a dreamer. Money made everything happen: a few blocks away on Wall Street, and even here among the dregs of the earth. *Particularly* here.

"Goddamn son of a bitch!!" Lonnie's Tennessee wail suddenly pierced the night. He was across the park, screaming, yelping, and bludgeoning something with a tree limb. At first it looked like the kind of makeshift cardboard shelter that dotted the lawn every night. Then Larry realized it was one of the new sculptures. There was a public art program in New York, and these things were likely to turn up anywhere. This one, installed last week, was a miniature version of one of the great pyramids of Egypt, painted orange for a reason known only to the artist. For a while Lonnie had been eyeing it as a possible domicile. Unfortunately, large as it looked, it was apparently just shy of being able to accommodate a stretched out human being. It was all a perfect example, Lonnie was screaming now, of how the poor get screwed. "You know how much they paid for this damn thing?" he drawled. "You got a million people sleepin' in the streets, they're layin' out the taxpayer's money for this piece of shit that won't accommodate a single human bein'!"

By the time they got to him, he had hacked it to pieces.

Larry knew that Tom Sligh, the black parks department worker, would cover for them and pin the destruction of *Eyeless in Gaza*, as the work was called, on unknown vandals in the night. But Larry sensed something ominous. This was the first note of discord in several days, and it accompanied a change in the weather—a hazy evening, a promise of the heat July had to bring, sooner or later.

Larry settled Lonnie down but could spend no more time on the matter. He was late for the Dinkins affair. "I'll take care of it," said Duke. As Larry moved off toward the fountain to clean up, Duke watched him go and wondered why he, too, had not been invited to the posh night out.

As Larry sponged and preened, he thought about Ellen McCarthy. Would she be there tonight? Probably not. Too bad. The romance had reached the thrilling phase of about-to-happen. Every meeting between them was a moment of redness in the face, of racing hearts. Whenever they were remotely near each other, even with backs turned, each sensed the movement of the other exactly.

He put the finishing touches on his wardrobe with a flourish. Why *not* a dandelion in the buttonhole? Lately his head had been full of delicious anticipations, right alongside the usual dreads. What would the night hold? What might the rest of his life? Something good, did he dare to hope?

As the sky grew black, he made his way across the street to the party. The small lights of the homeless camp receded into darkness, and he felt a twinge of guilt leaving Duke and little Art and Matthew to deal with Lonnie and Horace and the rats and all the rest of it. As soon as he entered the Municipal Building, all such thoughts disappeared.

Larry Locke had often stared up at this columned, gilded masterpiece while lying on his back in City Hall Park. He had already roamed its corridors by day, but nothing prepared him for the night. He stepped into an elevator with several lilac-smelling woman in cocktail dresses and rode to the top. The doors opened to reveal the art nouveau offices of Borough President Dinkins, illuminated only by candlelight. Dinkins himself, in a double-breasted suit, was receiving his guests. Larry was almost embarrassed by the effusiveness of his own greeting; he had met the man only once, briefly, in the park. But the borough president put him immediately at ease; he had a graceful way about him, and great sad eyes.

And he seemed to be in his element. A three-piece combo was playing Duke Ellington's "Satin Doll"—a sweet gurgling piano, a lazy bass, a simple brushing of the drums. The chatter was muted but constant and almost sexual, more sounds than words, *mmmm*s, *ahhhh*s, and *oooooh*s. To merely exist at this gathering required a shifting of gears, a suspension of all anxiety, an easiness. This was hard for Larry to achieve. He was afraid he smelled and was frightened of getting too near anyone. The room was half full of black people, but even this did not put him at ease, because they were the most elegantly dressed, sweetest smelling ones of all. One woman looked like Josephine Baker, even to the detail of a feather in her hair.

A young white woman in a tuxedo approached him and asked him if he wanted a drink. Larry soon realized that she was a waitress. He asked her for a glass of gin with some ice, but she did not understand the order. A gin and tonic? A martini on the rocks? "Just fill up a glass with gin and drop some ice into it," he repeated, but she continued to look at him quizzically, and now he felt as if half the room was staring at him, even though he had done nothing more than order the standard libation of Fayetteville, North Carolina. Finally, mercifully, the woman disappeared and came back with the drink. He gulped about half of it and very soon felt better, as he knew he would.

Now another white woman threaded her way across the room to him. Larry recognized her as Amy Foster, an acquaintance of Marc Greenberg. Greenberg had introduced him to many influential people. Hopefully this would not end on account of his pique about the stolen flute.

"Larry!"

He braced himself. He did not care for the woman personally but knew she controlled several million dollars worth of foundation grants. For that kind of money he would be, for a few minutes, the Nubian slave giving Cleopatra a milk bath.

"Ms. Foster . . ."

"Do you believe what that prick did to us?"

"Uhh . . ." Larry searched the day for the particular prick and the particular offense.

"I think he should be executed," continued Amy Foster. "I'm quite serious. As long as people are yakking about the death penalty, *and he's one of them, for chrissakes*, what about HIM!! A hundred thousand people are homeless, he wants to keep the goddamn buildings EMPTY!!!??? . . ."

Ahhh. Now Larry was clued in. Warehousing was the issue, and Peter Vallone was the prick. Vallone, who was the city council president, was sticking up for his constituents, many of whom were small-scale Queens landlords who wanted to retain the right to move their apartments on and off the market for strategic reasons. The practice was called warehousing, and in the era of homelessness there was something grossly callous and possible criminal about it, like hoarding food during wartime. But it didn't shock Larry Locke, even though he was the victim of it. He had seen Vallone in action, and when all was said and done, the man was simply protecting his own shit. Larry understood that. You had to protect your own shit, be it your life in the army, your shoes in a city shelter, your votes in an election.

Larry got Amy Foster's point, but not the moral indignation she brought to it. He was just beginning to grasp the idea of liberal guilt but still missed the advanced corollary: the less Amy Foster (who had a divine co-op) was actually affected by something, the more angry and vehement she became.

In fact, her vehemence made Larry Locke uncomfortable, particularly when she started calling people pricks. Larry had always been a regular guy, but even in the army he could never get used to that kind of language, constant and numbing though it was. From white men in particular it embarrassed him. Most black men knew how to curse lyrically and almost sweetly, and even some cracker boys, too, some of those noncom Georgia Whites. But coming from most whites, it just didn't play well. And coming from white *women*, it was like fingernails on a blackboard. Maybe it was family training. Had it been old Charles Locke listening to her, Amy Foster would have been left alone with her drink after the first words out of her mouth.

But Larry endured her tirade, agreed with her, and watched her leave the party, her voluptuous hips moving easily underneath a floor-length cotton peasant skirt. For an instant he imagined her naked, then turned his attention to the bar. The party was thinning out, and Larry moved to freshen his drink, to use a term he had just learned. He was getting the hang of all this.

As he moved to the tableful of booze, manned by a quartet of clean-cut white aspiring actors, he caught the eye of a figure he had been dimly aware of since his arrival—standing around on the fringes, drawing the party outward in surges, constantly transforming its shape. Occasionally they had exchanged looks in a manner that unnerved Larry. There was a generous dose of woman in this man. Though Larry was constantly defending Mickey and the other one or two homosexuals of Kochville, that didn't mean he had to like it. The spectacle of Mickey ambling by in his dressing robe always struck a nerve.

Yet Larry felt a bond with this strange partygoer. Both seemed out of place in these corridors of power. Neither had arrived in a flurry of handshakes and kisses. Both had displayed their personal sadness and confusion a little too nakedly. Clearly they were not political professionals, not even talented amateurs.

And then there was the matter of clothes. Larry was wearing a suit that smelled like it had been in a trunk for fifty years. A mayonnaise-stained tie was knotted mercilessly around his throat. He had thought himself terribly underdressed until he laid eyes on this other man, who seemed to stick out not by default but by design. He was wearing a loose, dense chemise full of erratic shapes and colors. On his feet were a pair of boots that looked like they had been skinned off a lynx.

All of this suggested to Larry that the man had power. Otherwise why didn't somebody throw him out? Larry's curiosity was about to be satisfied. David Dinkins was drawing people around himself. The big players were gone, at least the ones with morning appointments, and Dinkins was immediately looser and blacker, jiving and fooling around with Harlem Congressman Charlie Rangel. The two of them were assuming that anyone sticking around was interested in a nightcap, and why not? Why shouldn't the event take on a bit of the gaiety of the rent parties of Dinkins' youth? Hell, they *were* trying to raise some rent, namely on David Dinkins' occupation of City Hall. So Raise the Rent and Raise some Hell, as Cab Calloway used to say.

Larry was standing right next to the strange man with the strange boots, and Borough President Dinkins, ever the host, sensed that they hadn't been introduced.

"Larry Locke, Rudolf Nureyev," he said.

Later, when dawn began to crawl across the lawn of Kochville, Larry Locke would learn the whole story of this man—the midnight flight from Russia, the animal grace, the nearly frightening brand of genius. Right now there was only the wan chiselled face, the full lips, the dark eyes.

"Nice to meet you," said Nureyev in a broad, sensual drawl that seemed not of Russia, but of some other place where people said one thing and meant a thousand other things.

But Larry did not sense that the great artist was trying to pick him up. Rather, Nureyev seemed to be issuing some kind of warning. It was almost as if he was saying, with the eyes and the gestures famous to millions, though not to Larry, "We're not civilized, you and I. The rest of them have been tamed. Not us."

The prince-in-exile gathered his entourage and swept out. Larry was dazed for many minutes even by the afterimage. When he regained himself, he looked around and noticed there were few people left to network with, to use another phrase he had just learned. He swept a half-dozen hors d'oeuvres into his pocket and within minutes was down and out the elevator and crossing the street to City Hall Park. As he approached the green woods, he was stopped a moment by a feeling, an essence. The image of Nureyev returned uninvited, the dark prince dancing above the dark park. It felt like an invitation to genius, to daring, and yet to some strange caution.

In the two hours of Larry's absence, the camp had undergone a transformation, thanks to the arrival of one person. Rasta, as he introduced himself, was a young Jamaican with gleaming dread-locks and a streak of manic energy. Almost instantly he began talking nonstop. No doubt he was slightly mad, but his madness was not repetitive and irritating, like Mr. Cooper's. Rasta was mesmerizing. He had a mouth on him like a jazz drummer, wild convoluted riffs tumbling out of him, some of it drivel, some of it genius. "Blue night, green stars, crazy birds flyin' underneath the moon," he told people. "Stole us from our momma's titties, floated us down the river Zambesi and out to sea, dry-cleaned our souls pickin' indigo in the sunlight of five hundred degrees Fahrenheit, brought us up here to a stone plantation, slave quarters from Small's Paradise to the Audubon Ballroom, get our black asses downtown pickin' cotton in concrete rows . . . Sweet lavender nights, Rhythms of Arabia slicin' my throat in three-quarter time . . ."

Most people smiled in puzzlement. Horace, however, felt as if he was looking at the answer to his prayers.

At this point, the fact that Horace was still there was a mystery even to himself. It was because of the potential, he kept telling himself. At least there were no white faces currently in the camp, excluding dumb crackers like Lonnie and junkies like Matthew. That meant that something pure could still happen here, with the right leadership. Unfortunately all you had at the moment was a house nigger named Larry Locke.

Yes, it was an odious phrase, but Horace could think of no more accurate one. He had put up with people like this all his life. The house nigger was the lowest of the low. The white man threw him a few paltry bones, co-opting his anger and changing his loyalties. He talked a good game and thumped his chest and pretended to be Black when there was anyone around to listen. But when he was one-on-one with the White Master, he curled up like a pussycat.

Just why Larry Locke was even tolerated by the rank-and-file of Kochville was an irritating puzzle to Horace. Locke was a man of no political experience. Not a stupid man, granted. But one utterly without credentials, without portfolio. Hell, when Horace was getting his ass blown all over Jackson, Mississippi, by police fire hoses, Larry Locke was jerking off in a choir loft in North Carolina somewhere, a well-behaved little colored boy. Perhaps that was the very point. He was light-skinned and nonthreatening. Perhaps Kochville felt that this was the kind of person who could assuage the white man. Maybe if everyone were well-behaved enough, the liberals would simply give them a bunch of luxury co-ops on the Upper East Side.

Dream on. Horace had been many times around the block, and he knew that despite *Brown v. the Board of Education*, despite the Civil Rights Act, despite Martin Luther King and the mayors of Indianapolis, Newark, Los Angeles, and all the other house niggers, the black man only started to get some action in America when posters appeared of Huey Newton, the lean, unsmiling leader of the Black Panthers, sitting in a wicker chair with a machine gun across his lap.

The issue had been around ever since the first slave ship dropped anchor off West Africa. A few years ago, you had Stokely Carmichael and Malcolm X lambasting King as a gutless wonder, and before that you had W. E. B. Du Bois and Marcus Garvey ridiculing gentle old Booker T. Washington. You undoubtedly had two points of view in the holds of those slave ships: the one that said "Let's wait and see what happens," and the one that said "Let's turn the sea red with their blood."

Until now he had had no luck educating the shiftless citizens of Kochville. But here, at last, was Rasta.

He was a walking, breathing defiant symbol of victimization—not of the slow kind, like little Art, who'd spent his entire life in a tragic shuffle from Harlem to Vietnam and back again—but of the fast kind, the brutal kind. Rasta was one of the handful of survivors of the most violent racial confrontation of the eighties, the slaughter of the MOVE group in Philadelphia. This was a traumatic, mythic memory for every black man in America. Now, it was being fleshed out by a human messenger.

At Horace's urging, the benches were drawn into the traditional circle so that Rasta might narrate the tale. The bare facts were already known to most of them. Several Philadelphia city blocks had been cordoned off while the police firebombed a half-dozen black activists to Kingdom Come. It was as simple as that. What made it profound for Horace was that the whole thing had been sanctioned by the mayor of Philadelphia . . . the ultimate house nigger, a black man named Wilson Goode.

Rasta began, using the real events only as a point of departure. Soon he was into the realm of pure fancy, weaving threads of the Bible, the quasi-Islamic MOVE philosophy, and everything else under the sun. A single sentence included the names of Haile Selassie, Malcolm X, Hitler, and the Wizard of Oz. "Plastic Apocalypse!" he shouted. "Orange incandescence from the fifth tomb! Black moons descending, eating the corpses of mothers and children. Tears of the goddess cresting the river banks, drowning the white fatherland . . ."

At this point Larry Locke arrived back from the Dinkins fundraiser.

The camp as a group seemed to stiffen. Even Rasta sensed the change and went quiet. "Well, the nigger finally rollin' on in," said Horace after a while. "Done swept the parlor, shaved the massa, and finally rollin' on in." Larry steadied himself. He had a considerable buzz on, thanks to Dinkins' gin, and not much provocation was needed to make him forget himself and take a swing at somebody. Instead, he called the meeting to order.

"Already begun without you, massa," said Horace. "Somebody else already got the floor." Rasta flashed Larry a wild, vaguely evil grin, his dreadlocks throwing shadows across his face.

"Macedonia melting!!" he wailed. "Mists of the mountain come clear, and Hannibal leading twenty thousand elephants, fingernails painted the same color as the Temple of Luxor. Each beast carryin' the corpse of an African Queen . . ."

"Tell us about those funeral elephants!" screamed Horace.

The Jamaican beamed. "Huge essence, purple in their soul incandescence . . ."

"But who walkin' *behind* the elephants," asked Horace slyly, "with a pail and shovel to pick up that elephant shit . . . ?"

Rasta tilted his head quizzically, unaware of the political punch line implied by the tale. Horace turned the question to the general membership. "Is that by any chance *The Black Man* I see runnin' his sorry ass ragged to keep up with them rapidly shittin' elephants, that's carryin' the corpses of them African Queens!?"

The few men in the circle who got the point and didn't resent the manipulation mumbled "Yeh, that's who it is," and Rasta, finally catching on, took the idea as the seed of a whole new universe of images.

"Behold it!! Behind the biggest elephant be the Prince of Zambia, abducted from the Palace of the Moon by messengers of the white devil! Prince say, 'Arise, sparrows of Harlem, and peck out the eyes of—'"

"That's enough."

Heads turned to Larry Locke, who had spoken the words. "We need to get on to other things."

"I don't believe the brother is done yet," said Horace.

"He's done for now," said Larry.

"What did the Prince of Zambia say to the sparrows of Harlem?" said Horace to Rasta, as if there were no Larry Locke.

The Jamaican beamed. "Said, 'Peck out the eyes of your enemies! Let their yellow pupils clatter to the earth—'"

"I said that's enough." Larry was standing now and facing Rasta in the middle of the circle. All was quiet, except for the hum of cars on Broadway.

"Nigger said keep your voice down," said Horace to Rasta. "Nigger says you disturbin' the white man's sleep. He gonna come out of the big house and shut you up."

"Just sit down," said Larry to the Jamaican, who was frothing now, heart pounding loud enough to hear.

"Ain't no white man in a satin robe and mule slippers gonna shut *me* up," said Rasta.

Horace beamed. He had a true buck. Fearless.

"I'm the one who's sayin' you got to sit down," Larry said.

"Then you sit me, motherfucker."

Fffflittt.

Everyone knew the subtle sound. All eyes shot to the middle of the circle, where the moonlight was caught by a switchblade springing to life in the Jamaican's hand.

"Put that away," said Larry Locke, "or I'll take it off you and cut your heart right out of you and stuff it into your mouth."

Having spoken, the big man from North Carolina stood immobile in the dappled gloom. No one breathed. Rasta seemed capable of anything, sweating intensely, eyes wide. Larry's eyes were utterly placid, which was the most terrifying thing of all. He had said "cut your heart right out" with the same ease with which he might have given subway directions.

The arch in Rasta's back subtly collapsed. He pocketed the knife, then turned and ambled out of the circle, muttering incomprehensibly.

Larry stood alone in the circle. He had confirmed his right to rule in the ancient way. But the men could smell the gin on his breath, and the faint scent of lilac and women on his clothes. In the silence there was the unspoken question "When are we gonna get some of that?" behind every pair of eyes. Horace turned and walked away—to make a small show of disrespect, but also because he felt satisfied with the scene. Larry may have won the battle, but it was going to be a long, slow war.

"Now," said Larry Locke, "we gonna talk about the money." In the hours since the football game, and all the time at the Dinkins event, it had been working through him.

"Ain't gonna be no more money, just like there ain't gonna be no drugs," he said. "Somebody wants to give us money, they can write a check. Then Interfaith can cash it and give it to us." Then he looked over at Duke and added "This is sacred ground."

Dead silence.

Larry turned to the committee. Little Art looked away. Matthew walked away, in contempt. They were accustomed to being able to skim a few bucks from the big glass jar, just like everybody else. They did not want to be begging the likes of Marc Greenberg for cigarette money. Only Duke supported the chief. "Money done nothin' but mess us up anyway," he said. "You lookin' for money, you're in the wrong place to begin with."

"Money didn't ever mess me up," said somebody. "Bein' *without* it done that."

"Just the same, that's how it's gonna be," said Larry. "We ain't out here for money, like some whore or some organ-grinder's monkey. We're men."

He looked around the circle until he made eye contact with each man and did not move on to the next until he had confirmation that he had been understood. Then he walked out of the circle and unrolled his blanket underneath a tree.

Eight

As Rose Zulutoff Rifkin rode away from 850 Longwood Avenue on a summer afternoon in 1959, Victoria Hernandez waved until the car was out of sight. She would miss old Rose, with whom she had sat and embroidered in the evenings for hours on end. She would miss all the Jews. She was angry at them for leaving, but she understood, because in a sense she was one of them. Her father was a Spanish Jew from the Canary Islands, who had raised his family in Puerto Rico. He had made them all understand about being Jewish and about wandering.

Perhaps for that reason, the reason of blood, Victoria Hernandez had been accepted by the Jews. In her spare time at the record store, she made dresses that the Jewish women craved, and for a while she had actually carried on with a Jewish man. All of that helped, together with her naturally patrician bearing. She was different, felt the Jews, than the other Puerto Ricans who were moving into the neighborhood. But the Jews themselves were changing. Only the Jewish folk singers in Manhattan who Victoria met through the music world still seemed to care about the poor.

At least, thought Victoria, they were a gentle race. Up by Tremont Avenue, the Irish and Italians expressed their disapproval of the arriving Puerto Ricans with knives and chains.

So the world of Victoria Hernandez changed. Her Spanish music store, once such an oddity in a Jewish neighborhood, now became the cultural hub. Casa Hernandez presided over a thrilling time in Spanish music. Victoria took many of the great musicians under her wing, people like Noro Morales and Xavier Cugat, and guided them through the intricacies of American business. She became legendary for this reason and because of the continuing fame of her brother, the great troubadour Rafael Hernandez.

But as the influx of Puerto Ricans to the Bronx continued, Spanish music itself began to change. Though she had taught piano to Tito Puente as a child, she could not bear to listen to the work that was now making him famous. To her ear it was loud, insistent, cacophonous—so unlike her brother's, which had the grace of old Aragon about it. And was it because she was getting older, she asked herself, that the nature of her clientele seemed to be changing? Having been around the music business all her life she was used to the *perfumados*, the young dandies who breezed in smelling faintly of rum. But the new dawdlers in her shop did not have even that kind of liveliness; there was deadness in their eyes, not sparkle. If it came from rum, they must have been drinking oceans of it.

In many cases it came not from rum but from heroin. An opium derivative once entirely legal and available in a score of patent medicines, heroin had evolved along with the immigrant cultures that embraced it. Few did so as fervently as the Puerto Ricans. It provided them a lovely delirium and an escape from a grim reality. Just as push-button elevators, container shipping, motorized snowplows, and a host of other job eliminators were being invented, the Puerto Ricans arrived looking for work. They spoke no English, and their dark skin invited hostility, not only from whites but also from blacks, who now at last had someone to push around.

Bobby Ortiz, Victoria Hernandez's new upstairs neighbor at 850 Longwood Avenue, supported his family by selling drugs to augment his wages as a day laborer. Victoria was suspicious of the man's nocturnal visitors but nonetheless extended a welcoming hand. At least, she told herself, Bobby had a sense of family. There were many fatherless children in the neighborhood, the result of the Don Juan element of the Spanish culture.

But Bobby Ortiz remained with his family only long enough to extend it beyond reasonable limits. He gave his wife Irma six children, and then he left her. Six lightly supervised kids put an awful strain on a ceiling. They also put a strain on the plumbing, as all sorts of debris found its way into toilets. Eight-fifty Longwood Avenue was over fifty years old, and it was beginning to show it.

Emmanuel Margulies, the building's new owner, was doing his best. But even though he had subdivided the once spacious apartments, rent control was killing him. Where was he going to get the money to shore up the sagging infrastructure of 850 Longwood Avenue? The banks, wary of the changing neighborhood and the building's age, refused to give him a loan.

Slowly, Margulies began to diminish the services—the prospect that old Albert Brackman could never face. Margulies was less finicky. A little less heat, a slightly more infrequent garbage collection wasn't going to kill anybody. The more Margulies struggled, however, the less help he got from City Hall. In the liberal euphoria of the Lindsay Administration, every break went the way of the tenants. At one point, it was decreed that when a landlord was found guilty of a violation, *any* violation, the tenant was obliged to pay only one dollar a month in rent until it was fixed. A dollar a month!! There are very few buildings on Park Avenue that are not negligent of *something*, but only in the Bronx and Brooklyn was the bizarre statute enforced. Soon it was overturned, but not before the damage was done. In the middle of wrestling with all this, possibly because of it, Emmanuel Margulies had a heart attack and died.

The building fell to his younger brother Nathan, who had neither the talent nor the temperament for real estate. But the property was too large to ignore. In order to keep a close eye on it, the irascible, easily excitable man moved into a ground-floor office next to the Blue Danube restaurant, now under new ownership and renamed Danubio Azurro. The younger Margulies saw his mission clearly: to resist every entreaty for improvements that came from these people, but to get their rent, whether it came out of their pockets or the welfare office. This he continued to do, even as the services deteriorated.

Meanwhile, the prospects of the Puerto Ricans were not improving. They were not assimilating, like the Jews and Italians before them. Their fathers' jobs did not accrue to them because the jobs themselves were vanishing. The quality of education at nearby Herman Ridder Junior High was nonexistent. Having once taught bright and inquiring (if insolent) Jewish kids, the teachers now taught remedial reading to Puerto Ricans, with no reduction in the insolence. So the good teachers left, and Herman Ridder became less a school than a holding cell. The glee clubs and senior plays that had once engaged Jewish children were replaced, in the Puerto Rican street culture, by gangs. On the steps of 850 Longwood Avenue, where mothers had once dawdled with baby carriages, members of the Savage Nomads now loitered with spiked wristbands.

⸺

The moon had risen in the Catskills, announcing itself only by a silver haze that limned the hilltops. On nights like these, Marc Greenberg liked to sit outside his cabin and play his flute for hours on end, until the loons answered him. He did not do so tonight, because he had no flute. Nor did he have the lightness of heart.

As soon as he began allowing sick or disoriented Kochvilleans to spend the night at his apartment in the city, he knew there would be abuses. The homeless were no angels. It came as no surprise, then, when he got home one night and found his liquor cabinet empty. You had to be patient with them. Instant rehabilitation happened only in the movies. Greenberg had learned that years ago on his first day as a counsellor at a camp for the under-privileged. Five minutes after he got there a lovable, underprivileged child kicked him in the stomach and stole his radio.

But the theft of his flute was an offense of a different magnitude. It wasn't a thing, it was a piece of his soul. If they stole your money, they were saying "Look man, I need this and you got a lot of it, nothing personal." The flute, however, was personal. Immensely so.

Marc Greenberg was feeling like a chump, a frequent feeling among those who work with the poor. It prompted a jolting question: What if the right-wingers were right? Ronald Reagan was hung in effigy and ridiculed in every enlightened enclave in the United States, but what if the old bastard was right!? Social programs and welfare and Operation Headstart and everything like it proceeded from the assumption that people responded to kindness and second chances. But what if that was bullshit? What if kindness created a culture of beggars and wheedlers and lazy manipulators?

Even if you believed society had made monsters out of these people, the fact remained that they were monsters. And they were going to perform their monstrosities on *you* unless you got the hell out of the way. At some point, it was a matter of self-respect.

Kochville had broken Marc Greenberg's heart. There were nights, early on, when he had wept at the beauty of it all. Here were people daring to dream for the first time. You had only to look in Duke York's one good eye to see the magic. Suddenly everything was possible: justice, equality, happiness, you name it. Hell, they were like fifth graders getting their first civics lesson and *believing* it. And then, just when you got that dreamy look in your own eyes, they kicked you in the stomach and stole your radio.

Marc Greenberg felt suddenly exhausted and decided to turn in. All over the lake, people sat and waited for the moon to come over the hill. There was an innocence about this ritual, as if the people didn't know whether or not the old silver orb would make it this time. Marc Greenberg wasn't in the mood.

≡

Even as he sat and listened to the fiddlers in the Rollicking Molly pub, Ed Koch had a bad feeling. A politician knows when he's said the wrong thing, the same way a football placekicker knows instantly when he's blown a field goal. It's the way it comes off the toe.

Until this point, the Irish trip had been a miracle, a week of grace. The mayor had been to Europe many times since he first marched across France forty years earlier with the Allied Army. Frequently, these were gormandizing expeditions to sample the food in Paris, or Provence, or Tuscany. But the Irish do not cook well, and even if they did, that was not the kind of trip Cardinal O'Connor had in mind. The Cardinal was going from County Cork to County Down and every place in between, saying mass. And since the mayor was tagging along, he knelt in the front row, fingers moist from the holy water, and played along. It was an odd spot to find an old Crotona Park Jew, but what were his options? Was he going to repair to a local pub and gorge on fish and chips encrusted in fat, and wash it down with the despised Guinness?

No, might as well check out the competition, as old Rabbi Hershkowitz from the Bronx would have said. But a curious thing happened as Ed Koch knelt there, his arthritic knees paying the price of the wet Irish mornings.

His soul blossomed.

The mayor was a fiercely proud Jew, and on the High Holy Days he showed up at temple, threw on a yarmulke and a tallis, and moved his lips to the ancient incantations. But not for a long time had he sat in one of these huge empty spaces, be it cathedral, synagogue, or mosque, and simply let his soul roam through the silence. This he allowed himself to do in Ireland, in churches large and small, in town and country vale. So the trip had been a rare delight, a spiritual oil change for a man badly in need of one.

And then came Carlingford. This was an ancient little seaside town poised between the North and South of Ireland, and the venue of an informal mayoral press conference about the perennial troubles between the Protestants and the Catholics. The mayor shot from the hip, as usual. Based on his observations in the North, from whence he had just come, the mayor thought the rap on the British Army rather unfair. They were not a barbarous occupying force, as the rhetoric suggested. The mayor thought them more of a peacekeeping unit, like the U.N. occasionally deployed to the troubled places of the earth where people couldn't get along and needed adults to step in and take the guns away.

It was not long after the press conference, minutes really, before the mayor started to have a bad feeling. All through evening mass it grew, and now, during the furious fiddling in the Rollicking Molly, his mood was intensely worrisome. When the mayoral party emerged into the damp night air of County Louth, the ominous feelings took a human form. One of the mayor's aides was standing on the roadway with a tear sheet off a wire service. The mayor's remarks had been broadcast on the evening news in New York. The reaction had taken very little time to build to a crescendo of outrage.

A "peacekeeping" force!!?, bellowed an Irish assemblyman from upstate, whose great-grandfather had died in the potato famine, and whose nephew had been cut in half by a British machine gun. Perhaps, suggested the assemblyman, the mayor should have spent less time on his knees in church and more time in pubs listening to the lyrics of the songs. He might then have learned that the British bastards have been oppressing and murdering the Irish for three hundred years!!

The look on the face of the young mayoral aide on the dark streets of Carlingford said it all. Disaster. The Irish vote in New York was critical to anyone wishing to be elected dog-catcher, and the mayor had lost it in as much time as it had taken him to say "peacekeeping force."

The flight home the next day was a grim voyage indeed. Throughout, the mayor kept up appearances, so ensconced in his Irish souvenirs that he looked like some huge, demented leprechaun. But the gloom of the mayoral party was palpable.

The mayor touched down at Kennedy Airport as Michael Dukakis was being nominated standard-bearer of the Democratic Party. But none of the questions at the airport press conference had to do with that or with any of the dozen scourges that had befallen New York in the mayor's absence. There was medical waste washing up on the beaches of Long Island, including syringes. The Emergency 911 vehicles had been breaking down, and the whole fleet might have to be replaced, and there was no money to pay for it. Ordinarily the press would skewer him with these items, absolutely roast him on the sizzling summer sidewalks. Instead, they wanted to know only one thing: How did he feel about the threat of the Ancient Order of Hibernians not to invite him to the St. Patrick's Day parade?

The St. Patrick's Day parade?! The St. Patrick's Day parade was in *March*, for Christ's sake, nine months away!! But the reporters, of course, were right. The Irish vote mattered far more than syringes or doomed Greek Americans running for president.

Years earlier, the mayor had almost choked to death in a Chinese restaurant, and even as the Heimlich maneuver was being administered, he was trying to assure a group of Jewish observers that it was watercress, and not the forbidden pork, that was lodged in the mayoral throat.

This was a political creature.

For the week following his return to New York, the mayor was obliged to humble himself. Hourly apologies were issued from City Hall to every Irish police fraternal lodge and fife-and-drum corps in existence. A parade of windbags arrived at City Hall to "educate" the mayor about the history of Irish oppression. And greatest humiliation of all, the mayor was obliged to reverse his position on Joe Doherty, a member of the Irish Republican Army who was currently in custody in New York for killing a British soldier. Until now, Koch had made no secret of his contempt for the cowardly, murdering Doherty. Now, the mayor was forced to have a sudden flash of insight about Doherty's heroism. The mayor was almost choking on his own bullshit, and indeed the British tabloids and the American conservative press crucified him for his hypocrisy. But he endured it all and waited for the fresh headline that would mercifully change the subject. The nomination of Dukakis had not done so, the upcoming nomination of Bush surely wouldn't, but something eventually had to . . . didn't it?! He made a note to call Cardinal O'Connor and ask him what kind of miracle all his Irish praying now entitled him to.

When the event came that finally got New Yorkers off the mayor's case, he was vacationing in the Hamptons. Larry Locke was sitting in a meeting of homeless veterans and fantasizing about Ellen McCarthy, Marc Greenberg was back in the city trying to decide what to do about Kochville, and Duke York was sitting on a park bench listening to Matthew rhapsodize about the joys of an amphetamine high. The night that Tompkins Square blew, the lives of all these people would change forever.

Tompkins Square Park, on New York's Lower East Side, has meant different things to the different generations that have lived beside it. After the Civil War it was a militia parade ground. By the turn of the century, the newly arrived Ukrainian Jews were courting under its elms and talking politics in its gazebos. Forty years later, in the years just after World War Two, Charlie "Bird" Parker might be found on a bench next to other musicians like Charlie Mingus and Dizzy Gillespie, nodding hello to the new white hipsters, the Kerouacs and the Ginsbergs, the shock troops of the Beat Generation. Twenty years after that, in the sixties, Jimi

Hendrix stood on the bandshell playing a guitar with his teeth. Now, in the eighties, the park had become the front line for the great battle of the age: Land.

There was a homeless enclave in the park, not nearly so organized as the one in City Hall Park, but with a longer history. For years now it had coexisted with the burgeoning punk movement—assorted musicians and wild young things with hair every color of the rainbow. As it did in the forties and again in the sixties, the park represented a free zone, a place where misbehavior and free expression were a way of life.

Recently there had been a threat to all that. Inexplicably, there had been a tightening of the rules; more police, more arbitrary arrests, even talk of a curfew. Then it began to dawn on everyone: those well-groomed young men and women who occasionally walked their pure-bred dogs through the park were not tourists or drag queens with droll taste. They were yuppies, and they were moving into the neighborhood—mostly into the old tenements that cagey landlords had gutted and repackaged as luxury condominiums. The yuppies required cleanliness in their parks, and because their money exercised a degree of leverage with the police, they were getting it—at the cost of the bone marrow of the Lower East Side culture.

Nowhere were the class lines in New York more clearly drawn. The symbol of it all was the Christadora House beside the park—sixteen floors of polished granite adorned by seraphim. By far the largest and most splendid building in the neighborhood, the Christadora had been erected in the twenties as a settlement house, a refuge from the teeming Lower East Side. Here the newly arrived Eastern Europeans could read a book, play a piano in a room all by themselves (like the young Irving Berlin did on Wednesday nights), or climb to the roof to catch a breeze. But during the Depression the building began to decline, and finally, since the seventies, had stood empty. Now it had been re-incarnated as a luxury co-op with a concierge named Vidor.

At first the incursions against the Christadora had been slight; mottos like DIE YUPPIE SCUM spray painted on the building's marble façade. Soon the acts were bolder. On a recent night, a couple of punks screaming "Free the tree" had rushed the lobby, pushed Vidor aside, stolen a potted palm, and replanted it in the park.

All of this had stepped up the pressure on the police, and they in turn had tightened the screws on the park. It had to blow, and on August 6th it did. Trying to impose a curfew on a rock concert on a hot Saturday night, a squad of cops were met with a barrage of obscenities and finally with a rock. A nervous rookie then tossed some tear gas into the crowd, and now every rock in the park came hurtling back at the police. A call was made to headquarters, and a hundred cops arrived in riot gear. The punks, playing right along, gave them a riot. The event became a youth war. Some of the youths had pink hair, others wore police uniforms. Everyone was scared witless and swinging blindly, and blood ran in the gutters. The residents inside the Christadora trembled like Marie Antoinette before the guillotine. The New York City Police Department responded with everyone available, and by the time Mayor Koch was rushed back from the Hamptons in a limousine, the reporters were calling it a police riot.

The event had touched a nerve in the cops, be they trembling rookies or cynical veterans. The wildly immoral and disrespectful youth of Tompkins Square Park had given them a target for all their rage. Shaved heads were crushed with sickening thuds. Mounted police galloped chaotically through crowds of purple-haired children. The big brass of the NYPD, great warriors with chestfuls of medals and shocks of white Irish hair, were impotent to stop it. The troops were loose and swinging for themselves.

Everyone in New York was riveted to the event. The Lower East Side has more photographers and filmmakers per square foot than anyplace on earth, and they were all out snapping and shooting. The footage was replayed over and over. The heat of summer in New York brings everyone to the brink of madness, and here were people who had gone over the brink. For the old Jews on the Lower East Side, the nightmare was full-blown. The hoofbeats of the mounted police called up tales told by their Russian parents of long nights listening for the approach of the Czar's cossacks.

For Ed Koch, it was a mixed experience. First of all, it was a headline and the indiscretions of his trip to Ireland were now old news. But it also meant that force was no longer an option in dealing with the homeless. The police riot in Tompkins Square was ultimately tolerated by the public, but only because the public neither understood nor cared about the bizarre youth culture of the Lower East Side. But a group that evoked public sympathy, like the homeless veterans of City Hall Park, had to be handled far more gingerly.

The longer that gentle old David Dinkins remained in the upcoming mayoral race, the more clearly the battle lines were drawn. The issue was sensitivity. The mayor's abrasive personality, once such a bracing tonic to New Yorkers, had turned toxic. The city, rent by wars between races, between police and punks, between rich and poor, needed a healer.

With respect to Kochville, somewhere there was a kinder, sneakier option, and the mayor would find it. Perhaps not today, but soon. Now that he was back in New York, he would get Henry Stern focussed on this, no matter what that took. There was no longer a choice. With every new day of the group's existence, with every fresh feature story on an old soldier down on his luck, the mayor could feel a chip coming off his granitelike political base.

The task was now to get rid of them without appearing to get rid of them.

New York in midsummer is a test of survival. The ones who endure are the ones who give in to it, who embrace its sensuality, who move more slowly, who allow themselves to sweat. Ultimately, they know, there will be a breeze, a shower, an air-conditioned movie to take the pressure off.

The homeless do not have these options. When the heat settles in, it stays. A paste of sweat and grime clogs the pores; the clothes, which can never be discarded, seal it in. The homeless do not sweat. If they are lucky, they excrete a slow, reluctant ointment. They pray for the evening to bring a breeze, and when it does not, when it brings instead a darker heat, they find a way to manufacture a spiritual breeze.

Across the street from City Hall Park was a deli that carried ice-cold bottles of Colt 45 Malt Liquor. Around sundown, people wandered over to get some. The rules were clear on substance abuse; Larry forbade drugs entirely and demanded that drinking not take place within the strict confines of the camp. So people found a distant bench and drank until they reached what many of them called the Golden Hour. Then, the manic exhaustion of the day, the threatening mobs, the heap of public contempt, all of it fell away. They could think for a moment of their childhood, of their mothers, of their own children when they were babies. In the sweet twilight, not even the rats could bring them down.

But rats love darkness: only darkness-loving rats survive long enough to breed. When the Golden Hour ended and true night fell, the Colt 45 highs wore down, the rats got bolder, and all the other trouble began.

The moist, moonless nights of early August invited sensuality. But since sex was not an option, the men of Kochville had fights. If you swung at somebody or even got swung at, you sweated and you felt the flesh, and that would do for now.

There were different kinds of fighting in Kochville, just as under better circumstances there might have been different kinds of sex. Besides Mickey, there were a couple of other gay men in the camp, and something about them seemed to set everyone off. A psychologist would probably have theorized that the men of

Kochville were afraid of the woman in themselves. The Koch-villeans knew nothing of such theories; they only knew how sweet it felt to bury a fist in that soft flesh and watch a man in a dress crumple to the ground.

Weakness, frailty, the smell of blood . . . these were the tonics of August. Stan, a frail, white, Korean War vet, was one of the blood sacrifices. In general, white homeless men tended to keep to themselves, sleeping together in Bowery-style alcoholic clusters. Only the most fearless ventured into the shelters, which were a black culture. To survive in there, like in most prisons, a white man had to strut and not betray his fear, even for a second. Lonnie had perfected this, so much so that he actually had black men afraid of him. Not Stan.

Stan did not strut, he complained. Disabled by cataracts after thirty years as a longshoreman, Stan was now reduced to standing on welfare lines with black people, which he considered an indignity. Once, shortly after cashing his check, he was robbed by a black man. Now, he was forced to live among them in a public park.

All of this he felt to be part of a lifetime run of bad luck. As a child he had had to chase his drunken father down and beg him for child support payments. As an adult, his defining relationship was with a wealthy woman who constantly betrayed him. Every so often he would come home and find her in bed with "some socialite," as Stan put it. Once Stan pistol-whipped one of these guys, and the woman warned him that if it happened again, they were through. Figuring the only way to hold onto this broad was with dough, Stan set out to get some.

He robbed a bank, pretending that a vodka bottle wrapped in a towel was a bomb. Once he got the money he jumped into a cab, rode it a few blocks, then jumped into another cab, just like he'd seen in the movies. After a lot more of this maneuvering, with more cabs and trains and planes, Stan arrived in Las Vegas, where he was immediately arrested. It seems he'd dropped his driver's license at the scene of the bank robbery. He did a year at Attica and now here he was, complaining to black people about the bad luck of being among them.

Basically, Stan was pathetic and no one in Kochville intended to brutalize him. It began subtly, with people jostling him whenever he passed. He would complain, and that rated a little more jostling, maybe a punch in the back or a kick in the calf. Finally, Stan was just a welter of bruises. If there was a bloody wound, that would become the most tempting target. He was being picked apart. Finally he left, bleeding massively in several places and talking to himself. He disappeared into a VA psych ward and no one ever heard from him again.

Among themselves, the proud black men did not pick and jostle, they swung. The tail end of a drunken night was a good time to fight, because the booze acted as an anesthetic. Duke and little Art tried to control these fights or at least to prevent them from spilling over into the street. Every cop in City Hall knew that finding a legitimate reason to shut down Kochville would be warmly appreciated by the mayor.

But there was only so much Duke and Art could do, and many of the nights of August saw gross carnage.

＝

Most of the time during the violence of late summer, Larry Locke was nowhere to be found. He didn't return to the park until long after dark, usually because he was at a meeting arranged by Marc Greenberg.

After much soul-searching, Greenberg had decided to forgive Kochville for the stolen flute. He was not a petty man, and he would not allow his personal hurts to interfere with the movement. He threw himself into the education of Larry Locke, making sure the leader of Kochville was well versed not only in the mechanisms of government, but in all the habits of white men in high places. But Marc Greenberg was doing this joylessly and partially for his own personal goals. Even within the ranks of the nonprofit saints there are ambitious people, and Greenberg was becoming one of them. He was no longer the timid soul who had agonized over the ethics of putting the homeless in harm's way. Now he dared to ask the question "What's in it for me?" And if, as Greenberg hoped, Larry Locke became the most visible homeless spokesman in New York, then Marc Greenberg would be the homeless world's Angelo Dundee, the trainer of Muhammad Ali.

Larry was proving an apt pupil—not just about the arena of politics, but about the patient, minute world of forms and papers and regulations. He even wore the uniform of the job, a tie and jacket . . . all of which further inflamed Rasta and Horace.

"Motherfucker walkin' through here every day with an attaché case," Horace would whisper furtively through the camp. "People givin' donations to Greenberg, Greenberg givin' the money to Larry Locke. You think we ever see any of it?"

Whenever Duke York overheard one of these conversations he tried to intervene.

"Somebody got to be up there arguin' for us," he would say. "You think you're smart enough, why don't you do it?"

"Because," Horace would snap, "you ain't gonna get nowhere pushin' papers around a damn desk. You know how many goddamn empty buildings there is in this city? All you got to do is move in. Don't need to ask nobody's permission."

Indeed, the squatting option was becoming more and more talked about in Kochville, as it was in enclaves of the poor all over New York. The thousands of empty, tax-delinquent buildings cried out for some sort of faster occupancy than the lumbering city bureaucracy was providing.

"So why the hell don't we be doin' that?"

"I'm sure Larry got a good reason why we're waitin' on that," said Duke.

"Well, why don't we just ask him?" said Horace one night,

knowing full well that was impossible, since Larry wasn't home yet. "I'll tell you why," Horace continued, "because he off fucking that Irish bitch while we sittin' out here eatin' garbage. Gettin' himself a little piece of corned beef and cabbage."

Duke had no idea whether or not that was true, but he respected Ellen McCarthy, and he was sorely tempted to hurt the fat, helpless Horace. But his mission was to stop fights, not start them, so he ignored the remark. Frustrated, Horace turned the argument to the man he knew he could inflame. "Hey Lonnie," he said. "How do you crackers feel when you find out the white girls like the dark meat, huh? Because they do, you know. Miss Tennessee, I heard her blood bubbles when the dark bacon comes on the pan. She tired of all them tiny white peckers. Like yours."

And so the evening's fight began. Lonnie and Horace stood flailing at each other, as they frequently did. But because the gunpowder of Tompkins Square was still in the air, this night became more intense than others. Rasta started swinging at Lonnie. This brought Matthew in, who detested Rasta. Pretty soon, it was a melee. Only Duke and little Art tried to break it up; everyone else was swinging wildly. The women in the camp, the now enormously pregnant Princess and a couple of others, huddled together in dread. Tree limbs cracked, teeth flew out, blood sprayed. It was the worst anyone had seen. After a few minutes, most of the men were on the ground, crawling off to a corner of the park dragging a limp arm or leg. The ones still on their feet kept swinging madly, fists slamming broken noses until bloody membrane slid down faces and dropped into the dust.

At this moment, Larry arrived back in the park carrying his attaché case. He stared at the spectacle for a while, uncertain what to do. Then a fury began building within him and finally took over. He flew into the fight and began swinging. He was a physically powerful man who kept a lot inside; unleashed, he was frightening. Those who could, backed away. He was flailing like a windmill. His eyes were full of blood. He was starting to hurt people.

"Stop it!! You crazy niggers, stop it!!!" screamed a female voice. It penetrated everybody's consciousness, even Larry's. Females rarely asserted themselves in the camp. A woman no one had ever seen before was standing on a bench, hands on hips. "You lookin' like fools on a chain gang."

Everyone took her in. She was a slight thing, dressed in incredibly inappropriate clothes; some kind of old-fashioned dress far too delicate for the street. But she had a certain authority. She had stopped the fight, which Art and Duke had failed to do. And once stopped, it was the kind of fight that no one wanted to resume.

Larry sat on a tuft of grass, drenched with sweat and blood, and stared at the strange new woman. He heard her tell someone her name was Samantha. Ordinarily a new woman was a topic of fascination to Kochville, Larry included. But tonight he didn't care. Duke offered him a wet towel, but he refused it. Instead, he stood up and walked away and wound up down by the East River. He took a pint of milk out of his attaché case, poured some of it out, and poured in some brandy from a flask in his pocket. This was Larry Locke's version of Colt 45, a cut above the rank and file's.

He sat for a long time watching the river, feeling his wounds. For some reason, images of Newark came into his head. It was the first time he'd thought of that hellhole in a long time. He'd been ripped away from North Carolina by his bitch of a mother, only to arrive in a place where all hell was breaking loose, namely the Newark riots of 1968. As soon as he got there, he had to choose which side he was on, so he chose both. By day, he ran with the pack, looting hardware and appliance stores with his new friends. Then, by night, he would put on a choir robe and sing in his mother's church. He felt like he was living a lie both ways.

But the most awful memory was the last day of the riots. The madness was over, and peace had almost been restored. He was walking home with his best friend's mother, when suddenly an errant police bullet ricocheted off a sidewalk and killed her.

Sitting now by the water with his brandy and milk, he remembered the incident in detail for the first time since then. The dead woman lying there. Should that have been proof enough that the white man was evil? Were all attempts to fit in with him, to please him, to work with him, whatever, bound to end in sorrow . . . like the blood on the ground of Kochville tonight? Was it his fault? Should he have ripped off the choir robe in Newark and joined the revolution full time? Was he a house nigger then? Was he now?

He was not getting the buzz he felt entitled to after a pint of brandy and milk. Instead he was feeling the tie knotted around his throat. He ripped open his collar, popping a few buttons. He was feeling the need to run, which was familiar. This time he wanted to run from Jews teaching him about board meetings.

In her small Brooklyn apartment, Ellen McCarthy turned off the television as George Bush was accepting the Republican nomination for President. This was entertainment? Every four years she tuned into the conventions hoping for a little drama, but no luck. These things never went past the first ballot anymore. The most she could hope for here was an assassination, a hail of bullets piercing Bush's Yale blazer and sending his lifeless corpse tumbling into the sea of assholes below him.

She smiled at herself. That was a little unladylike. But she hated Republicans in almost a racial way. She hated the way they looked, talked, and smelled. Perhaps it was her Irish blood. George Bush reminded her of an Englishman.

Every day now, Ellen McCarthy found a new way to surprise herself. Even though she was a grandmother and it was 1988, she was living the sixties, which she had basically missed. She had married in 1955 and spent the next twenty-five years raising three kids and being a helpmate to a traditional blue-collar husband. Now she was letting it rip.

Shortly after her divorce, she had moved into a small apartment in Brooklyn and begun volunteering among the poor. Her kids were delighted that she was going to have something to occupy herself, but . . . the homeless? And did she have to be so tireless and dedicated about it? Almost immediately she became consumed by the work and gained a reputation as the budding saint of New York. Her own grandchildren didn't know she'd ever been anything else. Sometimes they'd be standing with her on a subway platform and homeless people would amble by and address her by name.

But the eighties were not the sixties, and the daily drudgery of ministering to the homeless was not like the thrill of flinging one's brassiere into a bonfire. That was the appeal of Kochville. The incredible innocence of these people! Learning about government, thinking they could influence it—all of it was old hat to everyone else, but not to Ellen McCarthy. And in the middle of it was this lonely, complicated man, Larry Locke. He symbolized it, and he suffered for it. She had a huge crush on him. If it were the sixties, she sometimes thought, she might have adored some young white boy who looked like Jesus Christ.

But it was 1988 and she was past fifty, which also meant she understood the value of time. The romance with Larry had been a long while in the gestation. That was fine. She could wait. She had already waited.

She moved easily about her small bright apartment, dusting. That was another thing that separated her from the sixties. Her place was not adorned with black light posters of Jim Morrison or shredded American flags. In her two windows fluttered immaculate lace curtains, and the whole place glowed with a supreme tidiness. She finished up and opened a window to admit the breeze off the East River. A giddy, stupid, familiar feeling came over her that it took a while to pin down. In the years just after

World War Two, she and her prepubescent girlfriends would go on jaunts to the beach, looking for some gorgeous returning G.I. Suddenly there he was, the one you wanted, bouncing along the boardwalk in that olive uniform that had liberated the world. He raised his eyes and looked at you, and that's when that giddy, stupid feeling set in.

There was a knock on the door. At first she didn't hear it through the volume of the music she was playing—the Chieftains, an Irish instrumental group that reached back into the pagan tradition for their melodies and their instruments.

But the knock was persistent, and she knew, finally, who it was. To a sad air played by fiddle and tin whistle, she opened the door to Larry Locke. Not a great deal was said between them. She led him in, and they sat a while beside the window. It grew darker. Finally he took her hand and began turning it over gently, examining it, prodding it, as if she were a strange creature in a forest and he were another. She watched his face as he did this.

He closed his eyes and tried to separate things out: which was the joy of her touch, and which was the joy of any touch at all? Which was the joy of being in her house, and which was the joy of being under any roof, his cheek brushed by anybody's lace curtain? Finally he decided that none of that mattered. He took her face in his hands and kissed her.

Beyond the sofa were the dim outlines of a bed, of a quilt, of puffed-up pillows. This was a lady's house. Before he would foul it, he told her, he would take a long hot shower and scour himself clean.

As he stood naked in the steaming bathroom, ready to step under a stream of blessed hot water, she rapped lightly on the door and opened it a crack. In came her thin white arm, first bearing a candle, and then a glass of Irish whiskey with a cube of ice.

After Larry had been gone a few days, Duke figured the chief was off on a mission for the good of the camp. This habit of Duke's, of wanting to believe the best about people, made most of his acquaintances want to slap him. Duke simply had no instinct for survival. Around the camp he was thought of as one big pulsing heart—as opposed to a hard penis or a pair of fists, the body parts that more often symbolized the men of Kochville.

Whenever there was sickness or sorrow in the camp, it was Duke who bought the flowers or organized the trip to the hospital. When Mickey's mother died, who else would have put together the memorial service but Duke? Otherwise the friendless transvestite would have had to deal with it alone and homeless in New York.

Frequently, Duke's heart was so huge it was laughable. Already, the fish story was lore in Kochville.

Someone had put a pair of goldfish in the park fountain, and they had become unofficial pets. There was something peaceful about watching them swim around in there. Then one day the word came that the pond was going to be temporarily drained to repair a few cracks. What would happen to the fish? Duke wanted to know.

No one had even thought about it. Probably the fish would die, and if anyone really wanted more of them, then a couple would be found once the pond had been refilled.

This was not nearly good enough for Duke York. After several dozen frantic phone calls, Duke found a liberal supporter of Kochville with an aquarium in her home. On the morning of the draining of the fountain, Duke obtained a large, heavy duty plastic bag and filled it with water and the two goldfish. Carrying this thing, which weighed close to fifty pounds, Duke entered the New York City subway system, bound for the woman's home on Ninety-Sixth Street.

But by the time the train had gone a couple of stops, the bag had sprang a leak. By Fourteenth Street, it was losing water rapidly, and Duke realized they weren't going to make it. He bolted from the train and ran up to the street, desperately seeking another bag, a glass jar, anything. The large black man with one glass eye racing around Union Square with a bag sprouting water and screaming "The fish, the fish!!" was off-putting to passersby, and they cut him a wide berth. Restaurants that might have solved the problem with a vase or a new garbage bag would not let him in the door. Finally out of options, the bag almost dry, Duke exercised what seemed like the final option. Gulping water from a public drinking fountain, he put the fish in his mouth, puffing out his cheeks to give them a little more room.

Just how long he would have done this, or what he would have done next, is not known. Happily, a sympathetic, amazed oberver pieced the story together. She was on her way home with a couple of large mason jars for preserves. She let Duke have one, he filled it with water, and he and the fish completed their journey without further incident.

The story was oft repeated, lushly embroidered with each telling, and it never failed to produce gales of laughter. Less amusing, however, was Duke's human fish story: his endless, miserable relationship with Diane.

Duke never stopped moaning about her, and as the details of the romance became clearer to his friends in the camp, so too did the pathology. Apparently, one day Diane had grown so impatient with his gentle, unaggressive stance toward the world that she had laid down the law: wake up and get a real job. You have a wife and two daughters, and you spend all your time making music— beautiful music, granted, but music that you don't have the moxie to then go out and sell. What the hell is the point of spending eight hours a day dubbing and redubbing these eight-track tapes if you don't get them out into the world?

Because, Duke would explain, money wasn't the point. There was a spiritual element to it that Diane wasn't getting. What she wasn't getting, she said, was money to feed their daughters. And so the argument raged, until Diane reached her limit. One winter night Duke came home to find her sitting in front of the fireplace, staring at the flames. Melting and burning were his tapes— all of them, his life's work.

To Matthew, who listened to all this one day, the tape burning was not even the most horrifying part of the story. Far worse than that he *forgave her for it*. "You gotta understand where she was coming from," said Duke. "She had her own anxieties." Maybe that was true. All Matthew knew was that at that point he would have beaten the crap out of her, or left, or at least not continued to go around moaning about how much he still loved her.

Certainly, thought Matthew, a fool like this should not be running Kochville. Nevertheless, after Larry Locke had been absent a few days, that is the position in which Duke York found himself. He was the obvious choice. He was a passionate orator with a tremendous capacity to feel—but not necessarily to act.

The timing could not have been worse. The bloody battle earlier in the week had begun a strange, trying period in Kochville, and it demanded a strong leader. It was more than just the fighting and drinking and rats. The intense heat and exhaustion was creating a sort of group mental illness.

City Hall was a little too quiet, as they say in westerns. People knew that Ed Koch was planning to somehow dismantle them, but they didn't know how or when. For the moment, Big Mouth was sleeping, but only because some subtler, more venomous thing was about to happen. Frazzled by the worst heat of summer, Kochville began to imagine things. Were the drinking fountains poisoned? Were there cameras inside City Hall, infrared equipment that could record their movements in the night? Were the flower beds hiding microphones that picked up their every subversive word? New arrivals were scrutinized endlessly. No matter how bereft, ragged, or insane they appeared to be, they might be spies for the government.

It was chaos. Kochville appeared to be shredding and Duke

York couldn't stop it. The dream was dying, and he began to take the sadness and suffering into his huge body, which was his habit. The Catholics in the group said he was punishing himself like one of the famous martyrs.

At first he complained of headaches and listlessness. Then it got worse. He would lie all day on a bench, sweating and hallucinating. Finally it got so bad that he couldn't stand to be near anyone, so he crept away. First he isolated himself in a corner of the park, where he deteriorated further. Then he crossed the street to a rarely used subway station and descended into the darkest corner, wishing only to decay in peace.

Nine

By 1974, Nathan Margulies' solution to the disintegration of the Bronx was self-defense. To that end, he stocked the desk drawers of his office at 850 Longwood with weapons, from handguns to lead pipes. What choice did he have? he asked any sympathetic listener. No fat Irish cop was going to get himself killed screwing around with the Savage Nomads. One night he returned to the office to find a Puerto Rican kid rustling around in the dark. According to neighborhood legend, Margulies grabbed a lead pipe and bludgeoned him senseless, only stopping when he realized it was his secretary's son, picking up some keys she'd left behind.

The building buzzed about the incident for a while, but it was insignificant in the larger, grimmer apocalypse. It was enough, however, for Victoria Hernandez. For a while she had grappled with the question of whether to stay or go. Her brother Rafael was ill with cancer back in Puerto Rico. Should she nurse the dying man or remain in New York, championing his music? The Margulies incident pushed her over the edge, and she sold the business to another Puerto Rican, a talented young musician named Mike Amadeo. The only good-bye she dreaded was the one to the abandoned wife of Bobby Ortiz. Victoria was now godmother to the woman's youngest, and frankly, Irma Ortiz was a bit helpless and a bit mad. She had filled her apartment with votive candles and dozens of plaster saints, as if that could somehow mitigate the vast misery of her world. Victoria felt deeply for her, but not enough to remain in the hell of the Bronx. With a long embrace she left Irma Ortiz and young Juan, her godson, and went downstairs to a waiting car.

Victoria Hernandez had arrived in New York in 1924 in a sailing sloop, and she was leaving in 1974 in an airplane. She had been on planes of the propeller variety before, but this was her first jet. As it roared off the La Guardia runway, it veered first to the northwest and gave her a parting picture of the Bronx. The faraway houses were almost quaint, and the evening seemed the perfect peaceful height of summer, studded with fireflies. It was only after several dreamy minutes that she realized she was looking not at fireflies but at fires. The Bronx was burning.

This was no biblical apocalypse, but pure business. Many landlords in the position of Nathan Margulies were simply giving up on the idea of collecting any further revenues from their buildings. The only conceivable milk left in the cow was fire insurance. All over the Bronx little conflagrations were erupting, many of them planned in an orderly fashion. Children excused themselves early from school so they could get home for the family fire. Firemen began to park the engines on the street rather than bothering to open, close, and reopen the firehouse door.

But Nathan Margulies did not have the stomach for arson. There was a Plan B for fed up landlords, and it involved the services of one George Montgomery, the neighborhood's best "finisher." In a more innocent time in the Bronx, that might have implied a star relief pitcher for the New York Yankees, a Ryne Duren or a Joe Paige. But George Montgomery was a different kind of finisher.

At some point after Nathan Margulies stopped paying his real estate taxes, the City would take over 850 Longwood Avenue. In the interim, Montgomery would do his finishing; that is, he would strip the building of anything remotely valuable, from the yellow brass plumbing to the polished brass doorknobs. Then Margulies and Montgomery would split the salvage money.

What caused Margulies to finally make his move was not a local but an international event. With the energy crisis of 1974, fuel oil prices skyrocketed and even the meager heat he was giving his tenants in winter became unthinkably expensive. It was time to walk away and to call George Montgomery.

When Montgomery arrived, however, he did not find the building that easy to finish. He had competition in the form of local junkies, who also prized the valuable brass pipes. Someone from Montgomery's staff was killed during a struggle for the fifth-floor plumbing, and Montgomery told Margulies he wanted nothing more to do with 850 Longwood Avenue. This was the last frustration for Nathan Margulies. He unloaded the building to a holding company for a song and walked away for good.

If Margulies had waited a few more years, the building would have been far easier to strip. By the late 1970s, the drug industry was changing. No longer was it dominated by the kind of desperate user-dealer who killed for plumbing. The sale and marketing of drugs was becoming a huge and sophisticated business: it could not be entrusted to someone high on drugs. The Bronx found itself in competition with places like Washington Heights, where commuters to or from New Jersey could pull off the George Washington Bridge and score quickly and easily. In order to survive, Bronx dealers had to run a trim, lean business. Anybody who gummed up the works was instantly dispensable.

In 1980, a druglord named Guiterrez became a familiar figure on Longwood Avenue. A dapper Dominican, he strode about like a dictator, throwing money to the children who danced and trailed behind him. It was understood that he asked for nothing in return but their loyalty; perhaps if a wealthy stranger wished to know where a certain substance might be obtained, the child might be willing to point in the right direction. The dark side of Guiterrez, however, was swift and brutal. The price of disloyalty was death.

Guiterrez was not the only figure to rise to power over the barren landscape. In 1976 Jimmy Carter campaigned on the ruins of Charlotte Street, vowing to reclaim it. Four years later, Ronald Reagan shot a campaign ad on the same patch of rubble, claiming that Carter had reneged on his promises.

The South Bronx had become the most celebrated slum on earth. Dignitaries who toured it were agape at the sheer desolation and for comparisons had to reach back for images like Dresden or Hiroshima. A river of antipoverty money flowed into the Bronx, and petty politicians, suddenly faced with huge blocks of cash to divvy up, squabbled incessantly and in one case killed each other over it.

Everyone had a theory about what to do for the Bronx, and the most radical idea of all was terrifying for the good sense it made. Why not, suggested city planner Roger Starr, simply withdraw from certain areas altogether and let them go fallow? Why should subways stop in places where no one got off and no one got on? Why should banks have branches there? With this idea came all sorts of bizarre corollaries. If the Bronx then became completely abandoned in sections, why not take advantage of the open spaces and simply plant them? Why not, say, turn them into wildflower meadows?

The idea was fantastic, but because it appealed to both environmentalists and very pragmatic politicians, it was actually tried. Young idealists poured into the Bronx and spent their days mixing compost out of decayed vegetables from the Hunt's Point market and animal feces from the Bronx Zoo (zoo-doo, for short). Sitting on a rock reading a newspaper and trying to keep his shoes clean was a ward machine politician who knew nothing of horticulture but was being paid to simply sit there.

The beneficiaries of all this, until it proved totally impractical, were the kids of Irma Ortiz. For the first time since Albert Brackman's halcyon days, there were patches of green to run through. The joy of the Ortiz children was always short lived, however. At dusk the huge water rats emerged from the Bronx River and virtually chased them home.

When they got there, they faced a grim reality. Eight-fifty Longwood Avenue was disintegrating. The phantom owner to whom Margulies had sold the building wasn't even attempting to collect the rent. By now there was no heat and no water, and the stench of urine hung in every hallway. Most of the tenants had bailed out, but Ms. Ortiz remained with her three youngest children, largely because she had no money and no choice. By the early 1980s Juan was eight, and was beginning to be of some help to his mother. But this was more than offset by the new responsibility of Emilio, her seventh child, who was born nine months after a drunken late night visit by Bobby Ortiz.

No fancy politician ever visited Longwood Avenue, with one exception. One day Deputy Mayor Herman Badillo took some reporters through the neighborhood to show them what the city was doing for the poor. Standing on the street outside 850, the handsome, Harvard-educated Badillo saw some workmen hauling a radiator down the street and told the reporters that it was no doubt a crew from the Department of Housing Preservation and Development, on their way to install some heat for a needy family. Later, Badillo was embarrassed to be told that the people with the radiator were not city workmen but thieves, and that the radiator had just been stolen.

Irma Ortiz was a woman with a sense of humor, despite all her travails and all her dependance on plaster saints, and she found the incident amusing. Had she not been knee-deep in diapers, she would have invited Badillo in for coffee and told him a story of her own. Earlier in the week she had seen workmen tossing the rubble of a demolished building into a truck. She asked them where they were taking it and was told Pound Ridge, an opulent Westchester suburb. Apparently an architect had been searching high and low for just the right kind of nineteenth-century bricks for a multimillion dollar private renovation and had found them on the ground in the Bronx.

Larry Locke had missed several days of meetings, and Marc Greenberg was pissed off. He'd invested a lot of time in Larry, and this was the payback: no note, no call, nothing. All the feelings of the flute theft rushed back: Greenberg the chump, duped again. It was enough to make him wash his hands of the homeless completely.

Then one night, rummaging through some laundry in his closet, he found the flute.

Now he remembered: he'd hidden it there himself, wanting to keep temptation out of the way of his houseguests. He was mortified. He'd made an incredibly hasty and unfair judgment. He began to agonize over his behavior of the past month. Had he become callous for no reason at all?

Not entirely. It had been good for him to toughen up a little and start looking after himself. But the Larry matter had to be reassessed. Why assume that Larry was disrespecting him? That was like assuming the flute had been stolen. Perhaps there was a good explanation for Larry's absence. Maybe he was sick or had a family emergency. If so, Greenberg wanted to find him and hear about it. Immediately he set off for City Hall Park.

As he approached the camp, Greenberg realized he'd barely set foot in it for weeks. Apart from Larry, he had few real relationships with the men and in fact didn't recognize many of them. It took him a while to find someone to listen to his questions, let alone answer them.

"Ain't seen him for awhile. Thought you and him was livin' in a penthouse in Tel Aviv," snarled someone.

Greenberg bit his tongue and scoured the camp for a face he knew.

"Where's Duke?" he said finally, remembering the big black man with the glass eye.

Matthew and little Art looked at each other, each wishing the other would tell the story. Finally, they pointed sheepishly toward the subway station where they knew the sick man was languishing. They had not known how to handle it, they explained as Greenberg headed off. Duke seemed to want to be left alone, they shouted after him, so finally they had wanted to respect that.

Greenberg crossed the street to the subway station, so poorly marked he had never known it existed. Descending into the darkness, he felt nervous but confident. He was once more on a mission of compassion, where he belonged.

He made his way through the gloom, past walls of the elegant, filthy porcelain tiles that adorned the New York subways of long ago. For a while it grew very quiet, and then he heard a sound—more of a moan. There in a corner was Duke York, all but indistinguishable from the darkness around him. Matted with grime, his face, once a gleaming ebony, was now a kind of sickening ochre. He was the kind of homeless man who made even hardened New Yorkers wince.

"Duke?"

A yellow bloodshot eye looked slowly up at Greenberg. "What you want?"

Greenberg took a long time with the answer, because it had to go through a lot of circuits in his brain. He had a memory of this man as clear-eyed and passionate.

"What you want?" repeated Duke.

"To take you home," said Marc Greenberg finally.

He lifted the rank-smelling man to his feet. There was no protest. Struggling with the nearly dead weight, Greenberg managed to get him to the stairs and finally up to the street, where he tried to hail a cab. After about a dozen passed them by, a Haitian stopped and drove them uptown, almost gagging on the smell of Duke York.

Greenberg brought him upstairs past his horrified doorman, threw him in the tub, turned on the shower, and for about an hour scrubbed the man clean. The drain water was almost black. Then he put a clean robe on him, took him up to the roof, and let him sit and breathe the air for another couple of hours. Around dusk, he brought him back downstairs and spoon-fed him some broth.

The next morning, they graduated to fruit purées. Then, after another couple of days, solids. What surprised Marc Greenberg was how good it felt . . . to him. For too long he had been pushing paper and withholding his natural instincts. Now there was something and someone he could touch, and it brought out the mensch and the natural man in him.

Duke was something of a mensch himself, and Greenberg liked him. Until this point, he had never allowed himself to think in those terms. You did not necessarily *like* the poor. They were in bad shape, so you helped them, which was your duty. Truth be told, even though Larry Locke was Greenberg's protegé and he had pinned a lot of hopes on him, Larry was a bit remote for Greenberg's taste. Whereas Duke was a big, warm-hearted, passionate man and Marc Greenberg liked him.

To his profound embarrassment, Greenberg had to admit that he had no black friends. Among his relationships in the nonprofit homeless world, there were many apparent friendships with black people, but they were all somehow strained and careful. You wouldn't just call one of them up if you wanted to go to Lincoln Center and see a foreign movie, or even sit in a bar and watch a ball game.

But Duke York was becoming his friend. Greenberg introduced him to his favorite pastime, which was kayaking across the Hudson River. At first this struck Duke as absolute madness, but in the sweet clear days of early September, he began to see the point of it. The men would travel along the immense Jersey Palisades as evening fell. Duke spoke of Diane, and the sadness of being apart from his two daughters. Marc talked of the sadness of having no one at all, of having a parade of relationships that didn't stick. Duke pointed out that Greenberg seemed to love humanity in general but no one in particular. Greenberg agreed, and admitted how painful and stupid that was.

≡

In the absence of both Larry Locke and Duke York, the reins of Kochville's government fell to the other two members of the ruling committee, little Art and Matthew. They were a curious pair, the small, grim black veteran and the smiling, devious white heroin addict. Neither of them had much taste for politics, and they were content to allow Kochville to drift. The rules of the camp were relaxed and finally ignored. Pilfering and drinking abounded. Without the steel of Locke or the soul of York, Kochville was presumed to be on moral vacation.

But the newspapers were oblivious to all this and remained in love with them. The publicity continued, as did the invitations.

There was a request for someone from the camp to appear on the Mort Downey TV show, and little Art and Matthew leapt at it, especially when they learned it involved a limousine ride. To add a little class to their act they decided to bring along Samantha, the new woman who had so dramatically stopped the bloody fight the week before.

Since her mysterious arrival, everyone's fascination with Samantha had only deepened. The men were both puzzled and obsessed by her. She was sophisticated, intelligent, and immaculate. Every night she would lay fresh linen on the park bench where she slept—linen she got clean any way she could. If she could beg a couple of dollars she would wash her sheets at the laundromat. If not, she would scrub them by hand in the fountain and hang them out to dry on a railing. It was whispered that she would turn tricks to raise money for perfumed laundry soap.

191

Most people didn't believe that. Samantha was a proud creature, and a classy one.

The mystery lay in her sorrow. She was clearly an alcoholic. She would arrive sometimes stinking of gin. Nothing new in that. But her problems did not seem to be of the homeless variety. When she got to talking about them, she sounded like a rich white woman in a café, complaining about her clothes or her divorce. Art couldn't figure her out, but he liked her, craved her actually, and so she rode next to him in the limousine to the Mort Downey show.

Rarely did any of them get to put their rear ends in anything like the crushed velvet seat of a Cadillac, and they were having a ball. "Hey man, where's the nozzle?" asked Matthew.

"The nozzle?" The driver was puzzled.

"Yeh," said Matthew, "so I can spray some champagne into my mouth."

Even the driver smiled. He knew, however, that the smiles would soon be wiped off everyone's faces. Had Art or Samantha or Matthew owned a TV set, they would have known enough about Mort Downey to be less gleeful about the gig. Downey was a right-wing talk show host who specialized in throwing liberals to the wolves. He pandered to an audience of dull-eyed New Jersey teenagers who mistook his viciousness for wit. Today, Matthew and Art and Samantha were the designated victims.

When they arrived, the audience was already shuffling and seething, many of them drinking beer out of cans in paper bags. Downey, a bloated former Irish tenor, was in his domain. His ego clearly at low ebb, he would settle for nothing less than complete ignition of his audience's pubescent rage. Within minutes, they were up on their chunky haunches, yelling "Get a job, you lazy scumbags" at Art and Samantha. For Matthew the white man, they reserved their harshest condemnations, of which "nigger lover" and "black butt-fucker" were the kindest.

The Kochvilleans did their best to defend themselves. Art, for one, asked the white New Jersey teenagers what suburban mall they were jerking off in while he was winning a Purple Heart in Vietnam. This threw Downey, who fancied himself a patriot. But the host soon regained himself and came back strong. Controlling the commercial breaks and the camera angles, he built to a final rant during which he spoke of his grandmother who arrived penniless from Dublin and worked herself into the grave scrubbing floors. Then he turned to his guests from City Hall Park and asked them why they expected handouts for lying around on a lawn all day. The audience roared, and the credits rolled.

Still, the ride back in the limo was not depressing for Art and Matthew. When you're homeless you live in the moment, and a fancy car is a fancy car. Only Samantha had been wounded. "I couldn't believe the hatred in that room," she said. Matthew and Art smiled sadly at each other. "You'd better believe it," they wanted to say to her.

They arrived home to find the benches drawn in a circle but empty. Someone filled in Art and Matthew on the events of the night. Apparently at about eight o'clock, just after their limousine had pulled out, Horace had called a meeting. His plan was to take advantage of their absence and effortlessly take over the government of Kochville. A bloodless coup.

Unfortunately for Horace, it was one of those nights when Kochville got turned inside out. No sooner did his meeting begin, when a half-dozen Puerto Ricans arrived. They had heard about Kochville from a feature story on the radio and immediately rushed down from the Fort Washington Shelter. It was mayhem. First of all, they were young, a couple of them teenagers, all of them wildly disrespectful. They took Kochville to be some kind of pleasure ground where they could misbehave with abandon. The mix with the middle-aged black veterans, who had paid such heavy dues, was like oil with water.

There were no physical fights, but barrages of traded insults, half of them in Spanish. Through it all, Horace tried to keep everyone focussed on the meeting. But even Rasta abandoned him, drawn instead into a mad theatrical screaming match with a Puerto Rican, imitating him, prancing around like a demented rooster. Horace retired to a dark corner of the park, alternately brooding and shouting at everyone.

Art and Matthew wanted no part of this madness. Still feeling festive from the limousine ride home, they went across the street for a couple of Colt 45's. Samantha retired to her bench, laid out her linen, and took from her possessions a small box inlaid with mother-of-pearl that had once belonged to her own mother. She liked to touch it when she needed to go inward and feel her strength. Downey's jackal shrieks were still ringing in her ears.

By and large, Kochville on this night was a portrait of poor people in chaos. Police officer Lee O'Brien, the City Hall cop who had recently been given the job of observing them, painted just such a picture in his nightly report to the mayor's office. Morale was low, he wrote. Violence was rampant, illness seemed to be in evidence, and hysteria and disorganization were chronic.

Ordinarily this would have been welcome news sitting on Ed Koch's desk in the morning. Unfortunately, before the mayor even got to see the good news, it was neutralized by a piece of bad news. According to the AP wire, Jesse Jackson had decided to make a political visit to New York, his first since the convention in Atlanta. And one of the first things he intended to do, he had told the Chicago press, was to visit the valiant homeless group in City Hall Park.

Ed Koch had known for a while that eventually he would have to deal with Jackson. At some point, the two of them would be obliged to make a public show of putting aside their differences and pledge their support for the greater good—the election of Michael Dukakis as president.

This, of course, was baloney. Neither of them cared at all

about Dukakis or his doomed candidacy. The point, for Ed Koch, was his own candidacy in next year's mayoral election. With the Irish vote in tatters, he could ill afford to alienate the black middle class.

Despite his bitter, public wars with the blacks, the mayor had managed to hang onto their votes. The most remarkable proof of this had come in 1985, when the blacks ran one of their own candidates, Denny Farrell. Naturally the mayor crushed him, but the most significant detail was the black vote itself, which the mayor had come within a couple of points of stealing.

As recently as January 1988, his approval ratings in the black community had been higher than ever, owing largely to his public demands for stiff sentences for the white punks in Howard Beach who had chased a black kid to his death on the Belt Parkway. Then, of course, the Jackson thing had screwed everything up. But what was he supposed to have said to someone who referred to New York as "Hymietown?" . . . "Thanks?" . . . "Welcome to the Big Apple??"

No, the mayor had played pretty square with the blacks for just about all of his public life. He was no limousine liberal, either. He had gone to high school with them in Newark, and he had served with them in World War Two. In those days the army was segregated, and no one was more vocal in his objections to that than Ed Koch. They were all in the same boat. In the army, if anything was worse than the racism, it was the anti–Semitism. One day he'd gotten the crap beaten out of him by a white southerner named La Rue, who took equal pleasure in beating up Jews and blacks.

By and large, the mayor didn't overdramatize his civil rights era experiences in Laurel, Mississippi, but they'd been pretty dangerous. He still had nightmarish flashbacks of walking across a town square with about twenty white farmers walking behind him, waiting for an excuse to pound the hell out of this gangling Jew who had come to turn their culture upside down.

Even as a New York congressman, Ed Koch had been a strong supporter of the Civilian Police Review Board, a mechanism to protect blacks against the whimsies of racist cops.

So what was the problem?

The problem, he felt, was ingratitude. Not long after he had supported the review board, he had been stung to hear blacks complaining about Jewish teachers in the public schools. "There are too many Goldbergs and Rosenbergs teaching in Harlem," said one genius. "The Board of Education looks like the Israeli Knesset." Well, maybe, thought Ed Koch privately, that's because the Jews are SMARTER THAN YOU ARE and are trying to teach you something!

Really, the gall of it!! It was no doubt the same outrage felt by Jack Greenberg, the wonderful Jewish lawyer who helped secure the landmark civil rights ruling, *Brown v. the Board of Education*, and was promptly dumped from the movement. That kind of thing, different from Jackson's "Hymietown" remark only in tone and degree, had finally prompted the Jews, after years of sacrificing for ungrateful black people, to say "Oh yeh? Well, fuck you too!!"

Far too many Jews, in the mayor's opinion, were more interested in saving the whales, or some other liberal cause, than in saving the ten tribes of Israel. At some point, you had to remember who you were. That was really all he had been doing when he opposed those housing projects in Forest Hills. Wake up, he'd been saying. *We're* the endangered species!!

Anti-Semitism was as fashionable now among the blacks as dreadlocks. Completely forgotten was the common bond of suffering. Yes, but you're all doing so well now in America, the blacks would moan. More self-pitying bullshit, thought Ed Koch. He knew of no Jew in the world who wouldn't trade his country club membership to reclaim the life of someone lost in the ovens. Case in point: for the life of his father's cousin, who had died at Auschwitz, Ed Koch would have resigned the mayor's office tomorrow.

"Sir, the car is here," announced the intercom. Time for the meeting with Jackson. He swung himself out from behind his desk, strode out of his office, clambered down the steps of City Hall, and rode his Lincoln Town Car down Broadway, repeating a phrase to himself almost like a mantra—Control Yourself.

The meeting was to take place in Governor Cuomo's office in the World Trade Center and would be presided over by the governor himself. The neutral site and the high-powered referee were proof of what everyone already knew: this was a volatile meeting between two borderline madmen and it could end in a hail of insults. With the press lurking around, no one wanted that.

The mayor entered the office alone, and the governor rose to greet him. Behind them was the harbor, the Verrazano Bridge, and the open sea. Nowhere was Jackson. Nonsurprise number one. The mayor was always grousing about the chronic lateness of black people.

Koch and Cuomo sat stiffly for a while. They had never been at ease with each other, even before they had squared off in a barbarically dirty gubernatorial race six years earlier. Now they could barely manage civilities. "How is Matilda?" asked the mayor of the governor's wife. The governor couldn't even respond in kind, since the mayor had no wife. The ensuing silence weighed a thousand pounds. The two of them were almost grateful when Jackson finally walked in.

He had with him an entourage of five, including Dinkins, Congressman Charlie Rangel, a couple of the Reverend Jackson's sons, and the Reverend Herbert Daughtry, a man who particularly irritated the mayor. Daughtry could always be counted on to appear with a long face as a "family advisor" whenever there was a highly publicized shooting of a black kid by a cop.

"Will you gentlemen leave us alone for a while?" said Jackson. Koch assumed he was talking to his entourage. After a couple of moments passed and nobody moved, the mayor and the governor realized the shocking truth. He was talking to *them*!

"Just for a moment, please, while I confer with my associates," said the reverend.

It was unbelievable. Cuomo was being thrown out of his own office so this charlatan could powwow with his so-called brain trust! Where were the mayor of New York City and the governor of New York State now supposed to go? Fortunately there was an anteroom of some size, and here the two men were again obliged to settle into their mutual discomfort. Jackson kept them there for almost an hour.

When the governor was finally invited back into his own office, the six black men had spread chairs around the room and made themselves quite at home. They were still smiling over a remark made just before the entrance of the white men. The subtext of all this, the way Ed Koch read it, was "we didn't really have anything important to talk about, but we just wanted to make you chumps cool your heels a while." The mayor could feel his bile rising.

It was time for the so-called meeting, the real test of Ed Koch's self-control. What the black men wanted to do, they said, was address a few of their concerns. Koch looked over at the pious face of Herbert Daughtry and wanted to smack it. *Concerns* was a code word for "unreasonable demands we want to blackmail you with."

Then they began to reel them off. Sydenham Hospital in Harlem, for example, was a concern. Why had the mayor closed it? The mayor's blood was boiling now. A better question was, Why was he subjecting himself to this indignity? The Sydenham closing was *years ago*, for Christ's sake!! So why were they breaking his balls about it now? Clearly a) for the sheer pleasure of breaking them, and b) because black people had never accepted his original explanation, which was that the goddamned hospital was ancient, and the city was losing millions on it, and other newer, smaller clinics could do the same job, only better.

Of course, no other politician would have dared close Sydenham. It was like an Indian politician condemning the Taj Mahal. But Ed Koch alone had had the nerve to do it, and so now it was a concern. Fine. Now what was concern number fucking two!?

Frankly, said the Reverend Jesse Jackson (and I would love to see his ordination papers, thought the mayor), there were concerns about the poor. "What concerns you about them, Reverend?" said the mayor between clenched teeth. The reverend went on to say that he worried about the mayor's attitude; that by keeping the shelters in such dreadful disrepair, the mayor seemed to be punishing people for being poor. And was it really wise, added Daughtry, for the mayor to go on TV and advise people not to give money to beggars and not to allow the homeless to wash motorists' windshields at stoplights? Didn't this exacerbate the gulf between the rich and poor in New York?

"You can't exacerbate a gulf," said the mayor.

"Excuse me?"

"A gulf is a body of water. Conceivably it could be widened or narrowed, perhaps by an engineering project. But you can't *exacerbate* water. You could boil it, perhaps."

What was the mayor doing?

"Excuse me?" said Daughtry.

"I'm merely trying," said the mayor "to use the English language correctly."

Control yourself, control yourself, control yourself.

"But that's not important," the mayor concluded. "Any other *concerns*?"

"Not for this meeting," said Jackson, coldly. "I have concerns for the homeless people in City Hall Park, but I'm going to meet with them tomorrow."

This rendered the mayor almost apoplectic, and Jackson knew it. Things were about to truly snap, and the governor had to step in. "Gentlemen, I know we all love politics and could talk about it for hours, but if the reverend has no more major concerns, I think we should call the press in and wrap this up."

Cuomo had taken charge, and within a minute the room was full of reporters.

"Mr. Mayor," said one, "did the reverend apologize for the Hymietown remark?"

"I think," said Cuomo, "that we want to talk in broad terms about what went on, not in narrow terms."

"Reverend, did the mayor apologize for saying that if you were elected president you would have disarmed the country in three weeks and bankrupted it in six?"

"I didn't know he ever said that . . ." said Jackson.

Cuomo headed this off quickly. "Gentlemen," he said, "we're getting very far off the point here. The important thing is that all of us have agreed to disagree on smaller points and still come together on the big point, which is the critical importance of electing Michael Dukakis in November."

Great politicians surprise, and surprise again. At this point, Ed Koch was seized with one of the extraordinary instincts that separate the champions from the kind of people who lose school board elections. With a dozen cameras poised, he reached out, grabbed Jesse Jackson's hand, and shook it. Before Jackson could extricate himself, the cameras went click and the event was history. Dinkins, Rangel, and Daughtry were in shock. That photograph, which Koch clearly needed so desperately to retain even a shred of the black vote, should have been very, very expensive for him. Instead, Koch was out the door, scot-free, before the flashbulbs cooled.

Larry Locke had not put on anything more than a terrycloth robe for a week. He was ensconced in a world of Ellen-ness. The apartment was a lace-curtain Irish paradise, a swirl of quilts and antimacassars and Waterford glass. When Ellen went off to work,

Larry remained, sleeping, smelling her smells, bathing, and making toast and five or six cups of coffee for himself in preparation for the real work of the day: watching soap operas and Donahue and Oprah Winfrey, and finally, while preparing dinner for Ellen, watching *Jeopardy!*

Lazy boy? No more so, he told himself, than a combat soldier surrendering himself to a week of R&R.

On the morning of September 4, having just seen Ellen off, Larry sat on her stuffed mauve sofa and riffled through the morning papers, as usual. Then he saw the article and spilled his coffee. That very afternoon, it said, Jesse Jackson was expected to visit the City Hall Park homeless.

Jesse Jackson!? Larry had issued the invitation himself!! A month ago!!! Anything you can imagine, you can do, Greenberg had told him. And so, among the other cockamamie pie-in-the-sky things he had tried, he had fired off a note to Jesse Jackson's church in Chicago, along with some newspaper clippings about Kochville. And now . . . this!!

He pored over the article to be sure he had it right. Jackson had arrived yesterday, had a meeting with Mayor Koch, and was scheduled to be in the park today at . . . noon! That was an hour from now!!

He threw on some clothes, dropped some paper towels on the coffee stain, and dashed off a note to Ellen that he hoped was coherent. Within minutes he was on the train to City Hall Park, where he hadn't been for a week.

When he arrived, it felt like he'd been gone for a year. He could get no sense of the state of things. That was to be expected. During the working day, the demeanor of the little strip of concrete and lawn changed radically. Finally Larry saw Lonnie but did not spot any members of the ruling committee or the man he was really looking for, Duke York.

Then the lawn began to take on a feeling of something-about-to-happen. Duke was always calling this sacred ground, and

Greenberg had called it a place of history. Larry had always pooh-poohed it all, but now he felt it himself. Photographers were arriving, as were people in expensive suits. Suddenly video crews were there, jostling office workers out of the way. A hum was developing.

Then Horace arrived. Larry had dared to hope that in the week of his absence Horace had dropped off the face of the earth. No such luck. Now the target of Horace's invective was Jesse Jackson himself. "Nigger say he cradled Martin Luther King's head in that motel in Memphis. Bullshit!! I seen the pictures. He wasn't nowhere near it!!" This was familiar rhetoric from the Black Left. Jackson was always aggrandizing himself, cashing in on his links to King. He had a star mentality, said his critics. In the time since the '84 race, when Jackson first ignited the black electorate, he could have been building a grassroots organization that would have benefited black candidates everywhere. Instead, he seemed to be interested only in his own bursts of incandescence every four years.

But none of that mattered. Horace was screaming against the wind, and Larry had to smile. Jesse Jackson *was* a star. He could have been a tax evader or a child molester, but the white heat of his stardom was all that mattered. And indeed, the park was brimming now. The man's aura was preceding him, and there was almost a sexual excitement around the place.

At that moment, barely visible beyond the throng, Ed Koch was hustling down the steps towards his town car. His instructions to his scheduling staff had been crystal clear: I don't want to be ANYWHERE NEAR HERE when that son of a bitch arrives. The mayor already had the photo of the handshake, at that moment being duplicated for a hundred-thousand campaign brochures. He did not now need a humiliating confrontation to neutralize it.

The mayor tumbled into his car, which swept out of the City Hall parking lot, narrowly averting a collision with the arriving vehicle of the Reverend Jesse Jackson, a modest blue Ford.

The grass practically lifted off the lawn. The man got out of his car and made his way through the crowd like Muhammad Ali moving towards the ring. He gave off waves and waves of high scorching energy. Men and women screamed, reaching to touch him. Finally he got to his destination, a single park bench ringed by thousands of people. He climbed up on it and flashbulbs exploded in clusters. The men standing close to him, among them Lonnie and Larry Locke, had never been in a manic press epicenter like this. People clawed towards the man. Microphones were pushed, thrust, even thrown. Then Jackson recognized Larry from the press clippings. He pulled him up on the bench and embraced him in front of the cameras. The homeless were all around them, their spines stiffening, their faces moistening, feeling the heat.

"They told Mary and Joseph to go sleep in a barn," said Jesse Jackson, Larry Locke right beside him. "And that's where the baby Jesus was born."

Yes. YES. The crowd was loving it.

"Let me hear you say it. I AM SOMEBODY."

"I AM SOMEBODY!" said many voices.

"I may be poor . . ." said the Reverend. "Let me hear it."

"I MAY BE POOR . . ."

"But I am somebody."

"BUT I AM SOMEBODY."

"I may be uneducated . . ."

"I MAY BE UNEDUCATED . . ."

"But I am somebody."

"BUT I AM SOMEBODY."

"I may be on dope . . ."

"I MAY BE ON DOPE . . ."

"I may have lost hope . . ."

"I MAY HAVE LOST HOPE . . ."

"But I am somebody."

"BUT I AM SOMEBODY!"

"I am . . ."

"I AM . . ."

"God's child."

"GOD'S CHILD!!"

A great din went up, and the faces around the bench glowed like the faces of small children on the most wonderful Christmas of their lives.

———

Arriving back at Gracie Mansion at dusk, Ed Koch climbed the curved stairway to his bedroom on the second floor and stepped onto his private porch to watch the evening sky. The only conceivable flaw in the fabulous mayoral residence was that it faced the East River rather than the Hudson, and therefore did not get a sunset. That didn't bother the mayor. Sometimes the eastern sky was more interesting at dusk, a subtler pleasure. There was a bit of a chill in the air and the mayor pulled his collar up around his throat. It was, after all, September.

At that very moment, a great peace came over Edward I. Koch. Why on earth was he torturing himself over what he would and would not do to rid himself of the homeless people in City Hall Park? True, for a hundred delicate reasons of public relations the cossacks could not be sent in, as they had been in Tompkins Square. But what about a strategy that had proved far more powerful for generations of Russians than all the cossacks and infantries and navies put together? What about the thing that had beaten Hitler and Napoleon and every savage that from time immemorial had ever laid siege to the great Russian empire? What about . . . the winter?

The first bracing nights of September would turn to the frosty harvest moons of October, to the cold starry nights and naked trees of November, and finally to the brutal deep freeze of December, January, and February.

When nature was acting in your behalf, there was really nothing to do but step out of the way. This the mayor of New York was only too happy to do, at long last. For the first time in three months, he put the matter completely out of his mind. He poured a Diet Coke into a glass, added a splash of Mount Gay Rum, put on a Judy Garland tape, and dreamed the night away.

The glow of the Jackson visit lasted all through the night, lighting up Larry's dreams. It was not until the next day, when he awakened, that he perceived the large changes in Kochville. But changes there had been: a week is a year in the lives of the homeless.

The population was still about thirty, but roughly ten new faces had replaced ten old faces. The most damaging loss was Duke. He had become ill, Larry was told, and had disappeared. This troubled Larry deeply. He loved Duke, to the extent that he was capable of loving anyone, and he also needed the one-eyed man to back him up. Refreshed by the time at Ellen's, he felt ready to step back into the government of Kochville, but he was not being invited to do so. Not enough people remembered him: he had lost his legitimacy to rule.

At the moment, the camp had a decidedly Latin flavor. But the half-dozen Puerto Ricans fought incessantly among themselves, so that even with the weight of numbers, they were too disorganized to step into the vacuum of power. It would have seemed a golden opportunity for Horace and Rasta, but apparently neither of them had a gift for leadership. Instead, their talent and passion went into making life miserable for whoever was in charge.

But who, exactly, was that? Little Art was a sergeant, a noncom who only wanted to take orders and to do his job. Matthew, brilliant and cynical, had no desire to preside over squabbling meetings of angry black people. The most powerful candidates, surprisingly, were Lonnie and Samantha. Lonnie's commonsense approach, government by drawl and twang, gave him a Lincolnesque quality. Samantha, with the powerful nurturing of a mature woman, was like a black Golda Meir. However the electorate was not prepared to accept a white man, much less a woman of any color.

So they finally turned back to Larry. One night Horace grandly announced that after a meeting of the provisional government (meaning him and Rasta), it had been decided that Larry Locke could resume his presidency, but only under certain conditions. He would have to acknowledge that time had passed and that in his absence there had been new ideas.

In a word, that meant squatting. Horace had been bellowing about it now for weeks. All over the Bronx and Manhattan were remarkable examples of what one could do with a little bravado and know-how. People had pried open boarded-up doors, run electrical wires in from lampposts, rigged sluice pipes from distant water towers, even rerouted steam heat underneath the sidewalk! If detected immediately by police, the squatters could be thrown out like any trespassers. But once they established themselves, they acquired a certain legitimacy and could only be moved if local public opinion swung against them. If they could prove they'd been there for ten years, they couldn't be budged by anything less than a constitutional amendment.

Backed by flowering rhetoric from the poets of the Lower East Side, the squat movement had overhauled its image. Squatters were no longer foul-smelling eccentrics clinging to some dreadful hole-in-the-wall. Now, they could almost be in beer commercials—young, intelligent, defiant, driven. The idea had arrived, announced Horace, and Larry Locke could no longer stand in the way of it. His solutions—talks, board rooms, attaché cases, negotiations—had all come up empty.

Listening to the fat man ramble, Larry almost exploded. It had been thanks to his sweat and blood that the camp still existed at all.

He needed to see Ellen. A couple of days had passed since he had left her place, and he missed her badly. Trying to put Horace out of his mind, he boarded an A-train and headed to Brooklyn. Once he got there and was holding her again, it all poured out of him. "Ain't gonna do nothin'," he said, "just because he tells me to! What the hell we been doin' out there all this time? What the hell I been goin' to these meetings for? We gonna throw it all away and crawl into some broken-down tenement like a pack of rats?"

Ellen listened patiently. She knew from the start that the romance would take sacrifices, that he would have to spend many nights in the camp to maintain his credibility as a leader, and that her role would be to stand by. This she was willing to do . . . to a point. Secretly, she agreed with Horace. Since leaving her middle-class husband, Ellen McCarthy's rebel Irish blood had begun to flow freely. She had transformed very quickly from someone who didn't care about politics at all, to someone who worked within the system, to someone who now wanted to rip it all apart. Squatting was not just an option, it was the *only* option; not just for Kochville, but possibly for all the homeless. Every day she passed a thousand empty buildings on the way to work, and then tended to a thousand shattered lives once she got there. If the city government wasn't going to wake up and put two and two together, then it was time for somebody else to.

But this had to be sugarcoated for Larry Locke, who was basically a conservative man. "You're right," she told him. "Follow your own instincts, no matter what." But, she added, a good leader at least looked into the things his constituents talked about.

As Larry considered this, she added that she had just run into a friend who was part of a well-known squat on the Lower East Side. The man had invited Ellen to drop by, and she now extended this invitation to Larry. The place was on Thirteenth Street, way over east near Avenue C. They could check it out, Ellen suggested, and at the same time have a nice dinner in a little place in the neighborhood. Larry agreed to it, if only to have a reason to spend the night with her.

They found a Ukrainian spot on Avenue A and had a few pierogi washed down by some chilled vodka, and all the magic of the prior week was back. They sat for an hour just looking at each other. By now it was clear to them both that this was a forbidden romance. Larry could not pass through the camp without whispers of "white woman" eddying behind him, nor was Ellen McCarthy's family going to like the idea of the Irish matriarch having an affair with a young black man. They would have to steal their moments when they could.

Still light-headed from the vodka, they walked east along Ninth Street past Tompkins Square Park, now riot scarred and nearly invisible behind police barricades. They turned north and finally they arrived at an abandoned building that showed no sign of life. They went to the corner and Ellen dialed a phone number. Soon a young white man in a bandanna arrived and led them back to the building. They descended to a basement entrance, and as they climbed a flight of stairs to the main floor, they heard music.

The room they entered was immense. The ceiling had been stripped of its plaster down to the studs, from which large tapestries hung. On many of the walls were candles in tin cans, illuminating the place like a medieval castle. There were many people, mostly young, listening raptly to an Asian man with waist-length hair play the piano. The instrument was old and out of tune, but the man played well and the event was magical.

Larry was powerfully affected. These people had taken what society had thrown away and made it beautiful. As a woman next to him observed, "We turn shit into gold." As a finishing touch, hanging from the wall was a piece of parchment signed by an American Indian named Chief Lenape. In a nutshell, it authorized the squatters of New York to take back the land stolen from his forebearers by the Dutch. The document was a fraud, thought Larry, but the point was well taken.

As they left, Ellen let him absorb the event in silence. She could see it was working on him. They walked all the way downtown and at the edge of City Hall Park they lingered a while in the darkness of the elms, touching and kissing and saying good-bye. Then Larry entered the camp alone.

The benches were drawn in a circle and people were shouting at each other. Standing with heads down in the middle of the circle, as if in stocks in the middle of a Puritan New England village, were the three young people of Kochville: Patricia, Lamont, and Tamara. The debate was whether to turn them over to the Bureau of Child Welfare in time for school. If that happened, some argued, the kids might disappear forever into a bottomless bureaucracy. But if they stayed in the camp, countered others, the price of freedom might be high: venereal disease, pregnancy, or rape by a middle-aged homeless man. Patricia and Tamara were pretty young things, and the sexually starved men were always tempted. There were leering remarks, and one had the feeling that someday, after one Colt 45 too many, someone would simply jump one of them.

Of course, young Lamont, the only male teenager, could have his way with them, and to the great jealousy of some of the men, Lamont was running amuck. He slept with both girls regularly, as well as anyone else remotely his age who wandered into the camp. Had he ever considered such a thing as a condom? Art once asked him. "Hell," said Lamont, "would you go swimmin' in a raincoat?"

This was a troubling remark coming from the youngster. In the confused sensuality of the summer, it had been tolerated, but now the nip of autumn in the air brought a sense of "back to school" to anyone with parental instincts.

Larry made his feelings known immediately. "What *about* school? You think they're learnin' anything here?"

There was such a hardened quality to Lamont, Patricia, and Tamara that it was hard to think of them as students. Yet Patricia, everyone had to be reminded, had not even entered high school. She was twelve.

Larry was joined on this issue by little Art, who for the most part kept his mouth shut. But when he took a strong position, the men paid attention. Everyone knew he had killed several North Vietnamese in hand-to-hand combat, and this gave all his pronouncements, even "pass the salt," a certain weight.

But Horace would not back down. Not when it involved an opportunity to challenge Larry Locke.

"House man's back, all right," said Horace. "Wants to lead the chillun' right up to the massa's house."

"What the hell else you want to do?" said Larry. "Let them run around the damn streets all winter? After a while these girls gonna do anything they can to stay warm. What you think that's gonna be?"

"Let me tell you somethin', nigger," said Horace. "You come back here stinkin' of Irish pussy, now you the king of the homeless again? You a tom-ass jive motherfucker. You got no idea what's even been goin' on here. We way past your bullshit now. I told you that."

Larry absorbed the barrage of insults, any one of which, a week ago, might have caused him to take a swing at the fat, pompous man. Finally he said, "Let me talk to you privately."

The meeting was adjourned, and Larry and Horace went across the street to the Greek place and sat down for coffee. It was the first such intimacy between them. Larry proposed a deal. This was another first; never before had he practiced the art of compromise. If the kids were turned over to the authorities in time for school, Larry said, he'd be willing to investigate a squat.

Horace was deeply suspicious. "When?" he said.

"We could start lookin' this week," said Larry.

Horace was still wary. "Where we gonna go?"

"I'll get a list of empty places," said Larry, "from the city."

"I got a list right here," said Horace, pulling a piece of paper from his pocket. "Got it from some cats uptown. Don't need nothin' from the damn city."

"All right," said Larry slowly, "we'll use yours." He took the piece of paper from Horace's hand and unfolded it. The first address was 850 Longwood Avenue, somewhere in the Bronx.

Ten

As the Number 2 train swept around the curve past 145th street, Larry, Samantha, and little Art stood pressed to the windows, gawking like tourists. Only Matthew, who had seen it all before, riffled through a newspaper.

Art was a native New Yorker, but he had rarely been north of Harlem. He had always assumed the Bronx was more of the same. What he wasn't prepared for was the emptiness. In the army he had crossed the country once on a train, and this brought it all back. The Bronx was like North Dakota—flat to the horizon. The difference was that instead of a carpet of prairie grass, what lay on the ground here were bricks. Once they had been houses. Vast stretches of rubble were punctuated by packs of gaunt, hairless dogs and by puffs of smoke. The sky was deep blue and huge.

At 165th Street, the four of them got off the train and descended the steep stairs from the platform. On the corner was a small café from which the smells of Spanish coffee emanated, which they could not resist. Once inside the tiny place, Larry took out a map to get his bearings.

Their destination was right across the street.

They peered at 850 Longwood Avenue through the restaurant's steamy window. The building was larger than they expected, running about half a city block. On the ground floor were several storefronts, but only one of them was occupied, by a record store called "House of Amadeo." At the front entrance to the building, near the corner, stood a dour Hispanic man. All of this the Kochvilleans took as reassuring; at least the building was not some burnt out hulk, abandoned for twenty years. The only disturbing aspect was the windows. Some were boarded up, but an equal number did not exist; even the sashes were gone, and they were merely rectangular holes in the building.

As the four of them crossed the street, the building only grew more imposing. On either side of the door was a large marble column. Against one of them lounged the Hispanic man they had seen from the café window.

"You need something?" he said.

"Need to have a look inside here, brother," said Larry in his friendliest, firmest manner. Art backed him up with a scowling look, and the Hispanic man stepped aside.

The hallway was dark, but the scant daylight illuminated several once-elegant features. The most impressive was the elevator, made entirely of wrought iron, with a dingy brass gate. There was no elevator shaft, only the poles on which the thing presumably travelled. Samantha's imagination surged; clearly as you rode this elevator, you could wave to people who were walking up and down the marble stairs.

Its cables, however, lay in a heap on either side of it. Art stepped inside and pushed the wooden handle back and forth, but succeeded only in disturbing the sleep of a mouse, who scurried up the stairs. They decided to follow the mouse and see what the building might hold for Kochville.

The going was slow. The marble stairs were cracked, and they had to move carefully to avoid dislodging chunks and creating an avalanche. Finally they arrived at the second floor and peered through the darkness. They began to get a disturbing feeling: other people were in the building, hiding.

There was a sound behind them and all four of them jumped. It was a small Hispanic boy, holding a child's orange plastic bucket. Art's spine stiffened. He had learned in Vietnam that children could be agents of death. The boy looked terrified and said something to the four of them in Spanish. Then a door opened a crack, and a middle-aged woman in a black shawl motioned intensely for the boy to enter. Beyond her, Larry could make out shelves full of plaster saints and lit candles. The boy ran to her and the door closed behind them.

Matthew led the way slowly up the next two flights, the crumbling stairs becoming more and more impassable. When they reached the fourth floor the true decay of the building became evident. Walls that had once defined rooms now barely existed. Lathe was visible through plaster, and piping stuck out like broken limbs.

By the time they were halfway up the staircase that led to the fifth floor, Art knew somebody was up there. Following his combat veteran's instinct, he got down low and crept up the remaining stairs alone. Then there was a burst of sound. Matthew, Larry, and Samantha remained frozen on the staircase. Art was screaming at somebody who was screaming back. Then there was silence. Soon Art's beetlelike head appeared around the corner of the stairwell. "This way," he said. When they got to the landing, it became clear that Art had interrupted a crack party. Vials and glass pipes were everywhere. A small fire smoldered in the rubble, an indication, said Matthew, that someone might also have been cooking heroin. "People all over here," said Art. "Maybe twenty."

Twenty! They stopped a while and listened to the silence, punctuated every so often by the rumbling of the IRT line. There was one more flight to climb, and Larry took the lead. Now the stairs no longer existed but were instead a graded stream of rubble. The visibility was better, but the reason for this was very bad news indeed.

The roof was open. Great gaping holes let in the light of a perfect day, as they had also clearly let in rain and snow. The floors were sagging badly. Samantha, a little sparrow of a woman, volunteered to finish exploring the sixth story herself. Treading lightly, she moved through a couple of rooms until she came upon a bathroom over which the roof had given way completely. The bathtub was full to the brim with debris, but what transfixed her were its legs. They were cat's paws, elegantly carved iron braces holding the porcelain belly of the tub. Samantha became lost in a fantasy of bathing in such a thing, of taking an hour to do it, of anointing herself with oils with French names.

Finally the voices of her companions summoned her back to reality and back through the darkness of the sixth floor. "We're going to the basement," said Matthew. He was the only one of them with any knowledge of construction. "We need to check out the boiler."

The going was even tougher downhill. At one point, they rocked back on their heels and simply skidded down the slope of pulverized marble and concrete. Soon they were back in the lobby, and Matthew located a narrow, dark stairway to the basement. When they were halfway down, they noticed a foul smell, and Matthew and Larry ventured the rest of the way alone. They descended in almost complete darkness, and with the last step they found themselves about ankle-deep in moisture, a sort of viscous slush. They took another few steps, and the muck was up around their calves. "What the hell is this?" said Larry.

Matthew did not answer, but instead began wildly pushing Larry back toward the direction of the stairs. His olfactory nerves had gotten the news first, by about a second. Then Larry's kicked in, and he began backing up desperately through the darkness.

They were in a lake of urine and feces.

The more madly they rushed for the staircase, the more they kicked up the sludge, and splattered and pasted themselves with it. The stench was unbearable. Finally out of it, they rushed up past Art and Samantha and out into the lobby. They went behind the elevator shaft and took off their pants and desperately tried to wring them out.

"Somebody must've ripped out the pipes," gasped Matthew,

"and the whole system went to hell." He could barely speak, and Larry could barely hear him. Their senses were shut down.

After several moments, Larry had the feeling they were not alone in the tiny alcove. He turned, and there, faintly illuminated, was a teenage Hispanic boy sitting in a corner. His eyes were wide open, and it took Larry a second to realize that the boy was dead.

He raced from the vestibule, pulling on his pants as he went, screaming for Matthew to follow. This Matthew did in his boxer shorts. The two men stumbled onto the street breathless, and Art led them over to a half-open fire hydrant and doused them, but he could make no real dent in the stench. He tried to get the hydrant open even further, hoping for a strong pressurized stream, but was unable to budge the big metal nut. Finally Matthew dropped to his knees and began vomiting in the gutter. Larry lay down in the shadow of the building and closed his eyes.

At this point the small boy they had seen a half-hour earlier on the second floor emerged from the building, again carrying a bright orange plastic pail. He held it under the hydrant until it filled with water, and then re-entered the building.

By now Matthew had regained himself and was staring at the child, wondering if he knew about the dead person behind the elevator. He and Art watched him disappear into the building, and then they revived Larry. Samantha arrived with Spanish coffee in paper cups. They drank it in silence, sitting on the curbstone. It was a long while before Art finally spoke. Clearly, he said, the building had no water, and this child belonged to some family that was desperate enough to still be living there.

Matthew and Larry did not respond, nor did they make any mention of the corpse. They continued to drink their coffee numbly. Finally they all climbed the stairs to the train station and waited for the Number 2 train to take them back to City Hall Park. They had the car to themselves the whole way.

Shhhhmmmmmmmmmaaaaahhh!!!! The ancient drone filled his soul. Ed Koch sat on a front bench of the Park East Synagogue, and let the sound of the cantor fill him again. *Melllllaaaaaaa-chooooooo-lummmmmm!!!*

He was moved by the timelessness of it all. These same melodies had been wailed by old men trudging across the desert, trying to outdistance the Pharaoh's armies. They had been sung softly in forbidden storefront shuls in Poland. They were part of Ed Koch's earliest memories, warbled by a minyan of ten *alte kakes* in the old synagogue at Crotona Park.

Where had it begun? It had been passed, orally, from one cantor to another since long before the days of the Second Temple, possibly for thousands of years before that. How ancient was the sound? Had it first emanated from the throat of a man or a beast?

Only Yom Kippur dredged these thoughts out of Ed Koch. While the Gentiles celebrated their New Year by getting drunk and dancing around with lampshades on their heads, the Jews went inward. On this, the last day of the year, the Day of Atonement, one fasted and meditated and purified. Traditions like these made Ed Koch immensely proud to be a Jew.

Recently, the mayor had had a revelation. The night the Mets won the World Series in 1986, the mayor had forayed into the winning locker room and gotten the traditional soaking by spewing champagne bottles. Immediately afterward, he jumped into his Lincoln Town Car and sped home, the quicker to shower and get the clammy paste of cheap champagne off of him. Too bad, he found himself thinking, that like John Lindsay, who had endured a similar dousing after the Mets' victory in 1969, I couldn't just sit back and enjoy it.

That's when it hit him: He had NO IDEA whether John Lindsay enjoyed getting sprayed with champagne. So what was he inferring? That the Wasps by their very grace and superiority could enjoy a champagne bath and that the clumsy, graceless Jews could not?

217

He underwent a curious soul searching. He found himself remembering the advice of David Garth, the media wizard behind the mayor's first victory in 1977. Can't you be . . . a little less Jewish? Garth had asked him. What did that mean? Koch wanted to know. Garth's reply was that Koch was a little like the uncle at the wedding who was so Jewish he embarrassed the bride. Unbelievably, Koch had *accepted that as an explanation!!* And he had then taken Garth's advice and outfitted himself with a dozen Brooks Brothers suits and various other accoutrements of a Wasp investment banker.

But why? For no reason unless Koch at some level really *was* ashamed of being a Jew. For all his bold political stands, like defying the integration of Forest Hills, for all his symbolic gestures, like taking the oath of office on a Jewish Bible that had been found among the dirt and ashes of Buchenwald, was the mayor apologizing for something?

If so, then no more. The older he got, the more deeply did he appreciate the depth of Judaism. His experiences in Irish churches this summer had only confirmed it. Where the goyim had superstitious rites, the Jews had prescriptions for living. Where other faiths said "Do this or else," the Jews said "Do this for this good reason." It was a religion of inquiry. Judaism sought to know difficult truths, not obscure them behind a fog of incense.

After his stroke in 1987, as the mayor lay in a hospital bed having narrowly avoided either death or paralysis, he was visited by a rabbi who introduced him to the concept of *mishbayrach*—thankfulness for the outcome. That was profound, as was the concept of *beshert*, loosely translated as "what will be will be." This was deeper than any thought he'd ever had in his head. A pardon from a lifetime of anal overachievement, it meant to do your best and don't worry about it.

This was the real reason to lash out at anti–Semites: they were trying to obliterate the earth's greatest wisdom. When Louis Farrakhan went around, as he was currently doing, proclaiming that

Jewish doctors were injecting black children with the AIDS virus, he was threatening to bury the world in ignorance. And when a bastard like Jesse Jackson. . . . No. The mayor felt his choler rising and vowed to think no more on Jackson. That was not a thought for the deep calm that was supposed to prevail on Yom Kippur.

But it was clear to him now that the lines of the upcoming election were profoundly drawn. It was not just about tax cuts and keeping the busses running. It was about keeping the Farrakhans and the Jacksons and the Dinkins of the world at bay.

Recently the mayor had seen a documentary film of the fiftieth anniversary of *Kristallnacht*. Roughly on this date in 1938, the Jews of Europe saw the grotesquely ugly face of Naziism for the first time. Throughout Germany and Eastern Europe there were anti-Semitic rampages, and Jewish shops and homes were vandalized and destroyed. *Kristallnacht*, or "night of crystal," referred to the thousands of shards of glass that littered the streets the next day. It was an obscene overture to everything that was to follow.

After the Holocaust, and to this very day, there were cries of "Never again," and "How could this have happened?" Well, thought Ed Koch as the hour for the blowing of the shofar approached in the Park East Synagogue, *this* is how it happens: when Jews begin to forget their history. He made a decision that the *Kristallnacht* film would be one of his inspirational campaign tools.

Eeeccccchhhhhhhooooooddddd!!!! He closed his eyes again and let the cantor's sound take him away.

About a mile away, another group of worshippers knelt before the Torah and bobbed to the same melodies as the mayor of New York. But in a sense this younger congregation, called B'nai Jeshurun, was singing a different tune.

Officially, Jeshurun was a Conservative synagogue: its adherence to the ancient rules, dietary and otherwise, lay somewhere between the Orthodox Park East's and most of the Reform temples of New York.

But there were other, more profound differences. The members of B'nai Jeshurun, like those of Park East and all Jews everywhere, lionized old Rabbi Hillel, the font of Jewish wisdom who had died almost two thousand years ago. The rabbi's famous remarks were many, and over the years had taken on a rashomon-like quality. They could be interpreted in many different ways, and there was one to fit every occasion.

The rabbi had framed much of his wisdom in the form of questions, and the members of Park East, for instance, had seized on his famous "If not now, when?" as a personal challenge to procrastination and a prod to achievement. In fact, the congregation contained some of the great movers and shakers of New York.

A congregation in a wealthy suburb, in contrast, might have taken to heart another famous Hillel question, "If I am not for myself, who will be?" as a way of justifying an insular community and the accumulation of great personal wealth.

But for the young idealists of B'nai Jeshurun, a third Hillel question burned. "If I am only for myself, what am I?" This was a call to arms for social action. Since the sixties, this kind of thinking had fallen out of fashion with Jews, but now it was striking a chord with another generation repulsed and embarrassed by the materialism of their parents.

In the back of the temple sat Duke York and his host for the day, Marc Greenberg. They were attracting much attention, not because black visitors were rare, but because Duke York was singing the hell out of the music. The old Sephardic melodies were kind of a moan, which Duke saw as an ancestor of the blues, and he was wailing on it.

Marc Greenberg was pleased, not because Duke was necessarily on pitch all the time, but because of the sheer energy the man was putting out. A couple of weeks earlier, he had been half dead.

Greenberg thought a visit to the synagogue might be a nice finishing touch to the rehabilitation, and it was working.

At first, Greenberg was afraid the High Holy Days might be
too heavy an introduction. As it turned out, though, Duke took
to Judaism like a duck to water. It required no translation. The
Jews had been slaves in Egypt and had been getting the shit end of
the stick ever since. What black man couldn't relate to that? But
the concept that Duke clasped most tightly to his bosom was
tikkun. This was an ancient Hebrew word meaning healing, and to
the youth of B'nai Jeshurun, it said this: the world has great pain.
Your only purpose on earth is to apply balm to that pain. That,
and that alone, is why you are here. "The meaning of the Talmud
is kindness," said Rabbi Avila, a contemporary of Hillel's. "All else
is commentary."

To this recognition of the great primal pain of living, the love-
racked Duke York said an emphatic yes. Contrary to everything
he'd ever been taught, the Jews had soul.

Marc Greenberg was feeling sadness beyond the solemnity of
the High Holy Days. The final hours of the outgoing Jewish year
were also the final hours of the intense time between the two
men. Duke York was now well enough to return to Kochville or
wherever else he wanted to go. Time had moved on. The light
slanting through the temple windows was autumnal: low, clear,
harsh. That is why, Greenberg thought, Yom Kippur was so well
placed in September. The light was suddenly clear in your own
head. You saw past your own bullshit.

After another hour of deepening dusk, the shofar finally blew
in B'nai Jeshurun, in Park East, and in a thousand other bright
spaces, large and small, throughout New York. The sound was no
less powerful now than when it had first drawn Duke York to the
overnight vigil three weeks earlier. It made the man tremble.

All around the temple, people shook hands and embraced and
made plans to celebrate, now that the day of self-denial was over.
It was time to eat and drink as only the Jews can. All over New

York, tables would groan with sable, whitefish, lox, potato ku-galeh, potato pancakes, blintzes, stuffed peppers, kasha var-nishkas, rugaleh, and above all, oceans of red wine.

Nowhere was this more true than in the home of Marc Green-berg's mother, a great mensch of a woman who had been cooking for three days. Duke was sated beyond his wildest dreams with the plentitude of food, wine, and love. It was a joyous punctuation mark to his recovery and to his friendship with Greenberg. At the end of the night, the two men drove the familiar route down Broadway toward City Hall Park, embraced, and at the dawn of the year 5749, said good night.

Duke took a step toward the park. Even in the gloom of night, he could feel a change. He couldn't put his finger on it until a leaf fluttered before his eyes and fell to the ground. Autumn. Immedi-ately he felt the chill and buttoned the top of his shirt. He trudged ahead another fifty yards to the row of benches that was Kochville. To his great relief, he saw several sleeping bodies. That was reassuring. It all still existed.

But something else had clearly changed beside the weather, and again it took a while to detect it. It was the noise, or the lack of it. Lamont, Patricia, and Tamara were gone. Young people laugh so easily, he thought, and that was the sound that was miss-ing: the quick burst, the crackle. Immediately he thought of his two daughters, Shianna and Across the Universe (contracted to Atu). Most people had condemned the latter name as a wild bo-hemian impulse, one that a child would spend a lifetime living down. Duke didn't care. Atu liked her name and was proud of what it meant. He didn't share the secret with many people, but he had told Marc Greenberg last week, as they kayaked under the shadow of Fort Tryon Park.

Duke decided not to make a big deal of his return and slipped unobtrusively off to dreamland. His usual bench was empty, and this gave him a warm feeling. No one had appropriated it in his absence, which was a show of respect in Kochville. As a deep sleep began to take him, he imagined he heard the laughter of Patricia and Lamont and Tamara and Shianna and Across the Universe and all children everywhere.

"How did it go?"

In another part of the park, Larry Locke lay with his eyes closed. Rasta stood over him, drunk, repeating the question.

"How did it go?"

Still caked with human fecal matter, the stare of a teenage corpse burnt into him, Larry was in a deep, merciful sleep. Finally Rasta left him alone.

Of the travellers to Bronx, only Samantha remained awake. Her body was different from a man's, she often thought. Probably all women's were. She could not sleep off an experience; not the Mort Downey show, nor this one. She had to let it sit inside her and do what it would until it was through. Process it.

However, the day had not been as horrific for her as it had been for Matthew and Larry. For her, the enduring image was not of death or feces but of the legs of a bathtub. Who would think to do such a thing? Who would spend the time to carve beautiful figures to be seen only in a bathroom? It meant that the world contained people of delicacy after all. She had always suspected this but had never had much proof of it on the streets of New York. She closed her eyes and summoned again the smooth porcelain tub, the graceful sweep of it.

"Samantha . . ."

It was Art, suddenly next to her on the bench. He had been courting her for a while, she felt, with looks and gestures. During the time in the Bronx he had been attentive, even chivalrous. Although she admired him and liked him, she did not care to have an affair with him. Art was cut out of very crude cloth. Perhaps that was unfair; no doubt they came from similar backgrounds. But one felt what one felt. She wanted something more than Art. She wanted the human equivalent of the tub with the paws.

"Want to have a drink with me?" he asked.

That was just what she wanted. Art had a private supply of Canadian Club whiskey.

"That place today would have taken a lot of work . . . lot of it . . ." he mused, shaking his head, rummaging in his pack for the liquor.

She wasn't listening. Her attention was riveted on his hands as he opened the bottle and filled two plastic cups. Her mother and sister back in Philadelphia would have been horrified. Complete teetotalers. But let them try living on the street, Samantha often thought, and see if they would still demur when someone tries to pour them a drink.

Thinking of those two Philadelphia ladies made Samantha smile. Her sister was doing brilliantly as a social worker now, which was reason enough not to go back—to avoid becoming her own sister's client! No, she needed to get herself a little more together before presenting herself in Philadelphia. Perhaps in the winter she would go.

She had Art's whiskey in her hand now, and not a moment too soon. The pain was kicking in. The bleeding had started again, and it was worse than usual. She had no idea what to make of this. At first she thought it was some strange reversal of menopause, a "last gusher," as a lady at a shelter had put it. But it was more profuse and painful than she remembered her periods being. These days, she often fouled her sheets, which she went to such lengths to keep clean. Until now the sole advantage of becoming an older woman, as Samantha saw it, was that it facilitated tidiness.

It was so bad tonight that she had to excuse herself from Art on the grounds of exhaustion. Art stood politely, as she knew he would, and offered to leave her with a little nightcap, which she hoped he would. As he ambled off, she spread her sheets, which she had risen at dawn to wash in the fountain. All during her time in the Bronx they had been drying to perfection, and now they snapped cleanly over the green park bench. She curled up under a tattered Hudson Bay blanket and sipped the whiskey till the cup was empty and the pain started to go numb. She thought again of the bathtub in the Bronx, of rising from it, drying herself off, stepping into a costume, and going on the stage, which was a fantasy she often had, although not as much recently. When she finally fell asleep, she was the last Kochvillean to do so, under a moonless Yom Kippur sky.

Burnout was the issue. Marc Greenberg understood it well. His only question was not "Why the conference?" but rather "Why not sooner?"

He scanned the brochure again for details. It was to happen at a monastery near Tuxedo Park, New York, a lovely wooded spot near a lake, part of the old Averell Harriman estate.

Specifically, the topic was "How much can you give and still have something left?" but it could be summed up, in Marc's opinion, in the one word: burnout. Time and again he had seen the giants of the homeless movement go off the deep end. If you worked among the poor and never took a break, you drowned in the muck. The despair came off on you. Greenberg himself had barely survived the flute incident. Sometimes he only got through the day by clinging to his distractions—his kayak and his revolving door of girlfriends. The conference was designed for him as much as anyone.

The guest list was impressive. Just about anyone who had ever put in any serious time on the homeless issue would be there. The headliners were spectacular. First of all there was Baba Ram Dass, formerly Richard Alpert, the Harvard professor who along with Timothy Leary had urged an entire generation to drop out. Leary's approach had been drug-oriented, Alpert's more spiritual. Finally Alpert had changed his name, explored every Eastern philosophy under the sun, and come to the conclusion that all of it was meaningless without action. Hence, as Baba Ram Dass, he was now concerning himself with the homeless movement.

Bernie Glassman was the other big name. Glassman had not changed his name, and in fact took a perverse pleasure in the Damon Runyon–like images it called up. But if anything, Glassman's credentials were even heavier than Ram Dass's. He was the head of New York's Zen community, and he too had come to the conclusion that spirituality without action was so much hot air. To that end, he had started a homeless bakery in Yonkers, and it had been a spectacular success. Not only did the homeless learn a practical skill, but the bread was actually good and the business turned a profit—all of which was then plowed back into the homeless community. Rather than merely preside over this, Glassman periodically put on his *shmattes* and became homeless himself, vanishing into the city streets for days at a time just to get in touch with the feeling. No doubt about it, having these guys at the conference was like having Ruth and DiMaggio run a clinic on hitting.

Greenberg was invited to come and to bring with him a head person from Kochville, which had by now acquired a national reputation. The morning before the conference, he went downtown to City Hall Park with the intention of inviting Duke, but as he approached the camp, the first person he saw was Larry Locke.

He felt a surge of anger. He had no idea Larry was back. He was still mad about Larry's desertion a couple of weeks earlier. There had been no phone call then, nor was there any phone call now to say he had returned. What kind of person was this? Greenberg had basically put his life on hold in order to train him, to dress him, to tutor him, to brief him, even to teach him table manners.

His first instinct was to stride over to Larry Locke and dump all his venom on him. But he didn't. The time spent with Duke during the High Holy Days had softened him. The idea was to forgive people for their frailties, not to be constantly disappointed or pissed off about them. Otherwise, you were in the wrong business. Clearly, Marc was going to have to learn this over and over again. If Larry had been some kind of reliable pillar of the community, he probably wouldn't have been living in a park in the first place.

In fact, thought Greenberg now as he watched Locke wring out a grime caked pair of pants in the fountain, maybe *he's* the one to take to the conference in Tuxedo Park. He probably needed it more than Duke, who seemed to be on a healthy track, at least for now.

Greenberg approached the fountain. Larry kept wringing the pants, barely acknowledging him. He didn't know how to deal with Marc Greenberg. He felt guilty about running out on him, but he also held him responsible for the house nigger accusations that kept raining down on him.

Greenberg stood there for a while. Larry was apparently going to say nothing, so Marc began speaking, and before he was through he had made the offer in its entirety—mountain air, good food, lakeside walks.

Still reeking of the basement of 850 Longwood Avenue, Larry digested the images of tranquility. Then he lashed out. Did Greenberg have any idea how hard it would be for Larry to maintain any credibility as a leader if he took *another* powder, this time to a resort in the mountains? It wasn't his fault Larry had taken the *first* powder, said Greenberg with a bit of an edge. And this wasn't a resort. It was a place where Larry would learn about leadership and make contacts and ultimately do some good for Kochville. Tell that to Horace and Rasta, said Larry. He would be glad to, said Greenberg. Don't bother, because they won't even listen to you, said Larry, because they already hate you and every member of your race.

Larry was embarrassed by his own outburst. But his head was swirling. He'd made vows to himself that he was going to spend less time in ties and jackets and more time with his men. But the day in the Bronx had been such a nightmare. Maybe that meant that at some point you *had* to put on a tie and jacket and get something done through channels.

Since no answer to the invitation seemed to be forthcoming, Marc Greenberg finally said, "Think it over," and left the camp.

Throughout the day, Larry thought about it not at all. But at nightfall, having a cup of coffee with Duke at the Greek place, it all came out. It always did when the two of them were together. They had been apart for almost two weeks, and Larry, though he had spent much of that time in the arms of a woman, missed the soulful presence of Duke York. When he found out how sick Duke had been, he filled with dread. The big man was the rock. Duke would sit there and listen to you, and pretty soon, if you were bullshitting, your own voice started to feel hollow. You couldn't stand the sound of it. Before long, you were talking about what really mattered.

"You out of your mind?" said Duke. "Somebody wants to take you to the mountains, you GO THERE! Get the hell out of New York!" He told him a little about kayaking with Marc Greenberg.

Larry went through all his doubts, about copping out on the men, being a house nigger, ties, jackets, all the rest of it. Duke continued to stare at him. He didn't believe Larry. He felt there was something else.

"Look," Larry said finally, "the thing is, I got a speaking thing coming up. I want to be ready for it."

". . . speaking?"

Larry had kept this a secret from everybody, even Ellen, but he couldn't withhold it from Duke. "Jesse Jackson's coming back to town to make some speeches. He's gonna talk at St. John the Divine. He wants me to say some things."

". . . When did you set this up?"

"When he left the park that day," said Larry, "he asked me."

Duke was thrown off balance. This would be good for Kochville. But why did no one ask *him* to make important speeches? He was the passionate orator. He had proved that, at the POMP hearings and elsewhere. He had not, like Larry, dried up at the press conference. Instead he had saved the day, eloquently.

He struggled not to be bitter. "If you go to the mountains," he said, "there'll be people there who can help you with the speech."

"I want to write it myself," said Larry.

"You can concentrate better there," Duke replied. As if to confirm this, a demented shriek came from the direction of the park.

Larry went up to pay the check, and Duke knew he had talked him into it. But as they walked together back into the park, Duke York continued to wonder why Marc Greenberg had not invited him to the mountains. He wondered if it had to do with his glass eye, and for the rest of the night he found himself pitched into angry memories of Diane.

≡

Every once in a while, Ed Koch forgot himself and actually supported a Republican. Very soon afterward, he paid for it. In the case of John Lindsay, whom Ed Koch once backed for mayor because he thought he was the best man for the job, Koch was repaid by treachery. Lindsay turned around and supported Koch's opponent, another Wasp, for the congressional seat Lindsay was vacating. The guy's name was Whitney Seymour North the Third, and he looked like he'd just finished singing a rah-rah song in an eating club at Princeton (where Ed Koch had once thought of going to college but abandoned the idea because they rarely let in Jews). Ed Koch took exquisite pleasure in trouncing North at the polls, but the supreme pleasure was yet to come. After the election, Governor Nelson Rockefeller, anxious to curry favor with the new congressman from the silk stocking district, had Ed Koch to tea in his townhouse. Apparently it was the cook's day off, and ROCKEFELLER HIMSELF was forced to scurry about with scones and milk and sugar. Oh, SWEETNESS!!

But moments like that were few and far between. For the most part, the mayor felt disrespected by Republican/Wasps (the two things went together, usually), and in fact carried with him as the most salient memory of the North episode not the image of Nelson Rockefeller in an apron, but John Lindsay's double cross.

Fool me once, shame on you; fool me twice, shame on me. In the eighties, Koch had said nice things about Ronald Reagan, primarily because Reagan was a friend of Israel. Koch took voluminous shit from the Democratic Party for being a turncoat, much as he had for backing Lindsay. And what was the reward for his integrity this time? The memo that sat on his desk. Washington was announcing a new policy vis-à-vis New York's welfare hotels. After thirty days of occupancy, it would no longer pay for them.

The mayor felt his blood boiling. The goddamn hotels weren't his idea to begin with! Forced by the advocates' lawsuits to put homeless families *somewhere*, the city had for years been paying exorbitant rents to fleabag hotels.

"President Reagan," the memo went on to say, "is shocked by the conditions in these hotels, and equally shocked by their price tag—$37,000 per family per year. 'For that kind of money,' the president is quoted as saying, 'why doesn't somebody just build them a house?'"

The mayor practically lifted out of his chair. Why doesn't somebody "just build them a house?" Because, YOU GODDAMN IGNORAMUS, the only one who can do that is the federal government, which has been doing it for fifty years, but under YOUR GODDAMN TIGHTWAD ADMINISTRATION DOESN'T DO IT ANYMORE!! AND NOW YOU HAVE THE GODDAMN GALL TO MAKE POLITICAL CAPITAL BY MOANING AND SHAKING YOUR HEAD ABOUT THE CONDITIONS IN THE HOTELS?!

YOU CREATED THE FUCKING HOTELS!

Enough. Relax, he told himself. He had a mechanism for simply disassociating himself from his rage. He called it his Rational Switch. Without it, this job would have driven him off the deep end long ago.

Nobody's heart bled more for the "guests" in the welfare hotels than Ed Koch's. He had no family, so where did he go on holidays? Where would he be this very Thanksgiving, in fact? Carving a turkey in a homeless hotel, probably the Martinique, a dreadful place where the smoked mirrors in the ballroom stood in cruel contrast to the current reality. The mayor had been there before and never managed to leave without crying.

Toilet paper was dispensed one sheet at a time. Mothers made dinner for their families on one-burner hot plates. They finished cooking the string beans, and then they cooked the carrots. They finished cooking the carrots, and then they cooked the rice. Meals took four hours, and by that time the kids were either asleep or sitting up on their beds afraid to step off of them, because after dark the rats came out. What to do about the rats? Smuggle in a cat, which was against the rules. How to circumvent the rules? Possibly by mom giving the security guard a blow job. Forget the kids doing well at school, or even getting to school half the time, or avoiding the stares of so-called normal kids once they got there.

Ed Koch knew the whole routine. And the last time he was in one of the hotels, he had almost had to be carried out on a stretcher. Someone took him to a frail old white woman who, it turned out, had not left the room she was living in since 1973. That was when her husband died, and one of the last things he told her was never to leave the place. By that he meant never to give up the room. But in her senility, the poor thing had muddled her last instructions, and had not physically set foot outside the squalid room for fifteen years.

It took the mayor, who thought he was calloused to that kind of sorrow, a week to recover. He'd been trying close these hellholes ever since. And here on his desk was this sanctimonious communique from Ronald Reagan, who it was rumored never visited New York without disinfecting his clothes afterwards.

Just "close" the hotels, eh? And put these people where, exactly? Unfurl a blueprint for a new shelter anywhere in New York and people bellowed that the "fabric" of their community was being threatened. What they were really saying, of course, was "Keep those niggers out of here." And if Ed Koch complained about it, people would remind him of Forest Hills and call him a hypocrite.

Homelessness was Ed Koch's Armageddon. It was a brain twisting puzzle that could not be solved, only managed . . . with endless hard work and a family-sized bottle of aspirin. To add insult to injury, humiliating offers of help now sat on his desk. A Japanese businessman who had been appalled by the state of things on a recent trip to New York had sent a $25,000 check "just to help out." A team of Israeli doctors offered to come and deal with the rampant tuberculosis in the shelters, noting that "TB, a nineteenth-century disease thought to have gone the way of scurvy and typhoid, is actually *on the rise* in New York City shelters." Marvelous. And stuffing the mayor's trash can were designs for cheap housing from every crackpot and yokel from Fourteenth Street to Davenport, Iowa. One genius was convinced the answer to New York's housing problems lay in tin Quonset huts, like the kind in which he had bivouacked during World War Two. A woman from Wyoming submitted the suggestion, and the design, for plastic igloos.

To all of them the mayor felt like spewing a river of obscenities. But he could not do that, especially when the ideas came from well-meaning if incompetent New Yorkers. One priest in the Bronx suddenly wanted to open a shelter but had no earthly idea how to run one. Should this man be given public money!? If he were rejected, the roar from the advocates would be deafening. A humble priest wished to open the doors of his church to the poor and the city was FORBIDDING HIM TO DO SO.

"The car is here, sir."

The mayor stiffened. He was glad to be delivered from his Housing Rage, as he put it, but he did not relish his next engagement. Contrary to his reputation as a tough guy, the mayor did not seek out confrontations, and he knew he was about to have one. This morning was the dedication of the new Mahatma Gandhi statue in Union Square, and Henry Stern would be there. For months, as he had issued his parks commissioner a stream of terse memos about the City Hall Park matter, the mayor had said to himself "When I see Henry, I'm going to kill him."

Larry rode up the mountain in a Mercedes convertible. Usually, the liberal supporters of Kochville had automobiles that were practical and drab. Often they had a small but chronic mechanical problem and were cluttered with tin cans and plastic bottles on their way to be recycled. Frequently there was a frayed bumper sticker about a grape boycott.

The maroon convertible of Dr. Ronald Colman was encumbered in no such way. As it began to creep into the foothills of the Catskills, the sun came out and the doctor put down the top. They climbed slowly around curving roads through one lush glen after another. The leaves, which were changing colors dramatically, were practically slapping them in the face.

Autumn was in full swing in Tuxedo Park, which was only an hour north of the city. On another day this might have alarmed Larry, for winter is the enemy of the homeless man. Today, however, even the short distance between this place and the Bronx was exhilarating. Eight-fifty Longwood Avenue no longer existed in his memory.

Until this moment, Larry had thought nature to be a thing of childhood. He had walked barefoot through endless fields of cotton and indigo, climbed cherry trees, and dived naked into the Cape Fear River. As a grownup, he had put on shoes and lived in places like Newark and Manhattan. That was about it, not counting the army. But now here was Doctor Ronald Colman talking about the country as a place to return to. "Man, am I glad to get the hell out of New York," the doctor shouted above the engine.

Larry considered this image for a moment . . . himself as a country gentleman. As they whizzed past the front gates of Catskills landowners, he did not see too many black faces.

"There it is," said Dr. Colman, pointing to a stone structure that hovered above a lake in the distance. "It used to be a very serious monastery. The monks would take vows of silence and not say a word for ten years at a time. Nowadays it's like a bed and breakfast. They have Easter weekend packages."

The approach to the place was endless, switchbacking up a sizable mountain. When they got to the front gate, several cars were unloading in front of them. Many of the people were wearing clothes of Indian origin, saris and robes and gowns.

Once inside, everyone was given a cup of herbal tea and ushered into a large room with an enormous roaring fireplace. Later Larry would learn that Dr. Colman's tale of the monks was barely exaggerated. For many years, even as the order dwindled, a handful of Eastern Orthodox brothers had shuffled about this enormous place in silence. The image was irritating to Larry. Counting the vast common rooms, dining areas, living quarters, and terraces, the place was twice the size of the Borden Avenue Shelter and theoretically could have slept a thousand people.

The meeting was brought to order and a convocation was delivered by a Jesuit priest who had once set himself on fire to protest the construction of a nuclear reactor. The man was a passionate speaker, and the effect of his words, augmented by the fire in the room, were powerful. One felt as if something important was about to happen.

The first official speaker was Baba Ram Dass, to whom Larry took an instant liking. The man truly seemed to be on some sort of quest, never satisfied, always checking himself out. Recently, he said, he had been on a pilgrimage to India that had involved three weeks of virtual starvation in a cave in a remote part of Bengal. Ram Dass had arrived home believing that he had ascended to a realm of pure spirituality. But in his next speaking engagement, telling a college audience about his experience, he found himself scanning the front row of pretty coeds and speculating which one he might wind up in bed with. This forced him to conclude that he had not ascended to anything at all, and he immediately returned to India to spend another month in the cave.

Many of Larry's friends would have considered this proof of the man's stupidity, but Larry was impressed. This cat was serious.

But Bernie Glassman, who followed Ram Dass, was intolerable. Perpetually scowling, Glassman seemed to believe that his occasional forays into homelessness made him morally superior to his audience. He spoke in grave tones of *johatsu*, a Japanese concept of the homeless wanderer as holy man. To Larry, this was absolute crap. Even Kochville, the cream of the crop, contained no holy men but rather an assortment of losers, junkies, winos, and madmen.

It was when Glassman got into some of his Zen philosophy, however, that Larry was forced to leave the room. Glassman introduced the idea that we all make our own choices, even to the point of when we are born. "We and we alone," said the rotund, pretentious man, "choose the moment that the sperm and the egg of our parents unite . . ."

What??!!! In that case, Larry felt like shouting at him, why the hell did I decide to be born into a racist society to a woman who ruined my goddamn life?!

He left the room, trying to be unobtrusive, but since he was the only black man there, everyone watched him open the big brass door and close it behind him. Screw them all, he thought, walking out of the stone archway and onto the huge terrace that hung over the lake. He was surprised at the intensity of his reaction to Glassman. The man's bullshit deserved a strong reaction. But Larry had never before thought in terms of his mother ruining his life.

Granted, she had put the kibosh on his first and only real love affair. Granted, she had ripped him away from his father and the only home he had ever known and at the age of fourteen brought him to Newark, New Jersey, for God's sake. Granted, she had suffocated him with her goddamn church, stuffing him into his Sunday suit and making him sing in the choir for ten hours at a time.

But had all that ruined his life? Had his life in fact been ruined? Was it over? And if so, where did her responsibility end and his begin? When he worked his way up to positions of authority and then screwed them up by getting high or getting drunk, whose fault was that? Anyone's?

None of that mattered anymore. The biggest opportunity of his life was in front of him, and he was *not* going to screw it up. He was going to be on a podium with Jesse Jackson—center stage of the whole world, at least the only world that he cared about. While the rest of the weekend monks agonized over their personal bullshit, Larry would walk these forest trails and compose the words that would electrify a nation.

<hr>

Ed Koch was the godfather of Henry Stern's older son Jared, and the Stern household gave the mayor the closest thing he knew to a feeling of normalcy and family.

That was why, as the mayor travelled toward the unveiling of the Gandhi statue and the long anticipated meeting with Stern, he had no stomach for a fight. Nevertheless, something had to be done. The mayor's Russian strategy in City Hall Park was not working. His deepest fears about the Jesse Jackson visit had been realized. Jackson had somehow given the homeless spiritual fuel to carry on, and now the mayor's enemies were drawing strength from it. "If these clowns can get under the mayor's skin," normally timid politicians said to themselves, "maybe I can too." For the first time since the scandals, there was the scent of blood. No one understood this better than Ed Koch.

The Mahatma Gandhi statue was coming into view, and the

mayor managed a smile. Clearly, it had been erected not because New Yorkers particularly prized barefooted humility as a virtue, but rather to acknowledge the city's burgeoning Indian population. The sculptor had the Mahatma naked except for his trademark loincloth and a garland of flowers around his neck. It reminded the mayor of a homeless madman he had seen on the way home last night.

Stern was already there, in a tattered corduroy jacket, leaning over a patch of weeds. No doubt, thought the mayor, he was making a horticultural observation incomprehensible to anyone else. That was fine. That was part of the eccentricity that people loved him for. What was not fine was his unresponsiveness about City Hall Park.

Much time had passed, and Stern was as wily as they came, which meant two things: he could solve the problem if he wanted to, and he fully understood the damage it was doing to the mayor. Therefore, Ed Koch concluded, Henry is doing more than playing games or merely asserting himself. He's trying to hurt me.

Stern saw the mayor arrive out of the corner of his eye. Some of the lackeys around the podium were popping up to greet him. Not Henry Stern. He'd found a rock outcropping uncatalogued in any of the city parks studies. That was what the job was about, wasn't it? Rather than glad-handing politicians? Much of the summer had been consumed in geological and botanical observations. Rocks and plants and animals had very few allies in New York, and in the end, protecting them was more important than electoral maneuvering. He had tried to help Ed with his political problems in City Hall Park. That had proven impossible to do, so he had turned his attention back to his real job. So what was wrong with that?

Slowly, reluctantly, he made his way to the podium and took his seat between a couple of big shots in the New York Indian community. A woman in a sari with a dark *bindi* in the middle of her forehead took the microphone and began the program. For the next half hour, Koch, Stern, Borough President Dinkins, and a group of other powerful people took turns praising a man who had conducted his business naked and crosslegged on a floor. As the mayor's old rival Charlie Rangel once cracked at the end of a long testimonial, "Everything has been said, but not everyone has said it."

Afterwards, Ed Koch finally made his way over to Henry Stern. Looking at the rumpled parks commissioner, forever tangled in his own neuroses and eccentricities, it was impossible to stay mad at him.

"I'm sorry I didn't get back to you on that City Hall thing, Ed . . ." he heard Stern say.

"That's all right, Henry. I've been away." Koch felt very like the big brother absorbing the stupidity of the little brother.

"I've been thinking about it a lot."

"I was hoping you had been, Henry."

"I was thinking that now that it's colder, it might be easier to remove them. For their own good. That kind of thing."

"Maybe you should try that, Henry."

"You want to drop over sometime this weekend? Margaret and the kids would love to see you."

"I'm going to Florida, Henry."

"Vacation?"

"Maybe I'll get a little sun."

Stern smiled. The mayor didn't believe in vacations. Once he had canceled a two-week idyll in Tuscany just to stick around Albany and argue about a pension plan. No, if he was going to Florida, it had something to do with the next election. Every Jew in Miami Beach had six relatives who voted in the New York primary. Florida was a repository of Ed Koch's people. It was as if you went to your aunt's house and just for showing up, she took your fat little cheeks in between her fingers and said, "What a good little boy!!" Koch needed that, politically. Whether it also did him any good emotionally, Henry Stern had no idea. The mayor seemed to have very few of those needs.

"Ed, look, I'll work on the City Hall Park thing while you're away."

"I wish you would, Henry. I really, really do."

Eleven

On a day not long after Larry Locke, Art, Samantha, and Matthew visited the Bronx, Irma Ortiz lost her sense of humor for good. Her teenage son Juan, the godson of Victoria Hernandez, was found dead in the alcove behind the elevator at 850 Longwood. Apparently the body had been there for days, even as Irma had been frantically inquiring all over the neighborhood. The boy had angered Guiterrez by not bringing home the money from a drug sale to a group of college students who had driven in from Westchester. Unfortunately for Juan, someone had observed the transaction. His mother had not even known he was involved with drugs.

A few weeks later, when she learned that Juan's execution had actually taken place outdoors on Prospect Avenue, she held a service on the sidewalk. This was fully sanctioned by her local priest, with whom she had a good relationship. She rarely went to church, but she appreciated the fact that it had never closed up its branch, like the subway and the bank.

She lit a candle, put it by the curbstone, and laid down some flowers next to a photograph of Juan. Then she signalled Emilio, her youngest, to set down his orange pail and push a button on a tape player. The music had been given to her by Victoria Hernandez, just before her departure from New York. It was one of the most beautiful compositions of Victoria's brother Rafael, now also dead and mourned throughout the Hispanic world. It was a sad melody called "Lamento Borincano," about a peasant farmer who goes to the city to sell his wares but fails to do so and bitterly returns home with his rotting fruit.

From this point on, Irma Ortiz teetered on the edge. She had endured all she could endure and still remain in contact with what people called reality. Her communion with her plaster saints was more or less continuous, as was the blazing of dozens of candles for both spiritual and physical heat. All that punctuated this existence were the comings and goings of Emilio, with water.

One day there was a knock on the door, an event that now terrified her. Only a few people could possibly be standing outside, and among the more likely candidates was her son's murderer, who still commandeered the building. The knocking became more insistent, and finally Irma Ortiz heard a woman's voice. With considerable trepidation she opened the door a crack. She saw a round olive face, framed in curls, and recognized her visitor instantly.

In the moments it took to unlatch the several chains, Irma Ortiz remembered the first time she had ever seen Eve Miranda, about fifteen years earlier.

It was at the height of the planned shrinkage movement, when the city planned to close the subway stops and plant the Bronx with wildflower meadows. One day, when a cluster of small buildings on Kelly Street was scheduled for demolition, a buzz ran through the neighborhood that something unusual was happening. Irma Ortiz walked over with her son Juan, then a babe in arms, to find a Mexican standoff, or at least a Puerto Rican one. The city demolition units were poised and ready. Holding hands and forming a ring around the building in question were its residents. Nobody was moving.

Irma Ortiz walked up to a teenage girl in the handholding circle and asked what was going on. If the city destroyed the buildings, said the girl, then they would have to do so over the corpses of its tenants. Irma Ortiz was both amused and disturbed by the bravado. Didn't they understand, she asked the girl, that as tenants of a demolished city building, they would go straight to the head of the list of public housing? They might find themselves on the top floor of one of the desirable new high-rise projects in Manhattan, perhaps even the one overlooking Central Park. If someone had offered such a deal to Irma Ortiz, she told the teenager, she would have been gone from 850 Longwood Avenue in about thirty seconds.

"This is where my father come to," said the girl. "Here I live." She went on to say, in Spanish, that mothers could not watch their children play from thirty floors up. That was not a neighborhood, but the opposite of one.

Admiring the girl's nerve if not her stupidity, Irma Ortiz withdrew and waited to see what would happen next. Nothing did. Finally, after squawking into walkie-talkies for a long time, the city demolition people withdrew. Irma Ortiz watched the residents, almost all Hispanic, file stolidly back into their buildings.

Years later, she would tell and retell the story. She had witnessed the birth of Banana Kelly. When she first heard the name, she couldn't get the image out of her mind of an Irishwoman with fruit on her head, a sort of freckled Carmen Miranda. But Banana Kelly was no joke. The name referred to the curved block of Kelly Street where the incident had taken place and the organization that it spawned: a group of Hispanic people who said to the world, as the world tried to burn, condemn, or otherwise forget the South Bronx, "Here I live."

In the beginning, a couple of young men on Kelly Street found a way to make use of its very desolation. As long as you lived on what had been reduced to a wind swept plain, why not reap the wind? They built a windmill, and that was followed quickly by solar panels. They had power, and very soon they managed to hook their water back up again. They even turned the wild, utopian, vaguely insulting idea of the wildflower meadows to their advantage. All the compost that had been collected from the

Hunt's Point Market and the Bronx Zoo could be used not to bury the Bronx in a meadow but to give people the means to raise their own food. Take that, Manhattan!! Anybody down there growing zucchini?!

"Don't move, improve" became the slogan of Banana Kelly, and soon pockets of resistance formed all over the Bronx. Irma Ortiz was always slightly bitter that Longwood Avenue was not among them, but was instead a forgotten corner of things. But perhaps that was no longer true . . . now that Eve Miranda herself was standing in the living room!

No longer the defiant teenager whom Irma had met all those years ago, Eve Miranda was now a mature, self-possessed officer of Banana Kelly and a major presence in Bronx politics. This was not the first time she had entered the building at 850 Longwood Avenue. One of her earliest memories of childhood was being taken by her mother in taffeta and patent leather shoes to the Danubio Azurro for dinner. This was a happy memory, but it co-existed in her mind with some grim ones. She remembered fearing not only the Savage Nomads but also the Young Lords, who took up the political cause of the Hispanics in New York. One day outside 850 Longwood, they almost clubbed the Miranda family car to a flat piece of metal because they thought it belonged to a gringo.

But no nightmare of the building's past, Eve Miranda knew, could compare to the present. This was the moral tumor of the neighborhood. By day, fifty people did their foul business in the various niches of the place—the gutted-out little holes in which one could smoke crack, cook heroin, count money, or threaten lives. At last tally, there had been seven murders in the building. At the center of it all was Guiterrez, with an arsenal that could equip a small army. Eve Miranda knew that whatever Banana Kelly's successes, fear still sat at the core of Longwood. And so she had come.

As Miranda sat down among the candles and the saints, Irma

Ortiz scurried off to make some *café con leche*, thrilled to be involved in a human, quasisocial event. But it was not merely social for Eve Miranda, or even merely business. As she surveyed the bewildering array of saints on the mantelpiece, and finally the urn that contained the ashes of Juan Ortiz, her anger and indignation grew. When Irma returned with the coffee, the look in Eve Miranda's eyes was very like those of the inflamed, uncompromised teenager of long ago. If it took the life out of her body, said Miranda, Guiterrez would be beaten, and the long, dark night would end.

≡

From its bluff on Morningside Heights, St. John the Divine Cathedral commands upper Manhattan. To the north and east lie Harlem; to the southeast, Central Park and the opulence of the Upper East Side; to the west, the student ghetto of Columbia University; and beyond that, the sparkling Hudson and the cliffs of New Jersey.

Over all of this St. John's sits like a fortress. In its vast yard lie great building stones as yet unerected. It is said of St. John's that it will never be completed, and that that is somehow appropriate for the world's largest church, for when is God's work ever done?

Few other churches on earth have interpreted the phrase "God's work" in such broad and practical terms. In various corners and niches of the huge compound are a homeless shelter, a nursery school, a vegetable garden, and a peacock lair. In its dank endless crypt, where the corpses of some of the city's greatest Episcopalians reside, may also be found an Off-Broadway theatre and a welter of nonprofit offices. But more than any of its lay enterprises, St. John's is famous for what goes on inside the huge cathedral itself. At fifteen million cubic feet, it is the largest house of worship on earth, its vaults and arches more like a low sky than a high ceiling. Its reaches are so vast, its entrances and exits so many, that people speak of the weather *inside* the church. It is beautiful beyond description, and if the purpose of a church is to make man feel his insignificance, St. John's succeeds to a terrifying degree.

The church serves New York by housing events of such size, emotionally as well as physically, that no other building can hold them, with the possible exception of St. Patrick's Cathedral. Duke Ellington's funeral was here, as was the memorial for the slain civil rights workers Schwerner, Chaney, and Goodman, and countless other events that cut to the soul of the city.

On the morning of October 10, 1988, Jesse Jackson, now the unchallenged leader of the black community in the United States, would give his first major address since the Democratic Convention from the pulpit of St. John's. His topic would be poverty and housing, to which the cathedral had a longstanding, passionate commitment. His introductory speaker would be Larry Locke, the leader of the homeless community in City Hall Park.

At dawn on October 10, the vast cathedral was empty, save for the dead bishops and the chambermaids vacuuming the altar. On the roof, however, a solitary figure paced the parapet. This was Larry Locke. The night before, Marc Greenberg had allowed him to sleep in the Interfaith Assembly office behind the altar so that he could prepare. The preparation would be emotional, for the text of the speech had already been set a week ago, in the forests of Tuxedo Park. Duke had been right. The serenity had been perfect. From beetles squirming up rocks and trees shedding leaves, he had taken his inspiration and his images. And he had slept, slept gloriously, both on hard monastic cots and on tufts of moss in the forest.

All he lacked was an opening image for the speech—a way to begin. He had thought to find this by soaking up the vibrations of the cathedral overnight. Unfortunately, the opposite was happening. The enormity of the place was intimidating him. So was the enormity of the moment and the city over which he now gazed. Everyone would be listening to him: from his Newark relatives, who would be sitting in the pews, to black people tuned into radios all over the country, to possibly even Nelson Mandela in his jail cell in Capetown.

Did he have enough to say? Did he have *anything* to say? He thought he did: just the simple story of who he was, and how he lost the roof over his head, and how he was fighting with heart and soul to get it back. He was going to tell them that no homeless person was any different, and that all of them were human. Fine. But how, exactly, would he begin?

As he wrestled with the problem, the sun came up over Harlem. It was a shocking, clear autumn dawn, and the sun was huge. It hit him almost brutally in the face. Then his eyes adjusted and he bathed in it. It was washing all of Harlem in a red-copper light. Even the broken glass shimmered.

This was his answer. This grace was everyone's, rich or poor. The light found its way into tubercular hovel and Fifth Avenue mansion alike. A new day is all we're asking for, Larry would say. Wipe the slate clean. Don't blame us for mugging your sister, we won't blame you for the slave trade. Fresh start in a new town.

Was it enough? Was he the first person to think of this, or the ten thousandth? Did it matter? No. He was feeling his power now. He walked to the western parapet just as a police truck arrived at the main steps below and unloaded hundreds of blue barricades. Across the street, the famous Hungarian Pastry Shop was gearing up. Larry realized he hadn't eaten in twenty-four hours. He descended the steep stone stairway and crossed the street to the little Columbia student haunt, curling up in a corner with a black coffee and a piece of strudel. By the time he finished and crossed back to the cathedral, people were already arriving.

The crowd was about equally divided between black and white, but some of the blacks were of the same ilk he had encountered at Dinkins' fund-raiser: rich and well connected, Harlem in ermine and pearls. Feeling a new wave of intimidation, he retreated to the back of the cathedral and sat in Greenberg's office collecting himself. The office was a mess, full of leaflets, half-eaten sand-wiches, coffee cups, and piles of clothes earmarked for the home-less. Why did Greenberg do all this? Larry found himself wonder-ing. By now, it was clear he came from a rich family and didn't have to. Maybe Horace and Rasta were right. Maybe Greenberg was doing this to *make* money. Maybe that's where the family money came from. It was rumored that Trinity Church had re-cently given the Interfaith Assembly a hundred thousand dollar grant. What happened to that money??

These were all distractions, and he put them out of his head. He went over the speech again. The sound of the crowd coming in broke up his thought patterns, and he had to start over. Now, suddenly, he was forgetting everything. Every word. Please God, don't let this happen. Now a phrase came back, but only a frag-ment. And not in the right order. What was happening?!?

"Larry . . ."

Dean James Morton was poking his head in the door. The Dean basically ran St. John's, steering its social policy and presid-ing over most of its huge events. "Just about any time now."

What!? Already!!?

"Jesse's been delayed in traffic near the airport, so we're go-ing to start without him," said Morton "The natives are getting restless."

Larry felt like he'd been punched in the stomach. He wasn't ready. Not only that, he wanted Jesse to hear the speech! He had, in fact, imagined Jesse's reactions to parts of it, the look on his face, the arched eyebrows.

He tried to absorb the disappointment. Maybe it would make him less nervous if Jesse *didn't* hear it. Sure. There would be time afterward to tell him about it, to get into the whole thing on a deeper level. Yes. Fine. And there were a lot of other people wait-ing to hear him right now, so he better remember the goddamn speech!!

Just how many people had never been made clear to him and

was not even clear to him as he walked out towards the altar. He could see a few rows of faces beaming at him, and that made him nervous enough. It was not until after Dean Morton had introduced him and he had climbed the steps to the sculpted, raised pulpit that he could see the size of the crowd. There were thousands of them. A sea of faces. The pews stretched infinitely back into the darkness, and all of them were full. He had never been in a place with this many people, let alone stood in front of them.

Morton's introduction hung in the room. Larry Locke. Larry Locke. Larry Locke. The reverb off the stone walls was intense. The roar of the crowd was astonishing. Whether they all knew who he was or whether any of them did, it was the single loudest sound Larry had ever heard. They were all looking at him. He looked up at the vast ceiling, praying to remember the words and trying to avoid the stares of the people. He felt they were examining him too closely, as if they were trying to find out what was wrong with him. Mercifully his opening words came to him now, and he began quickly.

"Good afternoon . . ." His voice felt light and thin. He felt empty, as if he had no power. It was the same feeling he'd had at the press conference on the City Hall steps in July.

"This morning, as the sun came up . . ." It didn't sound like his voice. ". . . as the sun came up, I saw Harlem from the roof of this building . . ." Building. He choked on the word, simple as it was. Why not just *church*? ". . . of this building and I knew that into every home . . ." It was better now. *Home* was a simple, strong word, ". . . every home the same sun was shining . . ." There was even a ripple of applause now, the sweetest sound he'd ever heard. It felt like a bowl of crack used to feel on a hot summer night, or a cocktail with a pretty girl. ". . . sun was shining just like it was on Park Avenue too . . ." that was a rhyme actually . . . *nue* and too. He was rolling now. ". . . Avenue too, and so I knew that all of God's children were feeling the warmth." Yes, that felt very good.

Now there was a large crescendo of sound. A little premature, he thought. He hadn't yet gotten to his first big point. If they liked it so far, they were going to *love* what was coming!

Then it became clear that the large sound emanated from a serious commotion in the back of the room. Was it a fight!? Heads turned to look. Larry turned to the dean. Should he continue? Yes, nodded Morton impatiently, stirring the air with his hands.

". . . so if all of us feel the sun . . . FEEL THE SUN . . ." Larry was shouting now, because there was tumult in the hall, and at last he could see why. Head bobbing a half-foot above everyone around him, Jesse Jackson was making his way down the side aisle. Scowling men were on every side of him, pushing people out of the way.

"Keep talking . . ." Dean Morton was now mouthing emphatically to Larry, who raced through his text as Jackson inched towards the front of the church. Finally the great man arrived in the sanctuary and Dean Morton embraced him, just as Larry was making his main points, shouting to be heard above the din.

"ALL A HOMELESS MAN WANTS . . ." yelled Larry, but now the dean was giving him a different sign than earlier, motioning to him rather frantically, running his finger across his throat as if to say "Cut."

Not on your life, motherfucker, thought Larry Locke. Not if you were God himself. And so he ignored Morton and kept talking. Now that Jackson was stationary, the crowd's attention was back to the pulpit, or seemed to be. It's a shame that Jesse hasn't heard most of this, thought Larry. It was a complicated argument he was building.

". . . and we have the same kinds of thoughts and feelings, the same kinds of pain, as anybody else," he said. That prompted a small burst of applause. Before Larry could continue, however, the old fox Morton bounded up the steps and grabbed the microphone. "Thank you Larry, that was very powerful!! And now we're going to hear from the man you've all been waiting for, the man this country has been waiting for, for a long, long time. I know he's on a very tight schedule today, so without further ado, I want to bring up . . ."

Jesse was already on his way up the steps. The crowd roared. Jackson shook Larry's hand warmly. Not the effusive hug of last month in the park, but these were different circumstances. There was a moment during which Larry was tempted to say "I wasn't finished yet . . ." but instead he surrendered the pulpit and climbed down the steps.

The Jackson speech was electrifying. Larry listened to the cadences rise and fall and watched the hand movements—few and far between, but always powerful, always hammering home a point, sculpting the air. The man was an actor. He let you know what made him happy and what made him sad. You wanted to comfort him, or take him home with you, or follow him into battle. Whatever he wanted.

When Jackson was done, the reaction was deafening. Every one of the thousands of people were on their feet, screaming. Jackson and his handlers began moving back through the crowd, and Larry got himself in between them, and the whole group just surged ahead, as if they had no feet but were like those boats that hovered above the sea. Finally they reached the front door of the cathedral and jogged down the steps, which were clear: the police were keeping the crowd inside.

When they got to the curb, Jackson and three other men got inside a limousine and Larry remained standing there. He didn't know whether to get into the car or not. Jackson seemed unaware of his position. ". . . Jesse!" barked Larry, loud enough to get his attention. Jackson turned and looked at him with a confused, pained expression that seemed to say, "I just can't." Then the door closed and the car drove off.

Now the crowd, released from the church, poured down the steps. Larry tried to absorb his disappointment and at the same time act adroitly enough to avoid being crushed. Finally he just let himself be buffeted. After a while the stream thinned out, and he was able to move up the steps and back into the church.

He plopped limply into a back pew. Up at the pulpit someone was actually speaking, a white woman named Bonnie Brower. She was a renowned housing expert, and Larry remembered now that she had insisted on speaking last. A dreadful miscalculation. No one followed Jesse Jackson. The woman knew more about housing than Jackson, Ed Koch, Michael Dukakis, James Morton, and Marc Greenberg put together, but she was speaking to an empty hall.

Just what Larry had hoped for he could not say, exactly. That he would become famous? That he and Jesse would wind up in Harlem at Sylvia's Restaurant, having cocktails? That Jesse would take him on as an assistant and that they would go around the country together, preaching like hell? No, none of those things. Just a conversation. Just a chance to utter the last lines of the speech he had never finished, which were, "I am Larry Locke. I exist."

＝

They took Samantha around midnight. She only had a few hundred yards to travel, but if the decent City Hall cop hadn't been on duty, as opposed to the bastard, they never would have gotten her there.

As it was, she'd already lost what the ER guys called an ocean of blood. Riding with her in the police car, Duke York was feeling what it might be like to be a woman. His intestines were tied into a knot, screaming for mercy. At first the doctors couldn't tell which one of them was sick.

His admiration for Samantha was huge. Through it all, she had been calm and even demure, combing her hair in the back of the car. When they opened the door, she practically floated out on her own discharge. Though he barely knew her, Duke stayed at her bedside until they took her upstairs to operate. There was something of his grandmother in her: clean, reserved, proper, but made of iron.

She was on the operating table for about five hours, and he stewed the whole time. The man was incapable of relaxing anyway, but this situation threw his bullish body into a mania. He walked around the block endlessly, checking in on every lap with the ER receptionist. That made about fifty-five check-ins.

"As I keep repeating, sir, there's nothing we can tell you until she comes back downstairs."

When she finally did come down, the presiding doctor, an Iranian named Kharrazi, approached the profusely sweating Duke with great caution.

"You are the husband?"

"No. Just a friend."

"I'm going to be honest with you. She was in very bad condition, and we couldn't afford to be subtle. We have performed what we call a gross hysterectomy. All her womanly parts, more or less, are gone. But she will survive. You can take her home. Perhaps tomorrow or the next day."

"She doesn't have a home."

Darkness crossed Dr. Kharrazi's brow. Duke read the subtext this way: "I break my nuts to save this woman, and now you're telling me she doesn't even have a clean bed to climb into and she's maybe going to die of some stupid infection?"

Duke spoke first. "I'll see that she's taken care of." After the doctor left him alone, Duke reviewed his options. He would have loved to consult Larry on this, but Larry was still in the mountains or was addressing St. John the Divine, Duke didn't know or care which. It was all on him now.

Clearly, the camp was no place for her. Larry's brief return had done nothing to reverse the downhill slide. People were drinking and whoring around. It was getting cold at night, and night came earlier, which meant the rats came out sooner and stayed longer. Even Horace and Rasta had lost their fire and were chanelling their energy into survival, not rebellion. There was a muted, stoic quality to things, a quiet bitterness, a frost, real and imagined.

A recent arrival named Joe was typical of the cold weather breed. Six feet four and a former master sergeant in Vietnam, Joe had been homeless for five years. He was not concerned with pieces of legislation or the names of politicians. He was concerned with getting something for himself or being carried out in a coffin, he barely cared which.

Into a milieu like this, Duke could not bring the post-operative Samantha. Instead, the night she was released, he took her in a taxi to the woman's shelter at the Seventh Regiment Armory. This was the strangest creation of the entire city welfare system. The armory was a rather elegant old building that actually fronted on Park Avenue. Mostly it housed the mementos of rich men at war—medals, elaborate banners, even symbolic coats of arms. All of the items were ensconced in trophy cases of glass and mahogany, with an occasional moose head mounted on a wall. On the top floor was a bar where only the highest-ranking officers were allowed to drink and presumably trade tales of sacrifice and victory. Crammed into the middle of all this, owing to some bizarre funding requirement of the government, was a woman's homeless shelter.

Duke arrived with Samantha around nine in the evening. The two of them were obliged to make their way through a reunion of a battalion that had landed together in Italy in 1943. The men were toasting each other with the regimental cocktail, a mixture of bourbon whiskey and Italian grappa. The combination both repelled and seduced Duke and Samantha, both alcoholics.

Finally they got to the shelter on the third floor. Duke had spent time in men's homeless shelters, and he thought he would never encounter anything as dismal. Now he reassessed his position. If the crudeness of homeless males was depressing, even more so was the absolute frailty of the females.

Duke was a man of the theatre, and he told himself he had

walked into a dormitory full of Blanche Duboises. They were all slightly or substantially mad: all shaking their heads over something that was or might have been. Some were potentially beautiful or once beautiful. Most were waiting for the next blow, like abused animals. The sound of the room was a collective sigh. Duke wanted to weep for them all, but he had taken enough of other people's misery into his body lately, so he settled Samantha in as quickly as he could and left.

On the Number 6 train back downtown, Duke wondered if there were indeed two types of people in the world: the ones who absorbed all the suffering, like him and Samantha, and the ones who dished it out, like his ex-wife Diane. Recently he had heard a quote from Ed Koch that stuck with him. "I don't get ulcers," the mayor had said, "I give them." Maybe you simply had to make a choice.

≡

Larry Locke remained in his pew in the back of St. John the Divine as dusk darkened the stained glass. It had been an hour since the Jackson speech, the place was almost empty, but Larry still had not moved. It was only at this point that Ellen McCarthy sensed the time was right to approach him.

"It was wonderful."

He looked up. She was wearing a dark red woolen coat that clung to her like the skin of a sea lion. Her lipstick was even darker, a maroon color. Her remarkable cheekbones were carved by the light of the tall candles just now being lit in the naves.

"You saw it?"

"Yes."

"I didn't get to finish."

"You can finish it for me now."

She held out her arm, and he rose and took it, and she led him out onto Amsterdam Avenue.

The city had pulled on the cloak of night. The sky was full of stars, and the cold autumn air smelled of perfume. She led him over to Broadway and down a couple of blocks to a new French restaurant she'd heard of, run by some Haitians. They sat for a while somewhat stiffly, as they always did after a separation. Ellen began gabbing to the black waiters with an ease that Larry envied. He sat there, keenly aware of the white patrons. An interracial romance was not big news on the Upper West Side, but there was always the infinitesimally raised eyebrow, the moment's hesitation before the smile. Ellen was sensitive to none of that.

Red wine arrived, Larry poured some for them both, and it wasn't long before the wine did what it was supposed to do. His miseries shrank, and he remembered that he was in the company of a mature and beautiful woman. They ate their salads and their sole meunière slowly and sensually, as if they were lying in bed.

As they rode home on the Number 2 train, the moment of truth arrived, as it had on other nights. Would Larry get off and sleep in City Hall Park, or would he keep riding, as every instinct in his body wanted to, all the way to Ellen's stop in Brooklyn? The park was no doubt freezing and filthy and riddled with tension and revolution. Ellen's was a fantasy of lace and warmth and flesh. What kind of a choice was this for a drunken man to have to make!!?

Against his deepest desires, Larry got to his feet and forced himself off the train. He waved to her and waited until the subway station was quiet. Then he climbed the stairs to the open air of City Hall Park. At the same moment, Duke York was arriving on the other side of the park, having deposited Samantha in the shelter at the armory. The two men saw each other and sat down together on a bench.

It was immediately clear to Larry that things had deteriorated even during his few days in Tuxedo Park. People he didn't recognize were drinking right on the benches, and even hygiene, once the camp's greatest point of pride, had fallen apart. Litter was everywhere.

Duke let him share his take-out coffee a while and then gave him more bad news.

Matthew, the white heroin addict, had betrayed them.

For a while some of the men had done odd jobs for various support groups around the park. One outfit, called the Food and Hunger Hotline, had hired a crew of them to paint the place. While they were on the job, Matthew had stolen five hundred dollars from somebody's desk. No one had seen him since.

It was betrayal on every level. The Food and Hunger Hotline, which had for months allowed Kochville to use their telephones and copiers and mailing lists, had been betrayed. The interracial government of Larry and Duke and Art and Matthew had been betrayed. And Matthew, who was no doubt getting high somewhere at this very moment, had betrayed himself.

Larry took a second to absorb the treachery. White men, ultimately, were white men. "Fuck him," he said finally. "What else?"

Duke told him about the sickness—not just Samantha's, but everyone else's. Shep, a bull of man, had come down with blood poisoning from the rusty park water. Big Jim, blind as well as homeless, had had a hernia explode on him. And the legendary Lonnie from Tennessee, who had seemed the hardiest of all, finally wandered away one night glazed and catatonic and had not been seen again.

The cold nights were lowering everybody's resistance, and people were checking into the Emergency Room at Beekman Hospital just to get warm and get a flu shot. There was no telling how much longer Beekman would keep admitting people who smelled badly and couldn't pay.

The two men looked at each other. In the great days of June, it was the moment they told each other would never come. They would stay here forever, they said. They would bring the city to its knees, they would get arctic parkas and build igloos if they had to.

That was the talk of a summer night. On the night of this conversation it was 35 degrees. Then it started to rain.

= = =

That Monday afternoon, the monthly meeting of the Interfaith Assembly was convened at two o'clock with a prayer by Sister Agnes O'Grady. Marc Greenberg stood and took the roll call of attendees. As usual, they included representatives of every major faith in New York, and several other people, like David Kirk of Emmaeus House, whose good works transcended all faiths.

The first order of business was new applications. The Fourth Presbyterian Church of West Seneca, the Union Theological Seminary, and the Zen Community of New York had all applied for membership. What this meant, among other things, was that Bernie Glassman himself might soon sit at this very table. The reach of Interfaith was getting broader every day.

The next item was antiwarehousing legislation. "Warehousing" was the issue that had so inflamed Amy Foster at the Dinkins fund-raiser months earlier. It was a classic battle of the rights of the business class against the general well-being of society, and Interfaith was throwing a lot of muscle into it. They were also alienating a lot of small realtors and big politicians. But Interfaith had no intention of backing down. Greenberg announced they were committing more of their resources to the fight than ever, and this brought cheers from the table, even from the normally reserved Sister Agnes.

As the applause subsided, the door opened and Larry Locke walked in. Instinctively, everyone stood. In the nonprofit housing world at this moment, there was no more recognized figure. Larry flashed a smile around the room; he had a nodding acquaintance with almost everyone here. This, however, was his first meeting at Interfaith.

"Welcome, Larry," said Greenberg. "What a great surprise! We're probably going to have to fight it out to see who gets to be the first one to tell you how great you were up there with Jesse on Saturday." There were convivial cheers around the table. Larry gave a small, grateful smile.

"So what can we do for you?"

"Well," said Larry, "I just thought I'd come to one of these things to see how it worked. Since us down there in the park is part of you, or you're part of us, or whatever it is . . ."

"We're all part of each other, right, Bob?" said Greenberg to Father Bob Davidson, the chairperson of the Assembly.

"Well, I don't know, Marc, maybe we ought to wait 'til those people from Union Theological Seminary get in here and they can tell us who's part of the larger what." More laughter. "Anyway, Larry, you're more than welcome. Please, sit. Coffee?"

"No, thanks, I'm all coffeed out today," said Larry with a smile.

"I hear that," said Davidson, grinning and giving a mock quiver of his hand.

After a little more banter, the meeting resumed with dry housekeeping matters of assembly business. Larry observed it all, occasionally dozing off. Finally there was a call for new business. A couple of people introduced things of minor consequence, and then Larry rose to speak.

"Folks, it's gettin' cold out there."

There were a couple of nervous laughs, and then silence.

"So what it is, we're startin' to think about the winter. Like to be inside somewhere by then. Be nice if we got inside even sooner than that."

No one knew quite what to say. The Vigil, as it was called in this circle, had been going on for so long that no one had given much thought to what would happen when it ended.

"I mean some of us," Larry went on, "feel like we could get a building or something and work on it. Not all of us got that kind of skill. But we been thinkin' all along that we'd get *something* before it got cold."

Now the silence was uncomfortable. This last remark of Larry's was to some degree accusatory. Some of the clergy heard it as "We've been out there all this time and none of you bastards have lifted a finger to try to put a roof over our heads."

Once the sting of that had been absorbed, the members processed Larry Locke's request in a variety of complex, individual ways. Generally, religions require people to die before they become saints. But if a practice were made of handing out sainthood to the living, a good case could be made for many of the people in that room. They were exemplary clergymen and clergywomen, and they went a lot further than that. They used the pulpit as a perch from which to do God's work on earth. They walked among the poor, fed them, housed them, and mopped their brows when they were ill . . . frequently at the sacrifice of their own health and in the final tally their time—the years of their lives, the nights of eschewing dinner parties for visits to dying old women in Spanish Harlem.

All of them heard Larry Locke's complaint about the cold. Half of them felt it in their own bodies, sympathetically. Most of them, however, had pragmatic sides. Otherwise, they would never have lasted as long as they had at the head of such large and powerful congregations.

Donations to the Interfaith Assembly were at an all time high, thanks largely to Kochville. Half the checks that arrived were actually earmarked for Kochville, and the other half were implicitly congratulating Interfaith for spawning the group. If Kochville disappeared, so would much of this support.

But money was not the real issue. These men and women certainly did not wish to line their own pockets, and their home congregations could probably be coerced into making up any shortfall. Interfaith would never go broke.

However there was a hierarchy among homeless groups, and for a while Interfaith had been at the bottom of it. The Partnership for the Homeless and the Coalition for the Homeless were far more well known and far more successful in attracting corporate and government funding. But neither one of them had created anything nearly as dramatic as Kochville. Nor would the great Bernie Glassman be applying for membership if Interfaith were not now the rising star that it was.

Prestige alone would never have motivated any of the men or women sitting at the table. But prestige brings other things: besides money, it brings power. If that power enables one to do good, good on a large scale, how significant is the suffering of thirty people? This was the real question for the Union Theological Seminary, or King Solomon, or God himself.

The long silence was finally broken by Lloyd Casson, the head of Trinity Church and coincidentally the only black man at the table besides Larry Locke. For months now, Casson had forced himself to stay at arm's length from the group on the theory that they didn't need patronizing advisors, black or white. Now that might have to change.

"We'll talk about it, Larry." said Canon Casson. "I promise you."

≡

"After the horror of *Kristallnacht*," the tall bald man in the yarmulke was saying, "a thousand Jews piled into a boat called the *St. Louis* and sailed from Germany in the middle of the night. When they got to Florida, they were turned away by the American Coast Guard."

The audience of young Conservative Jews, some with babies on their laps, gasped. They knew the story vaguely, but it had never been delivered by such a master orator.

"Those Jews," the speaker went on, "were the same Jews that walked away from the destruction of the Second Temple thousands of years ago, and they are the same Jews that sit here tonight. They are you and I. The event of last Thursday reminds us of who we are and where we came from. Let those who seek to destroy us today—those who did this horrible thing on Thursday night and those who stand on the pulpits of churches and refer to Judaism as a gutter religion and New York as Hymietown—let all of these people know that our memories are very, very long."

The audience stood and cheered, not just for the sentiments but because the mayor of New York cared enough to be there. The event of last Thursday night to which Ed Koch had referred was the vandalism of the Hillel Temple in Queens and the desecration of its Torah. In the morning the janitor had arrived to discover the sacred scrolls mutilated and defaced. The event had thrown the entire community into rage, fear, and ultimately a deep depression. But now the mayor had come, and like a good uncle, he had made it better.

As he shook hands and left, Ed Koch had never felt more fully alive, or more fully himself. A knowledge of Jewish history brought with it a certain pride and resiliency. But there were even deeper dividends. The fatalistic concept of *beshert*, with which he had become familiar after his stroke, was usually employed by the mayor as a sedative. *Beshert* meant RELAX!! Take a day off!! The world won't end!! Today, it would be put to a far sterner test.

A threat had been made on the mayor's life. There was nothing extraordinary in that. Every day some malcontent threatened to blow the mayor's brains out, and sometimes people arrived at City Hall with zip guns or Molotov cocktails. The city hall police handled these matters discreetly and sometimes brutally, often without the mayor's knowledge.

Today's threat, however, was of a different order. Recently a cop had been killed by a drug pusher, and the mayor, furious and ever protective of his cops, had declared war on the Medellin cocaine cartel of Colombia. He had budgeted a hundred million dollars for new antidrug units and backed it up with fierce Kochian rhetoric about foreign slime infecting the youth of America. The Colombians, ever anxious to reciprocate, had issued a death list with the mayor on it. "A list is just a stupid piece of paper," said the mayor, and so it was until the first two people on it were brutally murdered. Ed Koch was number three. Even so, the mayor had pooh-poohed the danger . . . until last night. Around midnight the police had pulled over a van on Amsterdam Avenue for want of an inspection sticker. It was found to contain several known Colombian assassins and several hundred thousand dollars worth of expensive electronic equipment and explosives. Upon arrest, the assassins had only smiled enigmatically and said: "There are more where we came from."

Today the mayor was scheduled to ride through Brooklyn in a funeral cortege for another cop killed in a drug bust, and Security was going nuts. For the cunning Medellin people, this would be like duck hunting. The mayor was going to be exposed for a couple of hours, moving slowly through a maze of hundreds of thousands of houses with low roofs.

"*Beshert*," said the mayor. The driver heard this as "Bullshit!" and off they went. The mayor was exhilarated and indignant. He never missed the funeral of a cop, and he especially wasn't going to miss this one. As he rode through Flatbush between two extremely paranoid plainclothes policemen, Ed Koch smiled benignly. He could never explain *beshert* to a couple of Irish cops, but at least he could loosen them up with a few dirty jokes. This he did, and what might have been a dreadful two hours turned into something sweet and fraternal.

Afterwards, as he rode home (this time at full speed, along the Brooklyn-Queens Expressway), his driver turned and complimented the mayor on the ice water in his veins. Ed Koch smiled humbly. Since the driver was a Jew, the mayor felt finally at liberty to share the lesson of *beshert*, and this he did. The driver was grateful for the ancient wisdom.

The car rolled through the gates of Gracie Mansion, and the mayor emerged to a particularly cold dusk. November was coming on. But as the days shortened, every day was more fully packed. He had begun with a workout in the gym before dawn. He had been to a synagogue in Queens and an Irish funeral in Brooklyn. In between he had fielded death threats and subpoenas. Would he ever tire of this? Could he ever give it up? Was this a way to grow old? Would wisdom accrue from such a life or just a sort of manic exhaustion?

Unfortunately, he did not have a moment of leisure to contemplate the question. He was obliged to jump into his tuxedo and be out the door to an affair at the Urban Center celebrating the upcoming renewal of Forty-Second Street. For most of recent memory, the fabled thoroughfare had been a freak show of junkies, whores, and losers. The corroding old theatre where Ziegfeld himself had spun his magic in front of a chronically depressed America, even this had become a twenty-four-hour porno house. Now plans were being hatched to renovate and restore it to its former glory. Ed Koch was responsible for that.

After the Urban Center event, it would be off to the Al Smith dinner, a quadrennial affair at which the two presidential candidates were hosted by the cardinal of New York.

The only antidote to an evening of George Bush and Michael Dukakis was late night at a place called The Ballroom, the mayor's favorite cabaret. There, in the shadows of Chelsea, he would have a couple of after-dinner drinks and listen to willowy, blowsy Karen Akers sing love songs. Mostly she favored the more acerbic tunes—the bittersweet work of Rodgers and Hart, and Kurt Weill. An evening like this would leave a couple of yokels like Bush and Dukakis flabbergasted, to say nothing of their dreary wives.

≡

Nothing. After a week of "doing their best," several dozen of the most powerful clergy in New York—bishops, priests, rabbis, shamans, and swamis—had come up with nothing. In the entire city, apparently, not one niche, corner, dormitory, church basement, gymnasium, or attic could be found in which to put thirty people.

"Bullshit," said Larry Locke to Ellen McCarthy. For once, she did not argue. They were sitting at her kitchen table on a Sunday morning, the East River glinting below. The fact that it was Sunday pissed Larry off even more. The sanctimonious bastards were no doubt standing in their pulpits at this very moment.

It always happened this way. You trusted white people, you started to believe what they were telling you, and then at the last moment, they said "Only kidding, nigger," and pulled the rug right out.

When he first got to New York, he had taken a job driving a Fink Bakery truck for a month. Almost a month, that is, because after the twenty-ninth day he was told his services were no longer needed. Why? Because, he later found out, after a month you can join the union and then they have to pay you real money. Solution? Hire another nigger for twenty-nine days. So you got mad, you vented to someone like Ellen McCarthy, she calmed you down, you swallowed your anger and tried again. You got some other job or trusted white folks in some other way, and then on the twenty-ninth day, they fucked you again.

He was running in circles. Now word had arrived that Jesse Jackson was coming back to town, this time to lead a huge housing march through Manhattan. Once again, Larry Locke had been asked to speak first. Another enormous honor, right? No. Jesse Jackson was no different than any of the rest of them. Just another bullshitter in a clerical collar.

Ordinarily Ellen McCarthy would have put balm on his cuts and then pushed him back into the ring. But enough was enough. Larry Locke was her man, and he was in a bad way.

"Let's talk about something else," she said.

"Like what?"

"Tell me about Locke's Creek."

The past was not something he liked to talk about. He didn't see the point. She kept prodding him, and after a glass of wine, without expression, he told her about the old house on the Cape Fear River, with the cherry trees along the dirt road. He told her about his father, the reclusive farmer who did his work, kept his mouth shut, and indulged himself by whittling amusing little wooden figurines. Larry showed her one, a half moon with a big nose. On it was inscribed the legend "Keep your nose out of my business." Larry always kept it in his pocket.

The last time he had seen his father, he told her, was the day of the County High School Football Championship. By that time Larry was already in the custody of his mother, who would shortly be hauling him and his brother and sister to Newark. He didn't see his father much in those last years, but old Charles Locke was proud of the way Larry played football. Maybe that was because Larry had had to overcome so much to do it. As a child, he had been so frail and bandy-legged it was hard to imagine that the beefy all-state linebacker was the same human being.

Larry could remember very little of that game, except for his father's face and the very last play. Larry's team was the Blue Devils, named after nearby Duke University, which none of them would ever attend, except as janitors. Their opponents were called the Redbones. On the last play of the game, the Redbone quarterback threw a game winning touchdown pass to a white kid named Jimmy Garrity in the end zone. Larry blamed himself, although everyone assured him that no linebacker in creation could have covered that deep a pattern. Nevertheless, he felt he'd let his father down. He did not see Charles Locke afterward. The old man was simply swallowed up by the crowd.

"That's the last time you saw him?" she said.

He drank a glass of wine in silence. Clearly, this was the part he didn't like talking about.

The last time, he told her finally, was a few years ago, after he got out of the army. He'd been working a night shift in a chemical plant in New Jersey, and there had been an accident and he'd hurt his leg. Several lawyers advised him that he could count on a hefty workman's compensation payment. While he awaited the hearing, he decided to go back down to Fayetteville to recuperate and possibly to reconnect with his father.

It was a wonderful, healing time. Father and son worked in the fields together, as much as Larry's injury would allow. They fished in Locke's Creek, as they had long ago. One day by the water, his father asked him a question. Why, now that Larry could make decisions for himself, did he not move back south? Here was family land, a natural wealth, a fiefdom almost, with all the dignity that implied. What was in New Jersey?

Just a very large legal payment to which he was entitled, said Larry. When that deal was done, he would very seriously consider Fayetteville. Perhaps there could be a partnership. Perhaps father and son could farm or paint houses together, or at the very least renovate several of the old houses that Charles Locke owned.

When the call finally came that the workman's comp hearing was imminent, Larry borrowed a few hundred dollars from his father for plane fare up to New Jersey. He was feeling like a big shot.

At this point, Larry stopped and asked Ellen if there was any more wine in the house. Since they had already been through a bottle, Ellen sensed that another painful part of the story was coming up. They got the bottle and climbed up to the roof, cold now in the late November dusk. Larry opened the wine and drank half of it, staring at the Manhattan skyline, before he began to describe the trip back to New Jersey.

"I get there, and they tell me my lawyer's on vacation, and some other guy gonna handle the hearing. Vacation! My man was workin' on it for a year! Why the hell didn't they change the hearin' or something?"

Ellen continued to drink silently.

"So we have the hearing, it lasts about twenty minutes, and the judge say, 'Give the man five hundred dollars.' Five hundred dollars!! I was thinking about twenty-five thousand, at least!! That's what the damn lawyers told me! I turn around to complain to my guy, but he's already out the door, to some other hearing! Five hundred dollars! That didn't cover the damn plane fare!"

He said nothing for a long time. When he spoke again, it was in shorter, unexpressive sentences. He could not go back to North Carolina without the money, he said. He couldn't bear the look in his father's eyes when he told him things hadn't panned out. He was always having to tell his father that.

Ellen winced. How many times on the job had she heard this story, or a variation, from some terminal alcoholic? She knew what was coming next.

New York seemed like the place to parlay small money into big money, so Larry arrived with the five hundred dollars and got a hotel room. It was a place in Harlem called the Carlton Arms, nothing fancy, but together with meals, fifty bucks a night. The first couple of nights, he figured what the hell, I'm in New York, and so he celebrated with a few cocktails and a bowl or two of crack, a custom he'd picked up in Newark from his unemployed friends. His cash began to run low, and somebody told him that there were city shelters that were free. He moved into one of them with the intention of getting a job and building up a little nest egg.

But getting a job with only the Harlem II Shelter as an address was next to impossible. After the legendary twenty-nine-day bakery truck job, he somehow managed to finagle a house painting gig, as an apprentice. But the money was pathetic. To get a place of his own, he needed to put down a security deposit as well as rent. Somehow, Harlem II never allowed money to accumulate. A twenty-dollar bill might be taken out of your pocket as you were shaving. Maybe you had to spread some cash around every once in a while to make sure that nobody bothered you, sexually or otherwise, while you slept.

You sat down and figured out that you'd have enough for an apartment after working sixty-hour weeks for a year, every night returning to the Harlem II Men's Shelter—taking a shit in a stall with no door, weirdos ogling you, eating cardboard oatmeal every morning, having to say "Yes, sir" to guards who were psychotic bullies, having to buy crack from them just to stay unraped. The weight of that reality caused you to smoke or drink something to take the edge off, which took a bit more out of the savings, and that meant a slightly longer stay at Harlem II.

"Why didn't you just get the hell out of there?" Ellen blurted out finally, "and go back to North Carolina?" As soon as she asked it, she knew the answer. The reason was asshole male pride. He couldn't go back to Charles Locke without the money.

She tried to understand that but finally couldn't. New York was the hardest place on earth. You didn't need extra handicaps. The man in front of her, whom she loved, was fading from the human race. She could feel him slipping away. "Why don't you go home now," she said, "for Christmas?"

Twelve

Eve Miranda, more than most of her comrades at Banana Kelly, understood that if the corpse of the South Bronx was to be revived, it would take money. The *venceremos* spirit had brought them only so far. The appearances by celebrities ranging from Paul Newman, who made a movie here, to the Bolshoi Ballet, who danced on the rubble, had commanded the nation's attention. Catholics, Buddhists, and Hare Krishnas had blessed the wasteland with incantations of every kind. Finally, however, bricks and mortar were not free.

While others learned bookkeeping and door framing and solar panelling, Eve had learned about the moral pressure points of people in high places. She stalked along picket lines outside banks and insurance companies. Why were they not giving loans or writing policies anymore? she demanded to know. Because, they replied, the Bronx was a nightmare of fire and decay and hairless dogs. But Miranda sought to call in moral debt; for decades these outfits had made fortunes on the Bronx. The insurance companies had cashed in on every generation of immigrants since the Jews bought burial insurance a hundred years earlier.

All of it was a tough sell, none more so than 850 Longwood Avenue. It was a huge, corroding den of debauchery and murder, and it would cost a fortune to put back together and insure. But Miranda persevered. Until it was reclaimed, she insisted, all other gains were temporal and flimsy. Nor could she forget her vow to

Irma Ortiz, who, as December 1988 approached, faced another winter without heat or water.

The holding company to whom Nathan Margulies unloaded the building had in turn passed it along to another phantom owner, and this process had repeated itself until 850 Longwood wound up in the hands of Arthur Management, which held a mortgage through the Bank of Tokyo. Whatever plans Arthur Management had did not materialize, and the Japanese bank now owned the property. The cost of buying it from them would be minimal: they would be gladly rid of it. The cost of renovating it and insuring it, however, would be in the millions.

And even more daunting than the numbers was the step that had to be taken first, before a penny could be raised—the expulsion of the junkies from the building.

A tough young black man named Carlton Collier was sent in as Banana Kelly's point man. Emerging ashen faced in a very short period of time, he confirmed the presence of Guiterrez and the murderous Dominican drug operation. The task of getting rid of them, he informed Eve Miranda, ought to fall to somebody who spoke the language . . . namely her.

With the whole neighborhood agape at her *cojones*, she entered the building one morning when she knew Guiterrez had already sent out his lieutenants to collect the rent from pushers on various street corners. She wanted to face him alone, although she knew that might be dangerous. She also knew that not all the remaining tenants were on her side. Some of them, their self-esteem at low ebb after years of domination, actually viewed Guiterrez as a sort of benevolent constable—keeping a dark order in the building, even occasionally bestowing a couple of vials of crack on somebody for mopping a hallway.

Eve heard music from somewhere. She peered up the forbidding stairway and began to climb, following the sound to the third floor. There was Guiterrez, sipping a cup of coffee and listening to quiet jazz as he did some accounting. This was no macho slob. Instinctively, she rejected her first strategy, which was to bat her eyelashes. Instead, she entered crying.

"What is the problem?" said Guiterrez.

She had known his sister in school, she said. She loved his mother and the whole family.

Why did that make her cry? he asked her.

Because of the rivers of tears they themselves would soon be crying, she said.

Why would his sister and mother be crying? Guiterrez wanted to know.

Because of the awful things, said Eve Miranda, that lay ahead for Guiterrez and his men.

His gaze left the sheet of numbers on his lap and he looked at her.

"What awful things?"

The *federales* were coming, she said.

He put down his pencil, and the color in his face began to change.

The government was renovating the building, she explained, and if anything got in the way, there would be a show of force—police cars, investigations, and perhaps even federal troops.

Federal troops!!? Guiterrez began to stammer, and finally to plead with her, as if she herself were the president of the United States. He was just a small businessman, he said, trying to turn a small profit in the face of terrible conditions, duplicitous employees, and customers begging him for credit. The economy was dreadful. Now the *government* wanted to hassle him too? Couldn't Eve Miranda, as an English-speaking person, intervene?

Possibly, she said. She excused herself to make a few important phone calls. Instead, she went across the street for a cup of *café con leche*. She returned in an hour and told Guiterrez she might have good news. She didn't think it was too late. Possibly if he got out soon, bloodshed could be avoided. Perhaps he could find another, distant neighborhood and relocate discreetly. (She felt a little guilty suggesting this, but after all, she was trying to save Longwood, not the world.)

The next day, an astonishing sight greeted the eyes of passersby. Looking like a bunch of Rotarians leaving a convention, a dozen of the most ruthless men in New York walked out of 850 Longwood Avenue with suitcases. What those suitcases contained, mothers did not want their children to see. But by noon all of it—and all of them—were gone.

Irma Ortiz celebrated by having a cigarette on the front stoop, something she had not done for fifteen years. Eve Miranda stood across the street and watched her. Through all her housing wars, this moment was among her sweetests.

This first, seemingly impossible impediment out of the way, everything else fell into place. The city as well as several community groups stepped forward with loans. Within two months Eve Miranda would have the financing to buy the building, and far more remarkably, to begin renovating it. For the first time since 1909, workmen would walk into 850 Longwood Avenue with the idea of doing something other than subdividing it or stealing the plumbing. The old people in the neighborhood spoke of it all as a *milagro*—a miracle.

———

Duke York did not begrudge Larry Locke his visits to Ellen McCarthy; if he had a sweet situation like that, he admitted to himself, he would have been all over it. But after Larry had been gone for another three days, his resentment grew. How many vacations was Larry going to take? Every day, the camp became more desolate. Horace and Rasta were gone, and Duke actually missed them. At least they were engaged, intellectually active humans. The stolid veterans who sat and froze in the park now, grunting monosyllabically, were not many steps above animals.

Finally came the moment that killed the dream for Duke York. Duke had always known that one day they would be gone without a trace, so he created a Journey Book—a large black notebook into which he put the press clippings, photographs, poems, and historical documents of Kochville. Pasted onto a page of its own was the Kochville constitution, written on the back of a grease-sodden pizza box. Little Art, as head of security, had always been the guardian of the book. One frosty morning, Duke awoke to find Art and the Journey Book gone.

Duke had seen it coming. Art was a military man, and while the structure of Kochville was defined and his duties were clear, he was happy. The cold hadn't gotten to Art, the chaos had. The Puerto Ricans had driven him nuts. Lonnie, with his slovenly white-trash lifestyle, had also gotten to him. But the final blow, thought Duke, was the rejection by Samantha. Art had fallen for her hard, but she wasn't interested. The night she got sick and the police car took her to the hospital, Art offered to go with her. She said no, she preferred Duke. From that moment on, Art had closed Duke off. The Journey Book had no conceivable value, except to wound the heart of Duke York.

It was the final disappointment and it was personal, as the worst ones always were. Now Duke was the only one of the ruling committee left, and as he gazed around, he saw nothing worth ruling over. In the end, Kochville was like all of life. Bright, hopeful things died a bleak, inexorable death. Always.

For a few days he lay on his bench, starting to get ill again. Across the street, the obsolete subway station beckoned, a siren of darkness and warmth. He knew if he went down, he might never come up. Finally he forced himself to start walking. Only by staying in motion, he felt, could he get through it this time.

On December 10, Jesse Jackson marched at the head of the Housing Now parade, the largest single housing demonstration ever staged in New York. Ten thousand strong, it began at Columbus

Circle, went down Central Park South, turned right on Fifth Avenue, and turned west again on Fifty-Seventh Street. By design, it passed some of the most valuable real estate on earth. The best seats for the parade were the Oak Room of the Plaza Hotel, for cocktails, or the Trump Tower, for the panoramic view. The parade ended on Fifty-Eighth Street, where a podium had been erected for Jackson to speak. But his opening act, Larry Locke, was not there.

Standing in the crowd and searching the platform was Canon Lloyd Casson. He was disappointed not to see Larry up there, but not surprised. When Larry burst into the Interfaith meeting a couple of weeks earlier, Casson had read the look in his eyes perfectly. Casson had been through exactly the same thing, off and on, for most of his life: black people calling you the house nigger, and white people, while grateful for a "civilized" black man, never really accepting you either.

There was much honest concern among the white clergy after Larry left, but all of it was tempered by what Casson saw as the racism that was like the earth's crust—it lay underneath everything. When all was said and done, even these, the most righteous white people in town, didn't feel that black folks needed shelter *quite* as much as white folks. Somehow they were built to take more punishment. Not that they didn't have a *right* to equal comfort. They did, and these truly pious people would have laid down their lives to defend that right. But was it really, just between us, necessary?

Lloyd Casson figured that if he himself didn't find a place for these freezing Negroes, it would be a long time coming. Fortunately, he'd made a lot of friends by spreading Trinity Church's cash around the smaller parishes and had a lot of favors to call in. One day a note arrived from Father Harvey, who ran a tiny church called St. Augustine's in a tough neighborhood not far from Henry Street. Harvey was moved by the story of Kochville and was offering the basement of his church for the winter.

At last. "It's a long hard row to hoe," went the line from one of Casson's favorite old spirituals, "and my back gwine be sore at the end."

He had arrived at the Jackson housing march to give Larry the good news himself. But not seeing him on the podium, or anywhere else, Lloyd Casson began to worry. The next morning, he set off for City Hall Park to find him.

The holiday season began festively for Ed Koch with Chanukah, the Festival of Light. As December deepened into the Christian holidays, however, the mayor's mood began to sour. Even his annual birthday fund-raising bash, on the twelfth of December, depressed him. Financially, it was wildly successful, filling the hall at one thousand dollars a plate. But something was missing. The mayor found himself thinking of a birthday twenty years earlier, when as a young congressman he and Bess Myerson and several other rising Jewish political stars had sat in an Italian place in the village all night long, drinking and behaving ridiculously. Now, the following Monday, he would have to testify at Ms. Myerson's felony trial.

The downfall of Bess Myerson was a tragedy not only for her friends but for all New Yorkers. Like Ed Koch, she was born in the Bronx to hardworking Jews of modest means. But Bess Myerson broke through into Wasp-dominated America far earlier and far more spectacularly. In 1944, she was crowned the first Jewish Miss America, leaving her corn-fed competitors in the dust. She had been to Music and Art High School in New York, and she had real chops as a musician. For the talent competition she played a Grieg piano concerto and topped it off with a Gershwin piece on the flute. The other contestants were tap-dancing or reciting poetry badly.

Add to this young Bess's remarkable body and world-class cheekbones, and not even a panel of anti–Semitic judges could stop her. It was a huge event for Jewish women in America. Overnight their image had changed from Lower East Side haus-frau haggling with the fruit vendor to ... Bess Myerson!!

Through the postwar years, New York had no more luminous celebrity. She was everywhere: magazine covers, TV panel shows, seminars on womanhood. Then, during the Lindsay Administration, she moved into politics, first as cultural affairs commissioner, and finally as consumer affairs commissioner. There seemed to be no limit to what she could do or be.

Enter David Garth. In 1977 the chubby, legendary media wizard had a problem. He was handling a mayoral candidate who was the original schlemiel. Ed Koch dressed like an undertaker from Queens and had about as much sex appeal. Wiseacre columnists wrote that his idea of a sexual thrill was shaking hands with voters at a subway stop. A woman who had been Koch's first (and only documented) girlfriend in high school gave a particularly demeaning interview about their prom night. "We were riding in the back seat of a car and he suddenly grabbed my breasts. It was horrible!!"

Sexual awkwardness Garth could have lived with. Far worse were the darker rumors swirling around confirmed bachelor Ed Koch—that he was a homosexual.

Again and again, the candidate suffered the indignity of having to account for his solitude.

Some people are not cut out for marriage, he would explain patiently. It was a comfort, but when one had a higher calling, one did not seek comfort as a goal. He had other ways of satisfying his need for companionship. He pointed with pride to his well-known dinner parties, where a half dozen of the people he was closest to sat for hours on end, trading deeply felt remarks on life, politics, and art—all with wit and candor and deep, abiding friendship.

But the sniping never stopped. It had gotten to the point where he couldn't sit over a cocktail and listen to the mercurial Bobby Short play the piano at the Hotel Carlyle without drawing a wisecrack. Not that there was anything wrong with homosexuality, he maintained. Or, he was quick to add, that there was anything right about it either.

Whether or not his candidate liked to sleep with women, men, or animals was irrelevant to David Garth. All that counted was the public perception. That was the moment the masterful idea was born. Koch and Bess Myerson had been friends since the Lindsay days. Why not manufacture a romance?

Garth had outdone himself—what the wrestling world calls a complete reversal. In one deft move, Ed Koch had gone from somebody with no girl to somebody with *the* girl, a goddess that most of the shmucks who criticized him couldn't get near in their wildest dreams.

On the stump she was magnificent: elegant when called for, gutsy when she needed to be. Once, at a campaign stop in Brooklyn, a bunch of tough Italian kids peppered Koch's speech with cries of "faggot!!" Upon leaving the site, Myerson leaned out of the car window and screamed "Fuck you, you assholes!!" and left her third finger trailing in the air. All of this worked to perfection. Koch was elected, and after a vigorous first term was returned to office with the biggest plurality in New York City mayoral history. But for Bess, things began to go backwards.

There were problems beneath the surface. Miserably unsuccessful in love, she had fallen for a younger man, a Long Island construction king who was married to somebody else. It had been a sordid, compulsive affair, and now Bess stood accused of influencing the man's divorce case by giving a job to the judge's daughter, an odd, overweight girl with no qualifications. Ever since the allegations had surfaced Bess's slide downhill had been rapid. In the interim, she had even been arrested for shoplifting a pair of panty hose. Shoplifting!! The Jewish Miss America!!

The mayor's response to all this was similar to his response to Donald Manes, Stanley Friedman, and the other figures in the corruption case of 1986. Quietly, discreetly, undramatically, he distanced himself from them. From close friends, they became, by stages, strangers. So it had to be with Bess.

Would it be painful, reporters wanted to know, to betray an old friend? First of all, said the mayor, you are not betraying anyone by testifying in a court of law. You are only betraying our remarkable system by *not* testifying. Secondly, yes, of course, it was distressing to see an old friend in such a bad way. After all, one was only human.

That was the official version. In truth, once again the Rational Switch was turned on and feelings were turned off. It was a matter of survival. Politics was full of treacheries, betrayals, disappointments, and double crosses. If you let each one get to you, you became a basket case and you lost your capacity to rule.

But it was a grim prelude to the holidays. Christmas was the toughest time for older men with no families, be they Christian, Jewish, or neither. Maudlin commercials with candles in frosted windows suddenly seemed something to aspire to. At least, thought the mayor, the time was all planned out, without too many holes to fill.

Christmas Day he would spend with friends, as always. The night before, on Christmas Eve, he would attend midnight mass at St. Patrick's Cathedral as a guest of Cardinal O'Connor. This would help considerably to restore the Irish vote, still in shards after the disastrous trip in July. To solidify his position on the homeless issue, the mayor had also scheduled a pre-mass visit to the John Heuss House, a controversial new drop-in center in lower Manhattan. What made it controversial was the neighborhood—Wall Street. The titans of the American economy, trading huge volumes of stock every day, would literally have to step over the homeless on their way to work.

But taking a shot at the high rollers would be a cagey thing to do at this point in time, the mayor felt. For one thing, they were on the way out. The stock market crash in October of '87 had caught a lot of them with huge, unrealistic holdings, and many of them had gotten creamed. So since the mayor's coffers were already full, and since these shmucks didn't have anything to give him anyway, it was time to jettison them and make some political capital in the process.

"If the 'Masters of the Universe' find it disturbing to step over the poor on their way to work," said the mayor, "then tough noogies!!" This he would repeat, as the cameras were rolling, roughly at about the time he was carving up a Christmas goose at the John Heuss House. Was it a goose? *Whatever* it was that the goyim ate.

Lastly, the situation in City Hall Park seemed finally to be in hand. The Russian strategy was jelling. Only a few of the men were left, and the really intense cold had not even begun. The mayor felt it was a matter of weeks, maybe even days, before there was nothing left out there but the squirrels.

The holidays were taken care of, then, except for New Year's Eve. But there would be all kinds of invitations, all sorts of fabulous things to choose from, so that too would be taken care of . . . until the stroke of midnight. Then, when people turned to kiss their mates or their dates, the mayor would have to go through some pathetic subterfuge. He would have to suddenly pretend to have to tie his shoelace or step out on the balcony. One time he had spent the critical five minutes in the bathroom, listening to the merrymaking. It wasn't so much that he himself cared *what* he was doing at the stroke of midnight. He had had his experience of the New Year months earlier on Yom Kippur, and it was far more profound than some Wasp ritual of blowing a noisemaker or stealing a kiss. He just didn't want anyone staring at him as the clock chimed twelve, and thinking "How sad—he's alone."

<hr />

When Lloyd Casson arrived at City Hall Park looking for Larry Locke, there was little evidence that the camp had ever existed. Gone were the placards and the leaflets and the banners with the housing slogans. Silent were the benches where heated debates had taken place. A row of sullen men sat along a bench in layers of army fatigues. A couple of them Casson recognized, most of them he did not. But the look in their eyes was familiar to him. He had seen it before, in prisons. It said "There is nothing more you can do to me."

Had it been immoral, Casson now wondered, to fill people like this with the preposterous hope that they could change anything? Was there some value in hope for its own sake?

He sat with his ethical questions for a while and then tried to get some information. This was hard to do, for the stolid, frost-bitten men reacted badly to the talcummed preacher in his fine woolen raiments. Finally one man begrudged the information that Larry had left, and no one knew where he went, and no one cared. Casson digested this and then asked about the other man he remembered from the camp, a wild looking man with one eye named Earl, or something like it.

"Duke," said a man finally. "He'll be around."

So Lloyd Casson decided to wait for him. He went back to the parish hall and got a few sweaters and an old jacket, picked up a cup of coffee to go, and came back to the bench. There he sat with the other men, waiting for the return of Duke York. After a while passersby could hardly distinguish one frightening, freezing black man from another.

The next afternoon, Duke York arrived back in the camp looking like a different human being. The walk had worked. Across the Queensborough Bridge, across Pulaski Creek, through Polish Greenpoint and Hasidic Williamsburg, through the wintry dead Botanical Gardens, and finally back across the Brooklyn Bridge, Duke York had walked and walked and walked, and expelled his demons. The lesson from Marc Greenberg had been well taken. Physical exuberance had restored him, as had the frenetic diversity of New York. His pendulum had swung the other way, towards a manic optimism. He no longer felt that Kochville was necessarily doomed. Thermal sleeping bags would be found. Fires could be built and maintained. Spring would come, at some point.

He found several people sitting along the bench, just as he'd left them. He was shocked, however, to find Canon Lloyd Casson. Duke's first thought was that the reverend had fallen on hard times, since he was swathed in about a half-dozen ragged sweaters.

The truth was that the canon had fallen not on hard times but on hard questions, as he always managed to do. After just a day and a half of sitting out here and absorbing the abuse of white office workers, Lloyd Casson had abandoned any notion that the world was changing. It was the eternal, vexing mystery. Thirty-four years had passed since *Brown v. the Board of Education*. Since that time, men had walked on the moon and computers had been invented the size of cigarette lighters, and yet the central problem of harmony between the races had only gotten worse. At the moment, Lloyd Casson's children were in private school. They were doing famously, and not just because a liberal ethos prevailed. They were brilliant kids with all the talent on earth. When they got out into the real world, however, they would be just a pair of niggers. Lloyd Canon winced, thinking of the day they would realize that. He wished he could take some of the pain of that discovery into his own body. Perhaps he already had.

"Reverend . . . ?" Duke approached cautiously. Did he have the wrong guy?

"Yes, Duke, I've been waiting for you." They said their hellos, and Casson suggested they go across the street for coffee in the Greek place. Duke could see that the canon was extremely anxious to get his ass out of the cold. When they sat down, Casson told him about the church near Henry Street. The men could move into it anytime they wanted to.

Casson expected some sort of mild hallelujah, but Duke said nothing.

The canon was surprised, and a little peeved. He'd busted his butt to find this church basement, modest as it was. Was he going to get a "Thank you," at least? At the moment, it was 20 degrees out.

Duke York was not ungrateful, just torn. Going indoors would probably save some lives, but it would also mean the dream of Kochville was dead. Officially. Death certificate stamped. This dream had endured a lot, and dreams were precious things. To Duke York, they were really the only things. Flushed with the triumph of his walk, Duke was now convinced that it didn't have to die. Possibly, he thought, if he didn't even tell the old soldiers about this offer, they would stay out there forever . . . if for no other reason than to say "Fuck you" not just to Ed Koch, but to all white people and to civilization in general. It was tempting to let them do just that.

But Kochville's decisions were not made by individuals inside warm coffee shops. They never had been.

Later that day, the benches were pulled in a circle. Duke York stood in the middle and spoke, sending vaporous clouds into the icy air. He told them that the basement of a church called St. Augustine's had been offered to them for the winter, and it was up to them to accept the offer or reject it.

Around the circle were nine faces, most of them protected by scarves and ski masks. Eyes peeked out. These were the toughest men on earth. There was no need to prove this to anyone. White men might have been stupid enough to prolong this display of bravado, eyes told other eyes, but not us. The road is long and hard, with farther still to go. It was a legacy as old as the indigo fields of Georgia. When rest is offered, it is taken.

≡

At first, the Seventh Regiment Armory was like being delivered into God's arms. The fastidious Samantha Jones was at last in a place where laundry was done, and things happened on regular schedules.

There was even a little gaiety from time to time. One night Samantha wandered up the stairs from the shelter to the top floor of the armory, to the cocktail lounge for former officers. In a clean dress and a playful mood, Samantha took advantage of her light skin and masqueraded as the wife of a colonel currently overseas.

To make the time pass for the attractive older woman, the young officers bought her cocktails, many of them. The whole thing brought out her theatrical instincts, and she turned into the boozy grand dame, admiring medals, downing martinis, growing sentimental about life in the regiment. It was a bit of a scandal when she was finally discovered and sent back downstairs. A few days later, she was officially expelled from the shelter. No tears were shed by the staff, even though it was Christmas Eve.

On the way out, she made a point of letting everyone know how much she hated the place. It wasn't that it was uncomfortable, she said. It was too comfortable. She told her fellow shelterees that they had simply given up. They were submitting to the place, she said, the same way they had once submitted to their abusive husbands.

Only when she was standing out on the street did she begin to think about her options. She remembered hearing that a new shelter had been built in her old neighborhood. Upon arriving downtown, however, she discovered that John Heuss House was not a shelter but a "drop-in center," a place where one could only temporarily escape the brutality of the streets. For permanent relief, you were supposed to go to places like the one Samantha had just left. Sleeping was not allowed in the John Heuss House, yet that was precisely what Samantha needed and aimed to do. She spread herself over three chairs and conked out. Several moments later, the mayor of New York walked in with a photographer and several aides carrying Christmas gifts.

A nervous official raced over and jostled her awake. Samantha sat up, grumbling. Eventually, though, she was seduced along with everyone else by the smells emanating from the steam table. Behind it were a few volunteers, including the mayor, wearing huge, ridiculous chefs' hats and doling out Christmas Eve dinner.

The mayor was in charge of the sweet potatoes, and Samantha thanked him for the generous portion and moved down the line. She then sat in a corner and consumed her holiday meal alone. From a practical point of view, she probably should have been thinking about where she was going next. She found herself instead thinking about Ed Koch. Tall, awkward, stooped over, he seemed almost to be apologizing for his height. He was a hugely successful man, but behind his eyes there was fear, as if it all might come down around him at any moment. Samantha knew the look, because she knew the feeling. In her case it was justified. Usually, everything *did* come crashing down around her. But it was a terrible feeling to live with. Silently she wished a peaceful Christmas to the big man dishing out the sweet potatoes. When she was done, she gathered up her things and went out into the night.

≡

Larry Locke was dropped off by a tractor-trailer in the middle of town shortly after dark.

Fayetteville, North Carolina, was no different from any other midsize American city. The old town square was a decaying hulk, an echo. The real life of the community took place in the big mall outside the city—the home of a Sears, a Home Depot, a Day's Inn, a Wendy's, a Shoney's, a sixplex movie theatre, and many other such enterprises.

The only reason anyone ever visited the town square was to have a gander at the building that dominated it, the Market House. Floodlit in amber, its gothic arches vaulting into the black sky, the old building was grand but divisive—infamous to the blacks, magnificent to the whites.

In the last century, slaves had been sold at the Market House. It had never been a brutal auction house, like the horrors in Mississippi and Georgia where families were broken up on the block. Market House was a more discreet place, where large estates were divided and disposed of. Sometimes, the property happened to be human. It was actually the white Ladies' Auxiliary of Fayetteville who had had the idea of promoting re-enactments of the drama of the "slave sellers" of Market House. The ladies were in friendly competition with the Charleston women's clubs, who had documented slave houses of their own.

Just why Fayetteville had ever wanted to win this friendly competition had always pissed Larry off—or at least it should have, he thought now as he stared at the mammoth, lit up structure. Tonight, for a Christmas Eve garnish, it was edged with red bunting. Larry felt like tearing it off. New York had made him more political in his thinking.

His eye roamed the empty town square, and there, almost invisible in darkness, was the car he was looking for, a 1960 Nash Rambler. It was just like his father, thought Larry, to just sort of be there, apologetically, in the shadows. In this respect, too, New York had made him less tolerant. He no longer understood the value of reticence or modesty. It irritated him.

As Larry trudged over to the car, Charles Locke watched his every step, trying to get a read on his boy. Ever since the phone call had come, he'd been thinking about him. He'd actually spent half his life trying to understand Larry and didn't have a clue yet. When the two men were seated together in the vehicle, Larry leaned over and hugged his father. This was another New York habit, the casual intimate gesture. It was not reciprocated. Instead, the old man stiffened.

They drove in silence out of town and over the bridge that crossed the Cape Fear River. Larry had always thought it a strange name for such a dull body of water. He had been taught in school that it was once hotly contested as a nautical passage to the seaside city of Wilmington, the site of a federal arsenal that had been captured by the rebels, recaptured by Sherman, and burned to the ground.

Since that time, nothing of a historical nature or any nature at all had happened here, with the possible exception of Fort Bragg. The construction of the huge army base outside of town had been a boon to the town's economy but had done nothing much for it culturally, or any other way. Larry had always hated the place, white soldiers lounging outside it, smoking cigarettes and grinning in vaguely evil ways at the black folks who passed by.

By the time they made the turn up to Locke's Creek some twenty minutes later, Charles Locke had still not uttered more than a couple of syllables to his son. They pulled up to the house, Charles turned the ignition key off, and the sound of water was deafening. To their left, the Cape Fear River rushed around a hairpin bank to the sea. To their right, separated from them by only a willow grove, was cackling Locke's Creek. Over their heads, the moonless sky contained about fifty billion stars. Charles Locke went quickly inside, since the night had a chill, but Larry stayed out a while to watch and listen. New York never gave you this.

When he finally went in, Charles Locke was waiting for him in the kitchen, which had not changed in the five years since Larry had left, or in the forty years before that. The walls were clapboard tongue and groove, painted a cracking beige enamel. An International Harvester calendar hung on the wall and a single light bulb dangled over the kitchen table, which was the same old oak masterpiece, carved by Charles Locke out of the ruins of a great river oak split by lightning.

Larry sat opposite his father and planted his feet on the floorboards under which he had hidden as a child in order to escape the constant tensions of the household.

After a while, it became clear his father had nothing to say. It was Larry's time to speak. He had left five years ago to do something for which Charles had given him plane fare, and now he was back. The question on the table was "How did it go?" That was how time worked down here. All the events in between—all of the fast life and the static and the madness of New York—none of that blurred the big picture for Charles Locke or answered his question.

Larry reached into his pocket and took out some photographs, and passed them across the table to his father. The old man pulled his pince-nez out of his vest pocket and examined the pictures. They showed his son in the pulpit of a church, shaking hands with Jesse Jackson.

Charles said nothing but turned the photos over and over in his hand, and so Larry filled the silence with a cascade of information about the speech, St. John the Divine, and fighting for the rights of the homeless. Still Charles said nothing, and Larry felt a small excitement. Was his father so full of pride that he couldn't speak?

"I once told you," said Charles Locke, "that trouble begets trouble."

Larry did not comprehend him.

"Your sister Reba," he went on to say. "That was a bad time."

Larry understood him now. Reba, as a teenager, had gone to a demonstration over in Fayetteville protesting the separate bathrooms for whites and coloreds in the town movie theatre. The event had turned ugly, and tear gas had been used. When Reba got back to Locke's Creek, her aunt washed her clothes for three days to get the odor out, as if the smell of the gas were also a stench of dishonor. Larry had felt just the opposite.

So what Charles Locke was saying to his son was "You think this is a photograph of you with a great man; to me it means you still haven't learned to keep your nose out of trouble."

A few days before speaking at St. John the Divine, Larry had sent invitations to his mother and his sister and brother in Newark. None of them had shown up. That didn't hurt nearly as much as this. He rose from the kitchen table and went outside into the night.

≡

Late on Christmas Eve, a final ceremony was organized in City Hall Park. A small Christmas tree was decorated with aluminum cans, the currency of the homeless economy. Uptown it was rumored that a former homeless man had rented a huge movie theatre and used it for nothing but the collection of cans, which he sold to someplace by the ton. He had a yacht and a home in the Bahamas now, the story went.

The City Hall aluminum can Christmas tree was lit with candles in the shadow of the huge Norway spruce that the mayor had lit several days earlier by throwing a switch. It was a clever juxtaposition, the final public relations coup by the talented amateurs. The handful of remaining Kochvilleans celebrated along with the half-dozen liberal supporters who braved the cold. Marc Greenberg was there, and together with Duke and Lloyd Casson, he organized a potluck supper and everyone ate, and the fellowship was warm and good.

Soon the supporters left, many of them to assemble the toys that their children would soon be awake and agape over. Once they were all gone, Duke and the remaining nine men of Kochville took a last look around. They secured the small tin can tree with cables so that it would stay in place at least as long as the mayor's. Then each of them picked up his duffel bag or black plastic bag. Nothing remained on the concrete or the frozen lawn to indicate they had ever been there.

Duke got that feeling often since he had become homeless. Everywhere in New York were dumb inanimate things, like fire hydrants or curbstones, that would long outlast the humans. Where were the faces of June? Mickey, big Annie, Lonnie, the ironworker from Wyoming, the bareback riding woman from Austria? Where were Matthew and little Art, Horace, and Rasta? Where was Princess? Where was her child? Had it ever been born? Who knew? Who cared?

The men got themselves into a loose formation, out of instinct. Before they could move out, they were surprised by the arrival of Samantha, fresh from her Christmas Eve dinner at the John Heuss House. She told Duke the story of her departure from the woman's shelter in the armory, and as the men waited silently, breathing the cold air, Duke told her where they were going and invited her to come.

"No, thank you," she said. The four walls of a church, just the image of them, suffocated her. She kissed Duke lightly and moved off into the night. He would have followed her, but he was in charge now of a small platoon. He looked behind him and they were ready. There was a certain excitement in their eyes at the idea of a warm bed, but a certain deadness also. This was the moment of retreat, and the old soldiers knew it.

Duke waved an arm, and they moved out.

≡

On Christmas Day a rare snow fell on Fayetteville. Inside the house on Locke's Creek, the large family gathering talked about when it had happened last. No one could remember a Christmas snow since before Aunt Min died, and that had been twenty years ago.

Outside, along the river, Larry Locke looked across to the other bank, where the elder trees were all finely limned with white. Around him was a grove of cherry trees. In the cold and the moisture, they breathed a cherry smell that Larry remembered from childhood. It was as sweet as the pie that sat on the table inside the house.

Larry wanted no part of that pie or of the women who baked it or the people who were about to stuff it into their mouths. He was feeling the warmth of home out here on the cold ground, beside the freezing river. He did not feel himself to be the child of the man and woman who were now strangers to each other. Rather he was a child of the earth itself, and he had no roof but the big cold sky.

Thirteen

Samantha Jones kept moving north, though she didn't know why. After saying good-bye to Duke on Christmas night, she went from Chambers Street to Chinatown, where she spent a few nights in an alley warmed by the exhaust from Hop Kee's Restaurant. From there she moved north to Thirty-Fourth Street, where she stayed a while in the vast, empty, out-of-business Altman's department store. When she was caught and thrown out of there, she moved to her present location on Fifty-Eighth Street, a vest-pocket park beside the East River. Sometimes people were like birds, she thought, and moved by instinct. But what kind of a stupid bird goes *north* in the winter?

She opened her bag and poked through it, being careful not to shred the satin lining. She loved this bag. It was some kind of carryall from the twenties, hard tortoiseshell plastic handle, big woven pouch, a pattern of grape arbors on a mountainside. Utterly impractical for a homeless woman, she knew, but critical for her state of mind. She found the gloves she was looking for and put them on.

The river was beautiful but cold. She would sit and watch it for a while, before the night came on.

The doctors had warned her that after her hysterectomy there might be fits of depression. Just the opposite was proving to be true. She felt rid of some weight, as if it wasn't her womb that had been reamed out, but her brain. She saw clearly now, without sadness, and beauty moved her more than ever. The sky was a hard, cold, deep blue. The lights on the Queensborough Bridge were on, and the East River caught them, in specks and sparkles. It would be lovely sleeping here, if it weren't so cold. She decided to try it anyway.

She climbed the stone stairway to the street level and stood at the cul-de-sac. The gods were with her. One of the townhouses along the river had thrown out a section of carpet, and right next to it was a huge discarded cardboard box from a TV set or some other appliance. A sporting goods store could not have provided better equipment. She hauled both items back down to her bench by the river, put the carpeting inside the cardboard, and climbed in. There was no wind, and her eyes closed quickly and she drifted off. Sometime later, perhaps an hour, she was awakened by voices. Some teenagers had arrived, drinking and carrying on. Samantha could make out their words, and to her relief, they did not seem to be thugs. From their inflection, given the neighborhood, she guessed they might be private school kids. Drunk, they were probably spoiled and nasty, but not violent. For this reason she decided to remain in her box and wait it out.

They stayed forever. One of them had been to Europe or was going to Europe, and talked endlessly and dully about it. Samantha marvelled at how someone so young could speak so casually of so great an adventure. Then they began to speculate about who was in the box. One of them thought it might be Jimmy Hoffa. Another joked it was the father of one of their friends, who always seemed to be losing his shirt in the stock market. One of the girls said she thought it was very sad and asked how anyone ever wound up sleeping in a cardboard box. No one could answer her.

Then the mischievous nature of one of the boys got the better of him. "I wonder if anyone's alive in there," he said. He flicked the outside of the box with his finger, then scurried away. Samantha wondered what to do, whether to give a sign of life, which might lead to a confrontation, or just to lie there and hope it would stop.

It didn't. The young people emboldened each other, and everyone took a turn at flicking or thumping the box. The reverb inside went from irritating to loud to frightening. It began to feel like blows to the body. Finally Samantha shouted "Stop it!"

Immediately, they did. She could hear them mumbling and whispering, then shuffling away. As they left, she could hear one of the girls say "God, it's a woman. That's really pathetic."

Samantha tried to fall back to sleep, but now she had to pee. It was freezing, and she hated to leave the box. She closed her eyes again, but her bladder was insistent, and her doctors had told her to obey this particular instinct. She squirmed out of the box and climbed into a large planter that contained a sort of dense oriental bush. She was obliged to invade it in a way that destroyed a few branches. She squatted and peed, trying hard not to wet her long johns, which were balled up around her ankles. A tugboat went by along the river. Samantha imagined it might be on its way to meet an ocean liner. She imagined a steamer trunk full of silk peignoirs. She imagined herself on deck, leaning over a rail, smoking a cigarette in a smart tweed suit, like the white movie stars of the thirties. She probably chose the tweed suit, she thought, because it was so GODDAMN COLD!! She very quickly snapped out of her reverie, wiped herself with a piece of clean newspaper kept in her shirt pocket for just this purpose, and pulled up her pants.

When she returned to the box, it was too cold to sleep. Once you've woken up on a cold night, you can pretty much forget it. She had to start moving.

She climbed back up to street level and walked out of her enchanted little cul-de-sac to Sutton Place. She turned right and walked several blocks, but soon her feet began to act up. In the hospital a doctor had told her she might have phlebitis, although that wasn't what they were treating her for and he didn't wish to get too deeply into it. Whatever it was, it made walking hard. She decided to do something she knew she shouldn't. She stuck out her hand to hail a cab.

Not many black homeless women could get away with this, but light-skinned Samantha dressed and accessorized herself with enough flair to stop a taxi. Fortunately, the driver didn't get to smell her first.

But it was the most dangerous kind of game, because she didn't have the money to pay the fare. This often led to disaster. Once a cab driver had beaten her up. Another time a driver had made her ride with him all night in the front seat and played with her sexually at his whim, even as unknowing passengers were in the back. Scrupulous drivers usually just turned her over to the police. That was almost the best case scenario. Rarely was she simply forgiven and allowed to skip away.

Despite all of this, the warm interior of a cab was too good to resist. It wouldn't be a Checker, with leather jump seats like in the old films, because they were extinct. But it would be warm. She continued to hold out her hand, and finally a cab pulled over. The driver was a thin, dark man with intense eyes, a Pakistani or Indian. She got in, leaned up to the plastic shield that protected her from Mohammad Babar, license 34667, and said, until she could think of something more specific, "North."

≡

On a January morning in 1989, Mayor Ed Koch rose in the City Council chambers to deliver the "State of the City" address. The real purpose, everyone knew, was twofold. Besides summing up the past year, the mayor would imply the future: the unprecedented fourth term for which he was about to run.

The expectation, therefore, was for a speech full of bluster. With the arrogance that was his alone, the mayor would exalt his achievements, lacerate his enemies, and begin to ferociously carve out his place in history.

Great politicians surprise, and surprise again. The mayor

began by asking everyone to stand. He introduced a frail black woman who was the recipient of every welfare program the city had to offer. He then asked her to lead everyone present in singing "Lift Every Voice and Sing," considered by many to be the black national anthem.

With even the cynical City Hall press corps dabbing at their tears, the mayor launched into a speech remarkable for its gentleness. In an era of power lunches and megadeals and fierce rhetoric and terrifying weaponry, he suggested, we have all but forgotten the lessons of people like Mahatma Gandhi, to whom the city had just dedicated a statue. The nineties loomed ahead with the opportunity for redemption. Meekness and humility would get us that redemption, not bombast. Whatever the new questions, love was the answer. "If we err," said the mayor, "let us err on the side of mankind."

For several minutes after the speech, the audience remained in its seats, stunned. Redemption? Mankind? Love was the answer?? Was he having another stroke? Had he lost his notes? Was he taking a bathroom break and coming back to finish the speech with a Kochian flourish?!

Apparently not. The mayor was done, and it was up to the Koch watchers to figure out what it all meant. Over the next few days, scrutiny of the mayor was intense. He flew to Puerto Rico for the inauguration of the new governor, but allotted only an hour to the pompous state ceremony. The rest of the day was spent in secluded talks with the widow of Roberto Clemente, the baseball great killed on a mission of mercy in South America. The mayor lolled about a small rural village, playing with her grandchildren. Was this truly a reborn, compassionate Ed Koch?

The mayor's enemies didn't believe it for a second. The more humble the communiques from Gracie Mansion, the more they sniped and snorted. Love? Humility!? GIVE US A BREAK!! To the Koch haters, this new tack was the most cynical and despicable in a long and despicable career. Koch was keenly aware of where the serious challenge would come from in the Democratic Primary—David Dinkins. Despite Dinkins' liabilities (and there were many; to begin with, he had "forgotten" to pay income taxes for several years), the man was formidable. He was no black lightweight the mayor could bury with a few naked appeals to the white ethnics. Dinkins had an impeccable war record as a sergeant in the Marine Corps. Nor could the mayor count on a sweep of the middle-class Jews in Brooklyn and Queens, his true power base. Dinkins had recently had the nerve to stand outside Madison Square Garden and denounce Louis Farrakhan, as Jesse Jackson had declined to do.

And last, but not least, Dinkins was a player. He understood the game. He was cut out of the mold of great Harlem politicians that included Charlie Rangel and the late Adam Clayton Powell, and they had all learned from the best—Raymond Jones, a.k.a. the Harlem Fox, the consummate artist of the back ward. Whatever lessons could be learned from the byzantine world of Negro politics in the twentieth century, Jones had learned them and absorbed them and passed them on to his protegés. Dinkins was one of the most astute, and now, from his perch as Manhattan Borough President, he was ready to take his shot.

He offered himself to New York as a healer. In a place where racial tensions ran high, an abrasive mayor didn't help. Let me bring us all together, Dinkins asked, and create a "gorgeous mosaic."

So the pundits and professionals began to realize what Ed Koch was up to. He was dealing with Dinkins' candidacy the way great politicians do—before it even began. If the issue was compassion, the mayor would become so compassionate that Dinkins would have nothing to complain about and would himself begin to sound like a shrill voice in the wilderness. To this end, the mayor spent much of early January shuttling from church to day-care center to drug rehab ward. Finally, the Koch haters braced themselves for what would undoubtedly be the most cloying hypocrisy of all; the mayor's speech on Martin Luther King Day.

The mayor didn't disappoint them. Drawing heavily on his own experience as a young civil rights lawyer in the South, the mayor praised the great sister churches, King's Ebenezer Baptist in Georgia and the Abyssinian Baptist in Harlem—from whose pulpit the mayor was regularly denounced. And then, as the final outrage, the mayor quoted King to the assembled crowd in the City Council chambers and gallery. The black politicians squirmed and fumed. ". . . I still have a dream," the mayor intoned, "a dream deeply rooted in the American Dream . . . that one day this nation will rise up and live out the true meaning of its creed . . ."

The Koch haters gagged; the mayor was actually imitating the King cadence, injecting soul and sorrow into words like *rise* and *creed*. It was like Barry Manilow doing a cover version of "Stand by Me," or some other black-as-the-night standard. Nor was the mayor apologetic. He finished with a benign twinkling smile, as if to say "Wasn't that convincing?"

And yet it could not be denied, infuriating as the man was, that he *had* put his ass on the line in Laurel, Mississippi, just weeks after the murders of the civil rights workers Schwerner, Chaney, and Goodman. He was fearless then, and he was outrageous now. He sent mixed signals, which is what made opposition to him always so futile and disorganized.

But in a corner of the gallery sat a small cadre of young black men in charge of the Dinkins campaign. At their center was Bill Lynch, who was a little boy during the civil rights era and who barely remembered it or Ed Koch's great sacrifices during it. Unencumbered by sentimentality or mixed messages, Lynch had only one goal: to turn the bastard out of office.

≡

Larry Locke moved north slowly through places like Duck, Kitty Hawk, and Nags Head. Mostly these were resort towns boarded up for the winter. Standing against the bleak Atlantic, they pretty much fit his frame of mind.

He wasn't sure where he was going. He knew only where he was leaving. The idea of family was a myth; he'd had it right the first time, as a child cowering under the floorboards of the house. All that existed was the Seven-Eleven in front of him and the dollar bill in his hand, with which he planned to purchase a jelly donut and a black coffee, his evening meal. He knew his dollar could buy him better nutrition, maybe an apple and a bag of nuts, but he didn't care.

As he sipped the coffee and watched the gray Atlantic turn grayer and finally black, he thought about New York and tried to think of a reason to go back. Being a vagrant in Nags Head was certainly easier. This was a rich town and many crumbs fell from the table, so to speak. On the other hand, this was the South and he was basically a wandering nigger. A rural northern environment would be better, but of course colder. California? Overcrowded. Every bum on earth was on the L. A. welfare line. Then there were places like Austin, a liberal college town, easy pickings. Measured against all this was the brutality of being homeless in New York. Since he'd washed his hands of all the bullshitters in the poverty industry, the only reason to go back there was Ellen.

He closed his eyes and called up an image of her. It brought mixed feelings. She was white, and in his mind she was lumped together with Interfaith, and twenty-nine-day jobs driving bread trucks, and all the rest of it. And yet he could remember her touch. He heard her voice in his head. But he also heard the voice of Horace; "Man, you are one dumb nigger. You gonna go a thousand miles for a white piece of ass?"

But he decided to do just that, because he couldn't really think of anyone else in the world who cared whether he lived or died.

≡

Samantha Jones was right to fear that the price of her cab ride might be high. Her directions were hazy, the first irritant to

Mohammad Babar. When they finally got to the godforsaken corner of the Bronx, well out of his route home and miles from where he would ever get a return fare, his patience was very thin indeed.

Suddenly she yelped "That's it, stop!" and the cab jerked to a halt. They were in front of a deserted movie theatre with a blank marquee. Babar asked her for the fare, which was thirteen dollars. She didn't have any part of it. That was the final straw. He had been duped into a joy ride.

Ordinarily, he liked to think of himself as a gentleman. Certainly he was the proud inheritor of a gentle culture. An argument could be made that Pakistanis were among the most refined creatures on earth. But at this stage of his life, Babar was trying to adapt to the American culture, which as he perceived it, was very intolerant of deadbeats who wanted to ride taxis for free. When a deadbeat also happened to be a homeless, middle-aged, black woman, it seemed to Babar that no more lowly esteemed creature existed in the New World. So if a man needed an outlet for the pressures that weighed on him (and there were dozens—mortgage payments, pediatrician's bills, car payments . . .) could he really be blamed for choosing such a likely target as Samantha Jones?

Still, he would live for many weeks in mortification of what he did that night, although there were colleagues in his garage who wouldn't have thought twice about it.

He forced her out of the cab and into the shadows beside the old RKO Franklin movie theatre. There he pulled down his pants, forced her head to his groin, and demanded that she give him pleasure. After that pleasure exploded out of him, he left her beside the theatre and drove away, his dark cheeks drenched with tears of shame.

After about an hour, Samantha struggled to her feet. Sexual assault, to which she was no stranger, was almost beside the point. She was numb to it. More than anything, she was tired. She felt like a sailor who had spent a day against a hard wind.

The irony of it all, she thought as she moved down the empty street, was that she wasn't even sure if she was remotely near her destination. Her directions to the driver had all been instinctual, picking shapes out of the darkness. Then she saw the building.

There were no lights on. It had been many, many months since her visit here with Matthew and Larry and little Art, but the bulk and sweep of the place were unmistakable. There were the fire escapes that looked more like stone balconies, and, barely discernable, the little oval window that perched at the top. It gave her courage as she approached the dark hulk of 850 Longwood Avenue.

The lobby was as desolate as she remembered. In the darkness she tripped over slabs of cracked marble, some of them floating in puddles of urine. The cables of the dead elevator were still wound around it like sleeping snakes. She began to climb the stairs slowly. Marble was crumbling underneath her, so she took off her shoes and gripped the powdery debris with her toes. It was critical that she not create a minor avalanche, or, for that matter, any noise at all. If there was anyone in these hallways, it was a good bet they were no gentlemen. She moved up the stairs with the stealth of a Lakota Indian, some of whose blood, she was once told, ran through her.

Finally she reached the top floor and moved away from the staircase and the scant light it provided. Through complete darkness, she made her way to a part of the top floor where a different light appeared, the light of the moon through a ruined section of the roof. Here, silver lit, was the mecca that had drawn her north and north again through the city—the bathtub with the cat's paws legs. Inside it was a dense pile of plaster and rock. She climbed on top, adjusted the rubble to the contour of her body, and was soon asleep.

Duke York was flabbergasted. The check looked real. It had two signatures, and it was large, far larger in size than a personal check. The numbers were generous, and they were typed clearly, not written out.

There was only one thing that wasn't clear.

"So basically, me and Larry are supposed to be . . . like . . ."

"Coordinators," said Marc Greenberg.

Duke looked confused.

"That could mean many things, at different times," Greenberg added.

"That's what I'm asking you," said Duke. "What am I supposed to be doing, say, right now?"

"That's up to you," said Greenberg. "This is a creative grant. You guys are supposed to be mature enough to see what needs to be done and do it. You've been around, you've met the people, you know the scene."

Duke kept trying to absorb it all. Sitting in front of him on Greenberg's desk was a check for him and a check for Larry Locke. Even though Kochville no longer existed per se, even though its members were now safely behind the walls of a small church on the Lower East Side, even though Larry Locke was nowhere to be found, the money was rolling in.

"Basically," Greenberg was saying, "Lloyd Casson got us this grant from Trinity Church. It's an acknowledgment that Kochville was a great experiment, and that it's ongoing. There are going to be lots of workshops for the guys in the church. Counselling sessions. Things like that. You and Larry will coordinate that, and you'll keep going to meetings with city council members. You'll be Homeless Spokesmen."

Duke continued to nod and absorb the warm glow emanating from the large number on the check. It was very warm and bright indeed.

"When do we start?"

"Anytime you like," said Greenberg. "Ellen McCarthy just

called me. Larry's on his way back to town. The two of you can start together."

Duke and Ellen met Larry's bus at three o'clock in the morning. Duke stood mutely aside as the two lovers greeted each other, and then they all repaired to a Dunkin Donuts across from Port Authority. Duke informed Larry first of all of the end of the camp in City Hall Park. It came as no surprise, but it stung. The dream, mottled, twisted, and battered as it had finally become, was over. It was probably just as well out of its misery. Still, they all sat in silence a while, like parents over the grave of a child.

Finally Larry asked about the people. Duke told him that many of them were in a church basement. Larry was surprised; the great white church fathers had come through after all. Then Duke told him the deal had actually been made by Lloyd Casson, and Larry smiled ruefully. He had been right the first time.

Then Duke gave him the last piece of news: they both had jobs, at a salary of $25,000 a year. Larry took a moment to regain himself. "What kind of jobs?" he asked. Then, for the last couple of hours before dawn, Duke and Ellen attempted to explain it to him.

Larry and Ellen went back to her place, she called in sick to work, and they spent much of the day remembering each other's bodies. By evening, they were still in bed. In the dark, he asked her to make the world clear to him. He had left New York in absolute disgrace, having let Greenberg down several times, the most public being his disappearance from the big housing march with Jesse Jackson. For this he was being paid?

"Kochville is part of history now," she told him.

He sat in the dark, absorbing this and drinking a glass of wine.

Kochville, she went on, was considered to have been the single most important grass roots homeless movement in the United States. And Larry, as its leader, was still considered homelessness' leading spokesman, even in his absence.

He didn't trust any of it. The deepest, truest instincts in his body told him to run the other way. He didn't even really expect the check to clear.

But the enormity of things will sweep a man up, especially when he doesn't have another gig. On January 19, a call came from public television. The next day George Bush was to deliver his inaugural address, and Channel 13 was rounding up a few prominent New Yorkers to comment on it. Would Larry be one of them? The following afternoon, he found himself in an extremely deep leather armchair around a wooden table not unlike the one in the kitchen at Locke's Creek. After David Dinkins and columnist Jimmy Breslin gave their opinions of Bush's speech, Larry was asked for his.

"I thought it was inadequate," he said, which was exactly what everyone thought he would say. He then added some of the things he had intended to say from the pulpit of St. John the Divine but never did. It didn't play quite as well as it might have to the live audience for which it had been written. This, after all, was television.

Later on that evening, he and Ellen went to a reception, a sort of anti-inaugural, at a liberal women's club. The event was black tie. Recalling his discomfort at the Dinkins fund-raiser months earlier, Larry vowed not to be underdressed. Ellen found him a tuxedo rental place, and Larry walked out of there like Noel Coward, even down to the pearl shirt studs.

When they arrived at the event, heads turned. Ellen was as magnificent as Larry, turned out in a velvet dress the color of turquoise, amber beads hanging from her pale Irish earlobes. They were seated at a table with three other couples, and Larry fell into immediate and easy conversation with the man next to him. The man seemed genuine for a white man, and Larry felt comfortable enough to ask him "What do you do?"

The man said he was in the insurance business. Then he asked Larry the same question. Larry was not prepared. Rather than give the real answer, which was "I'm a professional homeless person," he excused himself and went to the men's room.

Several miles away, in the basement of St. Augustine's church on the Lower East Side, the dozen or so men of Kochville's last stand sat around watching their TV. It was one of the comforts to which they had become newly accustomed. The room, like the other rooms in the church basement, were institutional cinder block painted lime green. The men seemed happy and clean, and many of them lounged in pressed pajamas and imitation leather slippers. Certainly they had never been healthier; St. Augustine's was providing balanced meals. Yet there was a glazed, medicated look to people. Thick with cigarette smoke, the place had the feel of a day room on the ward of a state hospital. The very air seemed somehow narcoticized. This was partially because some of the people were actually sneaking booze or hits of drugs.

There was more to it than that, thought Duke, who breezed through now and then from the rented room he occupied courtesy of his new salary. The thrill of battle was gone, at least the sexy battle against City Hall. Now they were all back in the old familiar battle against themselves; there was no glory here, only mud and barbed wire.

Larry's taped television appearance was broadcast late in the evening. The few men who remembered him were resentful of his self-importance. The rest didn't care. In the middle of it, someone changed the channel to a basketball game.

"Coffee," said a voice belonging to a woman named Connie, who lived in the neighborhood and volunteered one night a week at the church. Her last official duty of the evening was to put out coffee and cookies for the former Kochvilleans. Connie thought coffee to be a curious choice for a bedtime snack, but it was such a staple of the homeless diet that no one ever questioned it.

It was important to announce bedtime and to have some regularity to the moment of lights-out, because wake up time was immutably fixed. By day the basement of St. Augustine's was used for other things, for nursery school classes and Alcoholics Anonymous meetings and community groups, so the homeless had to be out by seven. No exceptions. The cots were folded up and put away, and for twelve hours Kochville-at-St. Augustine's ceased to exist.

Slowly the men shuffled to their assigned rooms, four beds to a room. At precisely eleven o'clock, Connie killed the lights. On this particular night, an older man named Marvin, one of the last arrivals to the camp at City Hall, was getting out of his trousers when lights-out came. He became tangled up in them, and owing to the darkness and a severe arthritic condition in his hands and fingers, could not extricate himself. So he simply tumbled into bed as he was.

He had trouble sleeping, however, because the air was stifling. He decided to open one of the windows. With his lower body bound up in his twisted trousers, he was obliged to crawl out of bed, dragging his ankles after him like a seal. When he got to the window, he found that it did not open. Rather than crawl back to bed, he decided to sleep on the floor, which he preferred to his sagging cot anyway.

━━

"How did this happen?" said the doctor to Larry Locke.

"Running," came the reply.

The doctor applied a gelatinous substance to Larry's ankle and ran a metal instrument over it for a while.

"I ultrasounded it," he said when he was done, "and now I'm going to wrap it. Try to stay off it. What kind of work do you do?"

Larry looked over to Ellen McCarthy.

"I mostly sit in meetings all day," he said.

"Good," said the doctor.

What Larry didn't tell him was that he twisted his ankle running from one meeting to another.

Larry was having trouble with scheduling. Ellen McCarthy was learning what different worlds they came from and with what different skills. "You can't leave a meeting at three o'clock on East Eighty-Third Street and go to a meeting near City Hall that begins at three o'clock," she told him on Monday. He tried to do it anyway, and wound up so frustrated and pissed off that he petulantly skipped all his meetings on Tuesday. He felt so guilty about that that he scheduled another impossible cluster of meetings for Wednesday and twisted his ankle racing from one to another.

Why he was trying to please everyone, he could not say. Nothing that he was finding out about white bureaucrats made him trust them more than he ever had. They spoke in a sort of shorthand; without a college education, you missed half of it. So the meetings were drudgery. He felt as if he and Duke were being paid just to sit there. A few months ago, they had swaggered into these offices like heroes, and people had hung on their every word.

One Saturday afternoon toward the end of February, the two of them were at a meeting of the Interfaith Assembly itself, and the subject turned to reports of drinking inside the basement of St. Augustine's. "I think the men are probably feeling disoriented, now that they're cooped up all of a sudden, and need to vent," said Sister Agnes. That's putting it mildly, thought Duke. The winter home of Kochville smelled like a distillery. Every five minutes someone was ducking out for a pint. Sometimes they didn't duck out at all but climbed up into the chapel itself and sat on the altar and got plastered.

Clearly, thought both Duke and Larry, the only way to deal with it was directly. "Anybody who has liquor on their breath don't get let in until they get it off their breath, even if it means they got to walk around in the cold for twenty-four hours," suggested Larry.

"Right," said Duke. "And anybody that gets caught with booze in the church, their ass is thrown out for good."

"Right," said Larry. This was good Kochville logic to both men.

"I don't know," said the Reverend Bob Davidson. "These men have been abused for so long, I'm not sure that harshness is the best way to go."

More of the usual bullshit, thought Larry. He looked across the table at Lloyd Casson, who nodded to him. They had discussed this. It was the kind of racism that rankled them both more than police dogs and fire hoses. Black people were handled gingerly, as if they weren't human, but some sort of species, fragile yet crude, that no one knew exactly how to deal with. No, thought Larry, he and Duke would go over there tomorrow and take care of it directly, in a way that would be understood and obeyed.

Riding the D-train back to Ellen's, where he was now living, Larry was in a state of mild agitation. There were things he'd rather do than face the men of Kochville. Most of them didn't even know who the hell he was. Among those who did, his memory was reviled. But why? This question always vexed him. He was the one who got them the damn space to begin with by storming into the Interfaith meeting and demanding it. Otherwise they'd still be freezing their butts off in 10-degree weather.

He reached over for a discarded newspaper and fiddled through the sports pages trying to get interested in the college basketball news, but unfortunately it was all about St. John's, a woebegone local team that didn't hold a candle to Duke or any of the real teams back in North Carolina.

As he put the paper back down, his eye caught an item in a box on the bottom of the front page. The headline said "Housing Activist Found Dead," and below it was a picture of a man who looked vaguely familiar. Possibly he was one of the blurred parade of white faces at the endless meetings.

The story itself was horrifying. The victim, whose name was Bruce Bailey, had apparently been a pain-in-the-ass to just about every landlord on the Upper West Side. He was forever organizing rent strikes, marches, sit-ins, etc. Then, yesterday, after his family reported him missing for a couple of days, he had been discovered in a clump of weeds in the Bronx WITHOUT HIS HEAD! Some retribution had clearly been visited upon him, but nothing could be proven at this point.

Larry put the paper down and tried not to think about it. For a while he stared at the advertising space over the seat opposite him. It was a new subway feature called *Poetry in Motion*. The poem was about blackbirds flying over a field in England. But Larry could not get his mind off Bruce Bailey. Then the train passed underneath the East River, a moment that gave him a kind of claustrophobic anxiety even in the best of times.

When the train finally got to Ellen's stop, he bolted out and raced up the steps. He reached the sidewalk sweating profusely, despite the cold night air. After a moment, though, the tree-lined street worked its usual magic. He turned the corner past the old brick nursing home and saw Ellen's nineteenth-century brownstone, and he knew that everything was going to be all right. He would close that thick door behind him and lose himself in her arms. Until morning, nothing could touch him. He was starting to feel himself again, even to the point of stopping at the corner store and picking up some flowers. Now that he had a salary, he could afford expansive gestures.

He climbed the steps to the top floor of the old building, once no doubt a rich man's townhouse. As he reached for the knob of her door, he noticed that his hand was quivering almost out of control.

Ellen McCarthy watched the doorknob jiggle and lit a cigarette. She knew it was Larry. But he had keys, he could figure it out. Lately she'd been doing a little too much rushing around to help him. She sank deeper into her stuffed woven armchair, once the property of her Irish mother, and took another long slow drag on the Marlboro. Guilty pleasure.

Maybe that's all Larry was. Often her friends gave her a look that said "What's it like to have a young black man in your bed?" Someone even asked her point blank once, and she refused to answer. The relationship was built on higher things: principles, common cause, poverty, homelessness, blah blah blah. But really, when it came down to it, romance was about flesh and heart. It was wonderful to have a young lover. But it was also a drag to have to mother somebody whose neurosis deepened by the hour.

It wasn't Larry's fault. He was being asked to do the impossible—to go to meeting after meeting and greet the world as a clean, punctual homeless person. That was a profound contradiction in terms. He was not a man who should be sitting in meetings or filling out forms at all. He was an exuberant physical person who should be building, jumping, sailing—anything but sitting. And he was a man with almost no tolerance for bullshit. Unfortunately, his profession was now to absorb it, often without a peep, and sometimes to sling it himself.

None of this was his fault, but it wasn't her fault either. She had her own needs. Every night Larry was a mess when he got home. Every night it took her an hour or two just to relax him enough to get ready for bed. She had to get up for work at six every morning. He of course could loll about until ten, or whenever his first "meeting" was. The whole routine was taking its toll on her fifty-five-year-old body. It was almost enough to make her think about her discarded husband, a dull hulk of a man who at least never fell apart on her.

At last the door opened and Larry let himself in. "Thought I lost my keys there for a second," he said. She looked at him. He was like a lost child.

"Got you somethin', though." He held out a fistful of daisies.

She smiled. This was his routine, to buy some flowers at a Korean place, throw away the cellophane and the paper, and just hand them to her with the stems dripping, as if he'd just ripped them out of the earth somewhere. You had to love it. He was a natural man.

She held open her arms to him, and he sailed into his safe harbor. He held her a while and smelled her modest Macy's perfume. Soon they completed a seamless journey into bed, and after making love, fell quickly asleep. Shortly after midnight, though, he awoke with nightmares. He was dreaming that his father was trying to cut off his head.

≡

Duke had to wait on the subway platform for a long time. Probably, he thought, Larry was late because he didn't relish the mission. As soon as they got to St. Augustine's, the usual accusations of betrayal and hypocrisy would rain down on them. For Larry, so long absent, the men would reserve a special venom.

Finally Larry arrived, frazzled and unshaven, mumbling apologies. They walked swiftly out of the train station and down Henry Street. When they got to St. Augustine's, Larry stopped at the window and looked through it. He could not go inside yet, he told Duke. He needed to walk around the block a couple of times.

It might not be as bad as he expected, said Duke. Larry replied that he was not afraid of being abused, he was afraid of crying. Already he could see the men through the window, shuffling mutely about. The great experiment of Kochville had somehow been neutered and reduced to this. It was heartbreaking. Duke assured him his sentimentality would quickly vanish. They were here in the capacity of wardens, or, to be even more cynical, zookeepers.

Nevertheless, Larry let Duke go inside alone and took a walk by himself through Seward Park, once a hotbed of Jewish intellectuals, now a sideshow of junkies and young Spanish punks. After a turn around the old wooded square he walked back up Madison Street to St. Augustine's. He arrived just as Big Joe was on his way in, smelling like a huge swab of cotton dipped in alcohol. Larry barely knew Joe, since they had overlapped only a day or two in City Hall Park, but he decided to confront him directly.

"That shit's got to go, man," said Larry.

"What shit you mean?" said Joe. "That shit walkin' around inside your suit?"

Larry felt his bile rising but was determined to subdue it. "Nothing personal, man, I'm just sayin' you're gonna get everybody thrown out of here if you keep doin' that."

"What you worried about us black folks for?"

They stood staring at each other for a few moments.

Alerted to the potential problem, Duke stepped outside. "What we're sayin'," said Duke to Joe, "is that we got a sweet thing goin' here . . ."

"*You're* the one got the sweet thing goin'," said Joe. "All that money come in to Interfaith for us, how much of it you think we see?"

Obviously, Horace and Rasta had left their legacy.

" . . . We don't see shit," Joe went on. "Motherfuckin' stewed prunes and Wonder Bread and Campbell's Soup. They keepin' all the money theyself, and throwin' you two a few bucks to keep your mouths shut."

"Look," said Larry, "you can't come in here drunk. You don't like the rules, you can leave."

"'When Irish eyes are smiling . . .'" Joe began to sing, moving his hips in a lascivious way, "'. . . all the world is bright and gay . . .' Man, I wish I had me a taste of that."

The big man stood there licking his lips and Larry just stared at him. Even in the park, no one had ever been this bold. Duke knew his friend well enough to know he was on the edge of doing something very bad.

"Get out of here, Larry," said Duke. "I'll take care of it."

"I can handle it," said Larry.

"Just go," said Duke. "Go on down to the Hotline. Just get the hell out of here."

Duke was right, and Larry knew it. If he started swinging he might never stop. Somebody would get hurt or killed. He took a long hard look at Joe, which made the large man quiver slightly, then turned and walked glacially off down the street.

When Larry was out of earshot, Duke turned back to Joe. "What you got to be insulting the man for?" Maybe he could reason with Joe. The two men had been civil to each other in the past. They had even managed to have conversations.

"I'm just sayin'," said Joe, "this crackhead comes around here and tells me to quit drinkin'? You kiddin' me?"

"Ain't no reason to call him a crackhead," said Duke.

"Why not?" said Joe. "It's true. Eddie seen him uptown the other day, gettin' high all over the damn place."

"Bullshit," said Duke.

"If you two wasn't bendin' over for each other, you wouldn't be missin' so much . . ." said Joe.

"Shouldn't be insulting me, either, brother," said Duke. He was trying to calm him down now. Drunk, Joe could become very self-destructive.

"I ain't insulting you, man. I think love is a wonderful thing. So does he give it to you in the butthole, or do you take out that glass eye and take it that way?"

Before Duke even knew it was happening, his right arm flew at Joe's face and knocked him down. Slowly Joe got back on his feet and swung wildly at Duke, missing him, throwing himself off balance and onto the ground again. While he was down, though, Joe's hands fell on a brick, which he flung backhanded. It caught Duke in the mouth and knocked out a tooth. Once Duke felt the warm stream of blood down his chin, he lost all control. He kicked at Joe's head and opened an immense cut above his eye. Within seconds, not only blood but a white membranous substance swarmed out of Joe's cut and down his face. Now Joe got to his feet, and both men began swinging. Both of them were massive, and each blow landed with a hard, crushing sound, or even worse, the soft sound of broken flesh or tissue. After only a minute, both of them were blinded by their own blood.

By now there was a crowd. No one had the nerve to step between the two huge men, but someone called the police, and soon there was the sound of sirens. At that point, Joe was pulled inside the church by a Kochvillean, and Duke lurched off down a side street.

He didn't know where to go for help. He wasn't thinking clearly. He decided to head for the Food and Hunger Hotline and find Larry. There was a first aid kit there, and Larry could apply it.

He was weaving. Joe was huge and had been swinging at him with everything he had. Duke felt like his brains had been knocked loose. Dizziness overtook him every ten feet and he had to stop. He was moving through Chinatown, and the small meticulous people stared at the bleeding, hulking man in horror.

Violence scared the hell out of him, perhaps because he knew what he was capable of. Once, when he had caught Diane with a hotel room key in her purse, he went berserk. She started making up excuses, but he knew she'd been with another man. He began to tear the house apart. At one point she tried to stop him and he pushed her, not that hard, he thought, but it sent her flying backwards across the room. Her head missed the radiator by about an inch. The two little girls, especially Atu, were in terror. It was the moment in his life he most wanted to take back.

Now, in Chinatown, his eyes filled with blood and he looked up at God and moaned for forgiveness.

"See your identification, please?"

There was a cop in front of him.

"I don't have any, officer. Sorry."

"Kind of a mess, aren't you?"

". . . Had a bad fall."

The cop took a long, hard look at him. There was a small amount of decency in his eyes, Duke thought, and he tried to connect with it. "Just waitin' to get to a men's room, clean up a little."

"Try to stay on your feet," the cop said finally and moved on.

Duke kept staggering fitfully south and at last reached City Hall Park. Even encased in snow and ice, the old place was familiar, and he started to feel better. Not far beyond it, he knew, was the Food and Hunger Hotline. Christina Walker, who ran the place, was some kind of a saint. Even after Matthew had stolen from her, she had continued to hand over the keys to Duke and Larry. On the weekends, when it was empty, it was a sanctuary.

There was a light in the window, which meant that Larry was still there. That was good, because Duke was getting wobbly; some of his cuts were huge and he was still losing blood. Larry was pretty good with antiseptic and bandages. He'd had a lot of practice.

It wasn't until Duke climbed the last painful steps to the fifth floor landing that he smelled the acrid smell. His first instinct was that it was a fire. But there didn't seem to be a lot of smoke. He took out his own key and let himself in, and there was Larry, his back to the door, his feet on the window ledge, rocked back in an office easy chair.

"Larry, you smell anything?" he said.

Larry turned a half turn, and that's when Duke saw the crack pipe in his hand. It took a moment to register then tears began to gush out of Duke's eyes. Mixing with his wounds, they created unendurable pain. He thought instantly of Diane's brutal lies.

Larry palmed the pipe, now gone ash-dead. "Look, man . . . this is just . . ." Before he could finish his thought, Duke York was gone, down the stairs and back into the gray dusk.

Anesthetized though he was, Larry felt as if a knife had been stuck between his ribs. "I'm sorry," he said in a low whisper. Then he screamed it. The first was an apology, the second was pure rage. Nobody understood the pain he felt. At least Duke had a family, splintered and fucked up as it was. Larry had nothing but suspicion and hatred from people. Why wasn't he allowed to get high once in a while? Hell, every day of the week the office towers around him were full of white executives going off for martini lunches, so why should Larry begrudge himself a little painkiller? He wasn't robbing anybody for it. It was coming out of his salary, for a job that was goddamn hard, impossible, in fact, since it was costing him his soul.

Why should Duke be so goddamn sensitive? Who asked him to take the suffering of the whole world on himself anyway? Were you supposed to feel bad every time Duke cried a tear?

Of course, Larry loved the big old one-eyed bear, and he didn't want this episode held against him. But he didn't want to leave here feeling bad about it either. He needed to stop feeling bad about things. He filled the bowl one more time. He needed to put a positive punctuation mark on the day.

He lit up, and the sky, murky until now, filled with color. He let out another scream. It came from the deepest part of him and lasted a long time. Had it not been Sunday and the office buildings empty, the sound might have scared a lot of people. As it was, the rock and the concrete absorbed it without a quiver.

Fourteen

In early March 1989, Eve Miranda offered the contract for the renovation of 850 Longwood Avenue to the Galaxy Construction Company.

Well-known in the trade, Galaxy was the creation of two very different sensibilities. Its president, Steve Zervoudis, was a burly Greek who had emigrated from a tiny Mediterranean fishing village at the age of sixteen. He had learned the construction business from the bottom and was now famous for forcing buildings into existence with the sheer force of will, often in impossible circumstances.

His partner, Rich Sica, had a Master's degree in City Planning from Columbia. He was the guide through the labyrinths of city housing law, and he brought both sophistication and idealism to Zervoudis's hands-on toughness. Together they had gone into some of the worst situations in New York, but none as daunting as 850 Longwood Avenue. Though the infamous Guiterrez was gone, the building's reputation still inspired fear throughout the trade and throughout the Bronx.

In order to decide whether to take the project on, the Galaxy partners went to have a look at it. Upon their arrival, they were almost killed. As they crossed Longwood Avenue, a car swerved wildly onto the sidewalk and missed them by a couple of inches. Tough guy Zervoudis found himself trembling in his partner's arms and they hadn't even been inside.

Once they were, 850 Longwood surpassed their nightmares. It was *Dr. Zhivago* relocated to a sewer. Zervoudis stubbed his toe on a piece of raw human waste, frozen solid. Before hammers or nails, he could see, they would need ice picks.

The walls were covered with all manner of obscene graffiti and odd little mathematical sums—the bookkeeping, Zervoudis would later learn, of the drug trade. There was no heat in the building. Every radiator in the place had been stolen, no doubt for the penny a pound the scrap cast-iron would bring.

The two men made their way through the dank rubble and finally came out onto an impenetrable airshaft piled high almost to the level of the second floor with garbage. Much of the stuff was rotted and frozen and suggested unthinkable odors, once it thawed. It was here, however, that the men had their first clue that the project might be on a different level, artistically, than most of the low-income jobs they handled. This was not merely an airshaft, it was a courtyard. If you squinted at it, editing out the debris, there was a graceful sweep to it. A bench even peeked out from the bottom of a mound of rotting orange rinds. The place had once invited people to come and sit.

As the men made their way back towards the vestibule, more clues emerged. Most of the apartments were small, clearly having been subdivided in the style of the late twentieth century. But one apartment in the rear was intact, and it appeared to have not only three bedrooms, but a kitchen, living room, and a couple of other rooms of no clear function at all. It was luxurious, even empty and filthy. The baseboards were all wood, as were the moldings. But nothing was as remarkable as the public hallway, revealing itself in the bright morning. From lobby to rear entrance, four feet of marble ran up the wall. Marble! It was staggering to contemplate. If all six floors contained four running feet of pure marble, here was opulence unseen anywhere north of Ninety-Sixth Street and very few places south of it.

What the men could not get over was the counterpoint between the elegant and the grotesque. In many of the rooms were the ash-cold fires of the junkies next to piles of human feces. It was as if cavemen had lived here.

Sica looked at his partner. It was time to address the question. "Should we take this on?"

Zervoudis said nothing for a while.

The old immigrant maxim, which even after twenty years was hard to shake, was that you never turned down a job. Once some-one had asked him if a building had a soul, and he had laughed contemptuously. One wrestled with cold mortar and steel for no other reason than cold cash. But Steve Zervoudis didn't truly be-lieve this. The home he was building for himself and his wife and four kids would have a soul; he was laying every brick himself in the Mediterranean style, to let them know where they came from. This building on Longwood Avenue would be dangerous and a pain in the ass, but it had a soul. So Zervoudis said yes, they should take it.

Before they left for the day, Zervoudis jury-rigged some pipes in the hallway so that at least people could get water without going across the street to an open fire hydrant with a pail, as a lit-tle Spanish boy seemed to be doing every ten minutes. But the matter of hot water would have to wait for another day. That would involve descending to the boiler in the basement, and Zer-voudis knew in his bones that would be a bitter trial—along the lines of cleaning out some famous stables in the Greek myths of his childhood.

One last chore for the first day, though, was taking a look up-stairs. Even from the outside, he knew there was a problem with the roof . . . like its absence. How much of a section was gone and how much integrity the exposed floor had lost he almost didn't want to know. But before going home, he felt obliged to find out.

What he discovered was more complicated than the lack of a roof.

The phone rang insistently in Eve Miranda's office, and even though she was on her way out, she had a feeling she ought to get it.

"Hello?"

"Zervoudis." It was his standard salutation.

"Yes, Steve. How is it going?"

"You better get over here," he began, and delivered some disturbing news.

Hurrying across Prospect Avenue, Eve Miranda played the conversation over in her mind. It seemed fantastic, but Steve Zervoudis was not given to fantasy.

Zervoudis was gone when Miranda arrived, but she was able to make her way up the crumbling stairs, thanks to the naked light bulbs that the Greek had already strung along the dormant elevator shaft. He was a gentleman.

When she reached the sixth floor she found a large arrow on the floor in masking tape, Zervoudis's way of pointing her in the right direction. When she got to the spot, the scene was immediately clear. On one pile of rubble were a few clothes and a bag. On another were the nubs of several candles. In a corner was a full chamber pot in lieu of a functioning bathroom. And lying in a bathtub, swaddled in burlap, was a black woman fast asleep.

The wake up was brutal, the conversation brief.

"I don't know who you are, or how you got here, but you have to go."

"I ain't gonna hurt nobody," said Samantha Jones.

"That's fine. I just want you to go."

"All right. Don't get your Spanish dogs on me. Me vamoose."

Eve bristled. Sometimes black people rubbed her the wrong way, especially when they insulted the dignity of Hispanics.

"And please don't come back," said Eve Miranda.

Picking up and moving on was a familiar thing for Samantha Jones, but she would have liked a moment to say good-bye to this place, which had been her home for a couple of weeks. Unfortunately, the Spanish bitch was clearly going to stand over her until she left. She got her things together and moved off down the stairs.

When she got outside, it was freezing. She reached in her pocket for a subway token. There was none. She looked around for shelter. There was none of that either. In poor neighborhoods all the habitable space is spoken for, and there are no philanthropists to give anything away.

Her eye was drawn to the corroding marquee of the RKO Frankin. She winced only slightly, remembering her experience outside it. She wandered over and tested all the doors and found one open in the back, probably the stage door from the theatre's vaudeville days. She entered and once again faced a world of darkness. As soon as her eyes adjusted, she moved along a corridor of rooms, possibly once dressing rooms, now filled with debris and the corpses of mice and rats. She moved out onto the stage, where the traditional single naked bulb shone from a floor fixture. Now, for the first time, she understood the purpose of such a thing: it illumined the entire vast space, no doubt for safety's sake. She could see it in all its early twentieth-century splendor, from the gilded balconies to the now-frayed velvet seats. Countering this impression was the ubiquitous mildew, the smell of urine, and the freezing air. It was hardly warmer than being outside. She climbed the steps to the balcony, which afforded a wonderful if dim view of the stage. So cold and tired was she, however, that she could not, even for a moment, enjoy a fantasy of herself moving across that stage in a cream colored gown, playing out a scene of romance and intrigue. Her fantasies were exhausted. She closed her eyes and let the cold numb her and take her.

Duke York could imagine Diane's reaction.

"You're *quittin'*?! First of all, you don't have a job to quit. They're *givin'* you the damn money!!"

Nevertheless, Duke York was now sitting in the vestibule of Lloyd Casson's Trinity Church office and trying to figure out how he was going to phrase it. He expected that Casson would respond pretty much the same way as Diane would have: in blunt terms, "Nigger, you're *crazy!!*"

The door opened, and Duke saw that Casson was not alone. Sitting with him was Marc Greenberg. This irked Duke slightly. Greenberg was his friend, but he didn't need any convocation of the great white father and the great black father to be sure the poor boy wasn't gonna do something stupid. Duke York knew exactly what he was doing.

"I asked Marc to come down when you told me what this was about," said Casson.

"Yeh," said Duke. "Well then, here it is. I don't want to work with the homeless no more. I mean the park, that was one thing, but I got two little girls at home, stayin' with their great-grandmother."

"You worked for a long time to get to this point," said Greenberg. "You've earned this job. You're entitled to the money."

"Yeh Marc, but see—"

"You need money to raise your girls, right? We're just trying to give it to you . . ."

"Yeh, but see, I don't *want* the damn money! I'm a damn artist!! I'm a singer!! I'm not a homeless spokesman!! I don't want to tell my little girls that's what I do!! Rather be a damn janitor!"

He began to cry. Casson and Greenberg were startled by the passion. What they didn't know was that Duke's tears sprang from an even deeper well. Just that morning, the last of twenty stitches had been removed from the fight he'd had defending Larry's reputation. As each one came out, Duke vowed never to be burned or duped again by anyone.

"Marc, I think we ought to respect his decision," Casson was saying now.

"But—"

"I really think it's better, Marc." Casson looked down at his shoes. The grants to Larry and Duke had been his idea. Once again, he had been seduced into thinking that money would be good, like water on a garden. Once again, he had been mistaken.

All three men were standing now.

"Don't get me wrong, I appreciate everything," Duke said. "For a while there, I was thinkin' we was gonna change the world."

"We all thought that, Duke," said Greenberg.

Casson smiled ruefully. He had never thought that. Lloyd Casson had stormed the barricades many times, when his hair was black and when his hair was gray, and the world hadn't changed. It just kept turning in that infuriating way. And if you took all the world's money tomorrow and divided it up evenly among everyone, within a year or two it would all wind up back in the hands of the same two percent of the people. There would continue to be a big, dull, bland, middle class, and the rest would be the starving, syphilitic multitudes. And Duke would be one of them. That was how it was.

Of course, none of that would stop Lloyd Casson from hurling himself into the barricades one more time. On Sunday he would climb into his pulpit and try to prick the complacency of his wealthy white parishioners, and tell the blacks in the back pews that anything was possible. That's what good theatre did, whether it was Barrymore standing up there or Paul Robeson or Lloyd Casson. You spun an illusion that sent the audience out transformed for a few hours. A few hours were better than nothing. There were less honorable ways to make a living.

Now Greenberg and Duke stood face to face, and Casson withdrew, leaving them the room. Friends were parting and ought to have their privacy.

"I don't blame you or nothin' for things not workin' out," Duke said when they were alone.

"I'm glad of that," said Greenberg. He had believed in their friendship. Though it had not continued with the intensity of September, there was no denying the power of those weeks. After a while, kayaking together, just walking along, they hadn't even talked but had just fallen into a silence that was both comfortable and infinite.

"So then, shalom, man," said Duke.

Greenberg looked at the hulking, one-eyed, extremely black man.

"Shalom," said Marc Greenberg, and watched Duke leave the office and walk into the street. The Wall Street lunch hour crowd was just beginning to pour out. Duke bummed a cigarette from a stranger and disappeared into the stream.

⬇

Bruce Bailey was widely mourned. Everybody knew somebody who had a problem with housing, whether they were at the center of some monstrous rent strike or just had a crummy apartment. Bruce Bailey, who had managed to get involved with crises great and small, was therefore a public figure on the Upper West Side and now a fallen hero. And so the public would be given a chance to say farewell in a formal way: the murdered activist would lie in state for several days in the Cathedral of St. John the Divine.

The ladies who cleaned the altar noticed that long after the milling throngs of the day had left, a solitary figure remained staring at the coffin. This was Larry Locke, who had become transfixed by the death of Bruce Bailey. He could not get it out of his mind that there had been no head on the body.

In his better moments—and he still had some of them, after a walk with Ellen by the river, or a cocktail, or a good night's sleep, or a secretive bowl of crack—Larry Locke was maintaining. With the resignation of Duke York, he was alone in the position of Famous Homeless Person, but he was continuing to struggle to the meetings and to be as affable as possible. In his worst moments, however, he was disintegrating.

He had been given a gift by a supporter of Kochville, a biography of Martin Luther King. No doubt it was meant to inspire, but instead it filled him with dread. He turned immediately to the end. From which motel window is my assassin watching me? was the question he now asked himself.

Certainly the men of Kochville, now in their church basement, had violent feelings towards him. But what about Interfaith itself? Lately, Larry had been raising hell at just about every meeting, demanding to see the books. He just wanted to make sure that all the money that was earmarked for Kochville-at-St. Augustine's actually *got* there. Sure, Interfaith were all priests and rabbis. But what if one of them had a secret to hide? What if one of them had been stealing? Rather than be disgraced in the community, wouldn't they want to silence the accusing voice . . . maybe even cut off the accusing head? Hell what about the other homeless groups, like the Coalition for the Homeless? They appeared to be civilized white people, but suppose some of the grant money that had poured into Kochville would have gone to them? Wouldn't they be pissed off about that? Couldn't they conceivably even feel *murderous* about it, if it meant that someone could no longer put food on his family's table?

And what about the murderers of Bruce Bailey!!?? Wasn't the message clear? DON'T FUCK WITH US OR ELSE! . . . SIGNED, THE LAND-LORDS OF NEW YORK. What might happen to a rambunctious nigger who didn't get that message, who insisted on giving speeches and making trouble?

And finally, what if—and it didn't seem so farfetched—all of these people *in concert* wanted to get rid of Larry Locke? They all had individual motives, but the collective motive would be to silence Larry before he stumbled on the greatest secret of all . . . that homelessness itself, so ballyhooed as a national tragedy, the scourge of the eighties, blah blah blah, was all a ruse? That's right, a fraud. By Larry's count, tens of thousands of people were employed in the homeless industry. There was a whole building

on Church Street that did little else but oversee the shelter system. There were thousands of employees in the shelters themselves. What about the doctors who treated the homeless sick
with TB or AIDS? Doctors always got paid, somehow. What about
all the charities that raised money for the poor homeless?
Weren't there salaried people on staff? Secretaries, fund-raisers?
The truth was that homelessness was a billion dollar industry.
What would happen to someone who stood up and exposed all
that? It wouldn't be just his head that would be missing. He'd be
spread out from Staten Island to Canarsie. A testicle here, a liver
there. A vital organ in every borough.

"Larry . . ."

His head jerked around.

"Over here."

He could see no one. His heart began to pound. Was the sound
coming from the coffin?

"It's me."

He was on his feet now, sweating.

"Somebody told me you were here."

There was a movement behind a pillar. Larry crouched, ready
to pounce. The figure moved out of the shadows.

"You scared the shit out of me!" shouted Larry.

"Sorry," said Marc Greenberg.

Both men caught their breath.

"What'd you do that for?"

"I said sorry. I didn't mean to." There was a brief silence. "You
want to come into the office for a while?"

"What for?" said Larry.

Greenberg bristled slightly. What for? Well, technically, Larry
was on salary, and if he was asked to do something, he ought to
do it, rather than snarl "What for?"

"To have a cup of coffee. Maybe we could talk about some
things."

Larry said nothing but continued to stare at the coffin.

Clearly, he was in one of his states. Greenberg thought about putting an arm under his elbow and helping him up, but he feared he might be violently pushed away. That's how erratic Larry had become. The Interfaith meetings were now incredibly uncomfortable. It was one thing to have Larry there as a corrective, as a real homeless person to keep the conversation grounded. It was another thing to have him calling priests and rabbis thieves.

To Greenberg's relief, Larry finally rose and followed him distractedly down the long aisle, across the nave, and to the crescent of offices that wound behind the main altar. It felt like they'd gone a mile down a country road by the time they were seated at Greenberg's desk.

"Coffee?"

"No thanks."

"There's a new program I want to talk to you about," said Greenberg. "I want to call it the Speaker's Bureau. Homeless people have stories to tell. I want to send them around to high schools and town meetings to talk about themselves. I want regular people to understand that the homeless are not all that different from them—that there are real reasons how they got the way they are."

There was a long silence.

"They get paid to do this?" asked Larry.

"A living wage," said Greenberg.

There was another silence.

"So what do you think?" Greenberg asked finally.

"I think it sucks," said Larry.

Greenberg was surprised. "Why?"

"That's no way to make a living, go around and tell people how you got so fucked up."

"I think it would be great for all homeless people if the rest of the world finally thought they were human."

"But what about *them*!" Larry was almost shouting at him

now. "That gonna be their profession? Stand up in front of people and be goddamn pathetic?"

"I think they'd learn how to present themselves, how to talk in public. I think it would be good for them."

There was a knock on the door. One of Dean Morton's assistants needed Greenberg's ear for a moment, so he excused himself. As soon as Larry was left alone, his eye fell on a memo on the desk. "Tell Larry to call Bill Lynch." Lynch was Dinkins' campaign manager, and one of the rising black stars of the Democratic Party. The memo was dated yesterday.

As soon as Greenberg re-entered the room, Larry said "Why the fuck didn't you tell me about this?"

Marc Greenberg felt like he'd been slapped. He did not like to be talked to like that. There were people so racked with liberal guilt that they more or less said "Let me have it, I deserve it." Greenberg was not one of them. Not anymore.

"I resent your tone of voice, Larry. My secretary must have taken it yesterday. I'm sure she would have let you know as soon as she saw you."

"I saw her a few hours ago."

"Then I'm sure it slipped her mind or just got lost on the desk."

"A lot of things get lost on your fucking desk."

Greenberg took a second to regain himself. "I told you not to talk to me that way."

"What the hell happened to that 501 (C)(3) application, for instance?"

Now Greenberg was reaching his limit. The whole 501 (C)(3) thing was Larry's paranoia in full bloom. A 501 (C)(3) was an application for status as a nonprofit corporation. Larry wanted one for Kochville so they could solicit funds on their own. Greenberg saw no reason for it, but played along and found Larry a lawyer to file it. The 501 (C)(3), however, was complex and took a long time to process. Larry claimed that Greenberg was stalling, out of fear that Kochville would lure contributions away from Interfaith.

It was madness. That anybody could suspect Interfaith, or Greenberg, of trying to rip off Kochville was insulting and utterly strange. The brilliant clergymen of Interfaith could think of no better way to make a living than to steal from Larry Locke??!! Marc Greenberg, the heir-apparent to a significant family fortune, had instead decided to go into antipoverty work so *he* could rip off Larry Locke?! It would be laughable if it weren't so disturbing.

"The 501 (C)(3) thing is going through, Larry. You have your own lawyer handling it now. Please don't hassle me about it."

"Anything you say, boss," said Larry mordantly, in the manner of a field hand. Again, Greenberg bristled. He didn't need this for another second. He got immediately to his main point.

"The reason I mentioned the Speaker's Bureau, Larry, is that we're going to do it. Definitely. Starting in the fall. That's where the Trinity Church money is going to go."

"So my job . . . ?"

"Will end at that point."

Greenberg expected an explosion. Instead, Larry Locke randomly grabbed a sheet of paper off Greenberg's desk (a rather important one), turned it over on its blank side, and scrawled a letter of resignation as of, he noted on the ancient clock on the wall, 7:01 that evening. Then he stood up and walked out of the room.

Greenberg expected to feel an emotional upheaval. This truly was the end of Kochville, the death of a very powerful dream that had involved many extraordinary people. Instead, he felt nothing. Kochville was over, and the Speaker's Bureau was a wonderful idea. High school kids in the suburbs would meet homeless people. One of society's terrible gulfs would be bridged. It would be a far more valuable way to spend the grant money from Trinity Church than to give it to a crack addict to attend meetings he barely understood. That was a harsh assessment, but there it was. Marc Greenberg was not nearly as naive as Duke York, and he had noticed the glassiness in Larry Locke's eyes and the raspiness in his throat long ago.

Maybe, Marc Greenberg would later think, it was his fault that Larry had taken such a bad turn. Maybe, as the one who groomed him for leadership, Greenberg should have had more of an "exit strategy" for him. But that was hindsight. The hard reality was that Marc Greenberg was not a therapist for individual homeless people but a strategist for the homeless in general. Sometimes you had to make a choice.

For an instant, he wondered if it had been anything personal. He'd never had the warm feeling for Larry that he'd had for Duke. It was simple chemistry, as friendship tends to be. So Marc had no temptation to talk Larry out of his resignation or to leap up and embrace him as he left. Instead, Greenberg remained at his desk and watched the big wooden door close.

<hr>

Everyone was against the run for the fourth term. The mayor's friends, particularly the professional couples for whom he played the role of eccentric bachelor uncle, felt the stroke had taken its toll and rendered him too frail. This was sure to be a brutal campaign.

For the political professionals, it was all about numbers. The coalition appeared to have shredded. The Irish vote was no longer solid, and the black and liberal votes were practically assured for Dinkins. Even David Garth, who had packaged and sold Ed Koch, knew that the time was past. The public was weary of the braying and shrieking.

For all of this advice the mayor was outwardly grateful, yet secretly contemptuous. Large decisions were made within, deeply within. The decision to run for governor back in 1982, ill-fated though that proved to be, had been a solitary one. Old Louis Koch, the mayor's father, had just died. The mayor was sitting shiva in the classic manner, unshaven, avoiding his image in mirrors, padding about the house in slippers, solemnly receiving visitors. It was then that the decision had come, perhaps because old Louis Koch would have wanted it. Whether or not it was to exalt the dreams of an old Polish peddler, it had been settled deeply, deeply within.

This decision was far less agonized. The answer was yes, of course he would run. Cynics claimed it was a pure stroke of ego, and indeed the mayor could not deny that the chance to make history, to surpass even the great La Guardia, was seductive. But there was more to it. If everyone was saying he could never win in an increasingly black and brown New York, the mayor's answer was "Oh yes, I can."

Nor was this a childish need to prove himself. At a recent party a friend told him, "Forget it, the city's going to hell, let the blacks and the Puerto Ricans have it." This deeply offended the old civil rights lawyer in Ed Koch. Never let it be said that he walked away when it wasn't worth having anymore.

So the campaign began in earnest. The first and most obvious way to address his "negatives," in the new parlance, was to march in the St. Patrick's Day parade, which after much debate the Ancient Order of Hibernians was allowing him to do.

It was like running a green gauntlet. Everywhere the boos cascaded down on him, and the ENGLAND OUT OF IRELAND banners rippled in a stiff March breeze. Nevertheless he got through it, and even managed to quaff a pint of the dreaded Guinness afterward. Within a week, the payoff showed up in the polls. It looked as if the Irish vote might hold after all. Where else were they going to go? The Irish view of blacks hadn't changed a great deal since the Draft Riots of the Civil War.

The next step was an even deeper indignity. For eleven years, Bess Myerson or no Bess Myerson, the mayor had endured the innuendos that he was a homosexual, a sodomizer, a necrophilic, a pedophile, a bestialist, and worse. His position had been to not even dignify it with a denial. But now he couldn't afford to lose even the handful of voters who mistook his silence for guilt. One night the mayor got on the radio and announced, for once and for all, "I'm not gay!!" Whether or not anyone believed him, at least that public excoriation was out of the way.

The mayor's main problem, though, turned out to be something nobody had anticipated; namely, what was he running on? What was the *positive* reason to vote for Ed Koch, besides the fact that he'd been there forever and his opponent hadn't paid his income taxes? Here on the brink of the chastened nineties, with the stock market crash of '87 still fresh and the streets filled with the homeless, it seemed ill-advised to gloat about all the new construction of the Koch era.

No, if gloating were to be done, it would have to be about *public* works. But the truth was that the Williamsburg Bridge was actually crumbling, and City Hall was still so hamstrung from the scandals of '86 that Alair Townsend, the mayor's brilliant deputy of finance, couldn't even OK a new water fountain without someone peeking over her shoulder to see if Meade Esposito, or some other boss, was going to profit by it.

So if the mayor could not run on his record, then in the old political wisdom he would run against it. He was reduced to promising things for the future, somewhat wildly, like some shmuck who'd never been elected to anything.

He seized on the city's decaying infrastructure and vowed to do something about it. Specifically, he was going to tackle the corroding, byzantine system of pipes and viaducts that brought New York its water. Much of it came from the Catskills, was stored in Westchester, and finally flowed into the city via a water tunnel. But the 1917 original and its 1936 replacement were in decay and collapse. Hence it was time for . . . the Third Water Tunnel!!!

The third water tunnel? To those who even understood what it meant (for many it called up dark science fiction images), it seemed like an oddly meek campaign theme.

Well, it was either that or the mayor's five-billion-dollar housing plan, but any mention of homelessness, even solutions to it, seemed to bring the negatives tumbling down on him.

Lately, just to stifle the hue and cry from the advocates, the mayor had gone against his own deepest instincts and actually begun moving the homeless into the empty, tax-delinquent buildings owned by the city. But the Norman Siegels of the world had insisted on fair hearings, which meant that you couldn't just assign a homeless person to an empty apartment. You had to give them the right to turn it down. Some did, for legitimate reasons. There were people with heart conditions who couldn't climb five flights of stairs. Fair enough. There was a mother who refused to move into a building because her daughter had once been raped a block away. Fine. But what about the people who just "didn't care for the neighborhood?" Last week, the mayor had met a woman who had turned down eighteen apartments. Eighteen!! Toothless and half-insane, the woman was behaving like Brooke Astor shopping for a country home.

It was all impossible. Privately, the mayor now traced much of the problem to bad appointments. Henry Stern had been a mistake. Personal things had gotten tangled up with professional things, and that was always a disaster.

But even worse was HRA.

The Human Resources Administration was the agency that oversaw welfare, the shelter system, and the whole mess of poverty that Charles Dickens made his living writing about. To run it, the mayor had appointed William Grinker, an irascible man with a quick and cruel sense of humor. It was like oil on fire.

Recently, a homeless baby had died while being shuttled from one city welfare office to another. The dailies had run with the story, and pictures of the tiny coffin were everywhere. "Perhaps," snarled Grinker in a memo, "we should have an anecdote of the week, where everyone could submit their story to an independent panel who would select the most poignant for publication in all the tabloids." The memo had leaked to the press and caused a furor. The heat fell squarely on the mayor, who then dumped a public ocean of bile on Grinker.

But the campaign absorbed its humiliations and its disasters and kept rolling, as all campaigns do. The numbers were low and there were huge problems, but it was early yet. Ed Koch had been given up for dead before, both politically, lacerated by corruption, and physically, rendered limp and light headed by a stroke. As his opponents would soon learn (although they should already have known it), he was going to be very, very hard to kill.

On the train home from his final meeting with Marc Greenberg, Larry Locke felt weightless. It was as if he'd been in a bad relationship for a long time and hadn't known it. But once out of it, the clouds lifted. He no longer cared about meetings, or church basements, or headless corpses. When he got out of the subway in Brooklyn, he decided to celebrate with a little cocktail at McNeely's, the pub on the corner. Sipping a gin with ice, he felt certain he'd done the right thing. The Speaker's Bureau was bull-shit. You'd have a bunch of Negroes making themselves as pathetic as possible and playing the act over and over and over again. Hell, that's what homeless people *did already*. What they needed to do was abandon that act, not tour it.

The late afternoon air was sublime. The worst part of March seemed over with, and scattered crocuses were even appearing outside the nursing home near Ellen's place. He took his time getting home and finally climbed the stairs and opened the door to find her sitting in the hall with a small bag packed. Dressed in black and smoking a cigarette, she looked like a pensive thirty-year-old model.

"I have to go to my daughter for a few days. She's sick," said Ellen.

"Uh-huh. Want me to come?" he asked.

"You've got meetings tomorrow."

Larry gave her the big news that he was a free man.

"I'd better go alone," she said.

"Uh-huh." He absorbed that for a moment. "Brought you something," he said finally, handing her a small bunch of blue crocuses. "Picked them right down the street."

"You shouldn't have done that," she said. "The old people love them." He began to get that hurt-little-boy look, and she pulled back a little. "But thanks, anyway. I'll go put them in some water."

She did that, and then came back and put her arm around his neck and kissed him on the mouth. "You've had a drink," she said. He nodded, smelling in turn her perfume, her mouthwash, her talcum, all her little scents.

"I'll call you in a day or two," she said, opening the door to go. Then, for a reason neither of them understood, they looked at each other in silence for what seemed like a long time. And then she left.

He watched her from the window as she moved down the street and finally disappeared around a corner. Then he turned and faced the empty apartment. He wasn't quite sure what to do with himself. He tried to watch some television for a while, but that didn't make him happy. He didn't feel like reading. He didn't feel like much of anything. He thought for a moment of returning to McNeely's, but then he remembered a half bottle of Chianti in the cupboard. He tried a glass or two of it, but it didn't have nearly the firepower to augment the gin high. He went into the bedroom and sat for a while on the bed. He saw his flowers sitting in a small vase on the bureau. Before he knew what he was doing, he grabbed the vase and flung it against the wall, shattering it.

Why did he do that? he wondered.

Possibly because he picked the flowers as an act of love, and she seemed to be more worried about the distress of some old biddy down the street. Well, that was just like a nigger to break an old lady's heart, wasn't it?

He stopped himself. That wasn't quite fair. Ellen was no racist.

However, he had just been left behind for the weekend, and there was no mystery as to why. What Irish Catholic grandmother wanted to say to her freckle-faced little grandchildren, "Tommy, Molly, this is your new colored grandfather!!"

No, no mystery there at all. So where did that leave him? All by himself, as usual. He continued to putter about, fingering her artifacts, so terribly delicate and white, so many gilded portraits of severe old Irish faces on her bedside table. He began to feel the eyes in the pictures follow him around the room.

He found a broom and a dustpan and cleaned up the shards of the vase. The Irish eyes were still on him. He turned off the lights. He picked up the tiny mangled flowers and placed them on her pillow. He went into the next room, but there was another pair of eyes in there, hanging on the wall. There was no escaping them, even in the dark.

He sat for a long time looking out the window but couldn't even do that in peace. The breeze kept blowing the gauzy white curtains in his face. Finally he stomped back into the bedroom and opened a drawer and grabbed a pair of clean socks and some underwear. This was all he could fit into his jacket pocket. He did not want to be encumbered beyond that, even by a plastic bag. On his way to the front door, he grabbed a tiny brass clock off a table. It might be worth something, and she wouldn't miss it. He took a last look around. The eyes were still on him. It gave him great pleasure to slam the door on them. He was beyond them now.

He entered the subway system and rode it to south Harlem, where Friday night was coming fitfully to life. He spent an hour searching out an old friend named James, and the two of them smoked a bowl of crack on the stone fence at the north end of Central Park. It was the first mild spring night, and this was a perch for dreaming. They looked up the famous Lenox Avenue, where the Cotton Club and Small's Paradise once shimmered in the Harlem night. James said his father had known people like

Langston Hughes and Zora Neale Hurston. Larry imagined this pair slouching around town in low-brimmed hats and chinchilla stoles. They smoked another bowl and basked in the warm glow of history.

Then the crack began to let them down, as it tended to do rather suddenly. They parted company, and Larry began to look for a place to stay the night. He had some money, and he settled on a modest dive called the Carlton Arms. It was only when he got inside and registered with the skinny clerk with a distinctive birthmark on the side of his face that he realized he'd been here before. This was the place he'd checked into the first night he ever got to New York, some five years before. It was from here, once his measly workman's compensation money ran out, that he had jumped off into the madness that was Manhattan and all that had followed. So he was back again. The strange-looking cat at the desk was to be his gatekeeper, coming in and going out.

Fifteen

Steve Zervoudis had been right to dread his journey into the basement of 850 Longwood Avenue. The level of fecal swamp had diminished not an inch since entrapping Larry Locke and Matthew several months earlier. If anything, it had become richer and more potent. For the boiler to even be approached, the whole place would have to be drained. There is a drainage hole on the floor of all basements, but clearly this one had become clogged. Someone would have to *dive down there* and unplug it. Zervoudis surveyed his quaking assistants. Finally his eye fell on Spiro, a young man just off the boat from Athens who very much reminded him of himself as an immigrant. In a gesture that was neither Greek nor English, that in fact required no translation at all, Zervoudis looked at the young man and simply pointed in a downward direction.

Spiro closed his eyes, trembled for a moment, and disappeared into the muck. A moment later he re-emerged, having performed one of the most heroic acts in the history of Bronx housing. Within an hour, the level of the roiling sewage began to sink, and by the end of the day, Zervoudis was able to approach the boiler. Miraculously, it was in good repair, and that night the handful of tenants in 850 Longwood Avenue were enjoying hot running water.

So the renovation process began, fitfully. After the basement episode, it was a week before Zervoudis' wife would allow him in the house. During that time, he slept on Rich Sica's couch and spent his off hours scouring the cosmetics counters of the Bronx for an ointment or a lotion that would get him back into his conjugal bed.

The original architect on the job, an Asian named Lee, was fired by Eve Miranda for reasons no one immediately understood. Some speculated that his cold, analytical approach clashed with Miranda's hot blood. True or not, a Greek named Michael Avrimides was soon hired, and he meshed perfectly with Zervoudis. From here the work went more or less smoothly through most of 1989. The only sour note was a melancholy shared by the two Greeks about all the compromises.

The marble was not confined to four running feet in each hallway. In the lobby and the vestibule, it ran from floor to ceiling! It was magnificent, but even as he registered amazement, Zervoudis knew it would all have to go. The marble was crumbling, and for the sake of safety and economy it would have to be replaced with something far less beautiful.

The elevator, dormant these many years, would no longer be able to creak elegantly up and down its brass spindle, its passengers visible through iron grillwork to the surrounding stairwell. Regulations now forbade such a thing. Had anyone known it was the first elevator in the Bronx, it might have been saved. With no such knowledge available it became part of the building's removable debris.

Nor was there any money to restore the Flemish oak baseboards or the bathtubs with cat's paws. Even the oval window on the top floor, the building's aristocratic signature, was compromised. Originally the glass had been curved, like the corner of the building where it sat. But where could anyone obtain such a piece of glass in this day and age? Instead, the oval shape was retained with a flat piece of glass. Even that much seemed a victory.

For Irma Ortiz, who for years had cursed the spasmodic avalanches of crumbling marble and the three-story ascent with bags of groceries, there were no mixed feelings about the modern touches. Every morning when Zervoudis arrived, a cup of hot Spanish coffee awaited him on his work table. At first the big Greek was slightly contemptuous of the sweet frothy brew, but in time grew to tolerate it and finally crave it.

Campaigning was why he loved the life. Some politicians found elections anxiety provoking, ordeals to be gotten through in order to do the real work of governing. Not Ed Koch. It was on the stump, with the election on the line, with the crowd hostile, with the PA system in disrepair, with the sky threatening to pour down rain . . . it was moments like these when he came alive. He would disdain the faulty microphone, come downstage and say "All right, you chumps, listen close, because I'm gonna tell you how much you need me."

The young campaign aides, the ones who'd never been through it before, were astonished by the energy and bravado. He went to the opening of a library in Harlem, and with David Dinkins sitting next to him on the dais, introduced himself to the crowd as the soon-to-be only four-term mayor in the history of New York. The nerve of it!! With the hard-core Dinkins people staring right at him!!

On the weekends, he scheduled days that exhausted the young aides even in contemplation. One Sunday called for a morning meeting of the Young Brooklynites for Israel at the Brighton Beach Baths, followed by a march down Madison Avenue in the Indian Day parade, followed by an anniversary celebration of the Seuffert Band (attended by every German in Queens), followed by a Puerto Rican street fair on 114th Street. And that was only the daytime schedule! As they rushed out the door to the first event, Ed Koch barked "Did you pack the Indian dress shirt?" A trembling young aide admitted he had not. How else, snapped the mayor, was he supposed to appear in the Indian Day parade? In a kilt?

Through June and July, the campaign seemed to be gathering momentum. As he reconnected with one ethnic neighborhood after another, he began to get the rust out and find his groove. Much had gestated since the last campaign, and in a sense he was four years older and four years better. There was less wasted energy now, and more precision in hitting emotional targets.

One afternoon the mayor addressed a crowd at the ribbon cutting of a new low-income housing project on Crotona Park in the Bronx. It had been such a whirlwind day that it took him a while to realize where he was—a block away from the house he was born in. Yet there it was, more or less the same, if a little dingier. Crotona Park itself, though almost sixty years had passed since he had skated on its lake and run through its grottos, was mythic in his imagination. Its shapes and shadows had not changed. Off to the right was the synagogue where the Koch family had gone to shul. Now it was a day-care center, and young black mothers lounged on the steps . . . somewhat disrespectfully, the mayor thought. The dais on which he stood was constructed over the very same huge rock, imperishable Fordham gneiss, where long ago the children would untuck their shirts and loosen their sabbath ties. Then, just when they all despaired of ever seeing their mothers again, the socializing outside the temple would end and Yetta Koch would come to find her little Eddie.

The ribbon-cutting program began, snapping the mayor out of his daydreams. It was a fairly standard routine. After blessing the new homes and giving the traditional gifts of salt and bread, the mayor made his remarks. He thanked the public officials involved, recited the major points of his five-billion-dollar housing program, and tried to whip up a little enthusiasm for the third water tunnel.

When he was done a small child walked to the podium and handed the mayor a letter. "Who is this?" he mouthed to an aide.

"Adopt-a-class," came the answer. The little girl was part of a program in which the mayor had participated along with several other city officials. The idea was to "adopt" a class of New York City youngsters and visit their school every so often to talk about government.

In the limousine back to Manhattan, he opened the letter. "Dear Mayor Koch," it began. "I would like to tell you that I think that the homeless need more help than you're giving them. You probably don't understand how it feels because you have a job and a home. I go to the New York City Kids on Stage summer program, and we're doing a show next Friday called 'Homeless.' I hope you can come and see what I mean. If you can't make it, please send me a letter telling me what you're going to do about homeless people. Signed, Aisha Ikram."

The mayor felt a sharp twinge of indignation. Apparently, little Aisha didn't understand the significance of the very event she was attending. Wasn't five billion dollars enough to give away to people too lazy to find their own lodgings? That was harshly put, but quite frankly he was at the end of his rope, mainly because the polls were showing the public to be full of little Aishas.

"Do you think the mayor is too insensitive to the needs of the poor?" is the way the pollsters usually put the question, and the answer, by a margin of two to one, was invariably "YES!" And nothing he had been able to do, from quoting Martin Luther King ad nauseam to talking about his own civil rights experiences to building methadone clinics to cuddling crack babies in his lap, had affected it.

Nor was he merely flapping his gums. "Money talks, bullshit walks," was the old expression. Wasn't FIVE MILLION BUCKS enough!? He was taking a hammer to the city's piggy bank to do all this. Firehouses had to close and cops had to be taken off the beat to pay for the building he'd just dedicated.

What hurt even more was that the mayor was continuing to hedge on his most deeply held principles. You were being evicted?

No problem. The city would pay your legal costs to fight it. You had no place to live? No problem. The city would pay a relative to take you in. You lived in a shelter and you didn't want to do the mandatory ten hours of work a week? Hey, forget it. If you don't feel like it, don't do it!!

Where was the morality in all this?! What message did it send to the poor bastards who worked their butts off trying to keep a family and a home together?!

The city was rewarding the scumbags.

The real crying shame was the buildings themselves, like the old homestead on Crotona Park. When he was growing up, it was unheard of for a landlord to lose a building by failing to pay his taxes. Lose it?! This marvelous piece of craftsmanship that contained the hopes and mementos and scars and echoes of so many people? A landlord would beg, borrow, and steal to find a way to keep it! He'd have nightmares that he'd forget a tax payment and somebody would come and take it away from him!!

Now, nobody wanted the goddamn things. Not the landlords, and certainly not the city. There were programs especially designed to get rid of them. EARP, DAMP, SHIP were their acronyms, although they sounded to the mayor like rude body noises and were about as attractive. They were official schemes to excuse landlords for the taxes they owed, to entice new landlords to take buildings for nothing, to loan money for repairs, to forgive those loans, and now the newest program of all: a gift of ten thousand dollars outright to anyone who would simply agree to take one of the buildings! In other words, like a variation of the old Hennie Youngman joke, TAKE MY BUILDING, PLEASE!!

Even as the mayor rolled on towards September 12, the day of the primary vote, the sickening feeling washed over him again and again like a badly digested meal. If the prize ultimately became his, it would be at the cost of virtually everything he believed in, all of which he'd violated in order to say, "Insensitive? Not me."

He was disgusting himself.

Then it all became academic. On the night of August 27, three black teenagers lounged in a Brooklyn apartment watching a video of *Mississippi Burning*, the story of Shwerner, Chaney, and Goodman, the civil rights workers who were brutally murdered by a white Mississippi mob. It was a story Ed Koch could have narrated himself.

When the video was over, the three kids hopped on the subway. One of them held a clipped-out newspaper ad they intended to check out—about a used car being offered very reasonably in the neighborhood of Bensonhurst.

Unfortunately for them, the place they were travelling to was in turmoil. A young beauty, half Spanish, half Italian, had been spurning the advances of the Italian romeos in the neighborhood. She made it abundantly clear that she preferred the company of black men. The blow to the collective manhood of the young Italian peacocks was intense. On this particular night, it all came to a head. It was the young woman's birthday, and the rumor had spread that she had invited a few black guys to her party. A mob of Italians gathered to give them a rude reception.

At this point the three kids arrived looking for the used car. Immediately they were mistaken for the party goers and terrorized. Two of them got away, but the third was cornered and finally murdered. The victim's name was Yusef Hawkins, soon to become as famous in the history of American race relations as Sacco and Vanzetti, John Brown, or Jim Crow.

The event galvanized New York, which had for many hot summers been heating to this kind of a boil. Were there now racial borders that could be crossed only at the cost of one's life? There were marches, riots, demonstrations, counter-demonstrations, and monstrous political fallout, all of it to the good of David Dinkins.

"You see," he was able to say finally, "for years an abrasive mayor has picked at our wounds. This is the result. I come with balm."

The entire Koch camp understood the dire portent, no one more so than the mayor himself. He plunged back into the fray. He haunted orphanages. He practically lived on the doorstep of Yusef Hawkins, attending the funeral, the wake, and paying a couple of condolence calls beyond that.

But it all seemed somehow hasty and insubstantial. The day before the primary, the mayor addressed a group of West Indian teenagers and told them that Alexander Hamilton had arrived as a youth from the Caribbean and done pretty well for himself. Even the Koch aides cringed. Was the mayor suggesting that the powder-wigged Hamilton arriving in colonial New York was somehow a model for a kid from Jamaica arriving in Harlem? The teachers in charge of the kids looked in disbelief at the mayor's aides, who looked away. It was some kind of tragic, absurd last monologue, proof of how far the balding old Jew on the podium had drifted from his constituency.

The day of the primary passed like a blur. In the morning, he conducted his only official business, the welcoming of two visitors. During the Tiananmen Square riots, the mayor in a burst of compassion had declared Peking and New York sister cities. Now two idealistic young Chinese men had sailed from China and bicycled across the United States with the official proclamation in their hands. The mayor received them cordially, but with considerable irony. No wonder the youth of China had been so mercilessly crushed, if they were as naive as these two.

There was a brief ceremony, but the mayor's mind was elsewhere. He went off to vote in the late morning, had a long lunch with his aides, and went home to watch the returns.

When Ed Koch had been a young congressman, old Sam Rayburn, the wily cactus of a house speaker from Texas, told him this about the voting public: "When they turn on you, you can feel it in your bones, like bad weather in Galveston."

He was referring to the dank, still air that preceeds Texas hurricanes.

When the early returns rolled in from Staten Island and Queens, they gave Ed Koch a sizable lead. But he was no less a master of the game than old Sam Rayburn, and he was starting to feel the humidity. Sure enough, Brooklyn put Dinkins even, the Bronx kept him there, and Manhattan crowned him . . . and buried Ed Koch.

The mayor's worst fears had been realized. The black vote had been almost unanimous, and the Puerto Rican vote, even the *middle-class* Puerto Rican vote, had defected in significant numbers. Apparently they no longer voted like white ethnics. Not that the white ethnics had delivered so magnificently either. The middle-class Jews in the outer boroughs had held, but the liberal Jews in Manhattan had fallen over each other to vote for Dinkins. The Irish had gone for Koch, but not nearly in the numbers he needed. The Northern Irish controversy, in the end, had lingered. The twelve-year administration of Edward I. Koch was over.

His aides quaked as they watched him absorb the meaning of the returns. How would the great man react?

Displaying no emotion, the mayor walked slowly out of the mansion and into his Town Car for the journey to his hotel headquarters, presumably for the concession speech. But at some point as he neared the Sheraton Centre on the night of September 12, 1989, Ed Koch was seized with a powerful instinct.

When Koch had won his first congressional seat twenty years earlier, his opponent had done a remarkable thing. Whitney Seymour North, on the night of his defeat at the hands of Ed Koch, defied political protocol by actually travelling to the Koch headquarters and conceding the election on Koch's very podium in front of a thousand jeering spectators. It had always struck Ed Koch as a remarkably classy, courageous thing to do. Whatever one might say about the Wasps, at certain moments that noblesse oblige surfaced and you could learn something from them.

So Ed Koch instructed his driver to take a right turn and bring him not to the Sheraton Centre but instead to the David Dinkins headquarters at the Penta Hotel. He would make the grand gesture and personally hand over the mantle of power, and the two old Democrats would reconcile with a bear hug as the crowd gasped and roared.

When the mayor arrived at the Penta, however, the Dinkins people told him to get lost.

Duke York's grandmother was a much discussed figure in the neighborhood of St. Alban's, Queens. As a teenager, Duke had been sent to her from Harlem in the hopes that the old woman would be a stabilizing influence. She did as much as she could, but the boy continued to be wild. At least he substituted the drugs of the white culture for the drugs of Harlem. Better hashish than heroin.

But people wondered how the old woman coped. She was a nineteenth-century person, and her charge was a strange kid almost inventing the future. What did she make of it when he sat up all night with two tape recorders, singing, playing different instruments as he rerecorded and re-rerecorded, winding up with an eighteen-track version of himself singing The Jefferson Airplane's "White Rabbit"? She absorbed it all with a smile, and people could only conclude that the nurturing art transcended styles and generations.

Through much of 1988 and 1989, the old woman was put to an even sterner test. In Duke York's absence during his months of homelessness, her great-granddaughters Atu and Shianna lived with her and perplexed her with the nihilism of yet another generation. But she loved them, and the three of them created a home where antimacassars and the rap sounds of Public Enemy co-existed.

When Duke York finally returned to Queens, though, the old woman feared the worst.

Diane, the girls' mother, was no good and Duke was still wild for her. His grandmother could see that the minute he walked in the door. He started talking about how much the girls looked like their mother. The old woman knew it would not be long before he got drunk and started moaning about her, and then they would all be pitched back into the old madness.

Almost immediately, he went to where Diane worked, just to "talk things out." Instead he wound up screaming at her on the street. He got terribly drunk and didn't get home until well after midnight. The old woman was long asleep, but Duke's daughter Across the Universe was still up. He steadied himself and tried to be the responsible parent. What was she doing awake at this hour? he demanded to know.

She looked up at him. He saw himself as she must have seen him: one eyed, drunk, wobbling, contentious. She could well have replied "Where the hell have you been for a year?" Instead, she told him calmly that she was writing poetry. Duke looked at her. She had ceased to be a child and was now a small person.

He picked up the lined school notebook and read, "An apple you can eat. Oh boy, what a treat. You can munch them in a bunch, you can crunch them up for lunch."

He began to cry.

She had witnessed some of the most destructive scenes that ever came down, and she was whole. She was not writing about giant sodomizing ants, but about apples. She sat now in a flannel nightgown, her hair braided and catching the amber light of a lamppost. She was an angel. He had not ruined her.

He asked if he might read some more, and she gave him permission. He leafed through the notebook, which had brightly colored drawings on every page in addition to the poems. He began to feel as if she might be gifted. By the time he got to the end, he realized that many of the gifts came from him. She had his knack for phrasing, for the sudden unexpected rhyme, and above all for seeing the magic in the humdrum. Her life, provided it didn't get wrecked by some swine like himself, might be a sane, even a blessed one.

"My daddy said," the last poem began, "that whenever it rains, angels are crying tears. But how can that be, when they live with God all those years?"

As it turned out, the warmth of that night did not transform Duke York's life. His obsession with Diane continued, and he never learned to protect himself from her cruelties, many of which he provoked. Some time later, she convinced him to drive her to California for an abortion, even though the child was not his. This he did, because he loved her. Upon returning to New York, she repaid his kindness by taking up with yet another man. He raged at her, threatened to kill the other man, and wound up wildly protesting his love. Why couldn't she love him back? he begged to know. Because, she told him, she was a thoroughbred and he was a pushcart horse. Friends to whom Duke told the story only shook their heads.

"You know what?" they would say. "She's right!! And you're a *dumbass* horse on top of it!" And then they would walk away from the poor devil.

But Duke York began to find that even the most horrible episodes with Diane could be endured, because there was a bottom to them. There were other women in his life, an old one and two young ones, to prove that not all females were treacherous. So he finally elected to rejoin the world, which after all contained a billion of these creatures. He got a job far below his talents as an aging bicycle messenger and began to chip in with the old woman for the rent.

After his defeat in the Democratic primary, Ed Koch became invisible. Whether it was the election night rebuff at Dinkins' headquarters or the unfamiliarity of losing or just a great weariness, no one could say. He continued to preside over the mad circus of New York, but as a phantom. At dawn he would arrive at his health club, do his time on the treadmill, and by 7:30 be in his office, from which he would not emerge except to go home.

The weekends offered the usual plethora of ethnic fairs, but to invitations on September 16 to the Vietnamese Festival, the Steuben Day parade, and the Flatbush Frolic—all opportunities for grandstanding and gourmandizing normally irresistible to the mayor—he said a muted "no."

Oddly, his first public appearance was at the opening of an Abraham and Strauss department store. Perhaps, thought the pundits, he was just doing his duty to the tribe of Israel, from which no amount of personal grief could excuse him. Several days after that, he appeared at an event for transit police officers. Unsteady on his feet and somewhat maudlin, he told them "This is the last time I will ever stand before you, but I will never forget you."

But that was all. In mid-September, as Jews all over New York sat in temples through the High Holy Days and chanted the ancient chants, Ed Koch sat in his own temple of seclusion, the fabulous old Gracie Mansion on the East River.

Some thought Rosh Hashanah mortified him, since he had come to see the campaign in such religious terms. Did he feel he'd let down the whole race by not defeating David Dinkins? Did he feel as if the gates had been trampled down, and barbarians like Jesse Jackson and possibly even Farrakhan himself would now maraud through the synagogues of New York and trash the Torahs and rape the women? Perhaps. But the Jewish faith, at its best, transforms anxieties like these. Sometime during or shortly after Yom Kippur, the mayor found the strength to re-emerge.

One Sunday, he appeared unexpectedly at a Polish event on Greenpoint Avenue in Brooklyn. Of all the ethnic celebrations in New York at which he'd posed and clowned and pandered, the

349

Polish ones were closest to his heart and to his blood. After feasting on kielbasa and vodka, the mayor was emboldened to say a few words. Up on the platform, he found himself speaking with a new freedom. Not that he'd ever been shy. But now there was no election to win and no one to worry about offending.

Koch watchers expected the long accumulated venom to spill out. Surely he had been feigning sensitivity for so long that he would take almost orgiastic joy in letting the liberals have it. His friends and aides rubbed their hands in anticipation of some well-aged bile. Instead, on that day and on days to follow, the mayor behaved with a totally unexpected gentleness, more so even than during the campaign.

He began by commissioning a statue of Racial Harmony to be erected at a future date in Brooklyn. Cynics thought this was intended only to show up Dinkins, but it soon became clear that the mayor was genuine. He had continued to befriend the father of Yusuf Hawkins, long after the case had left the headlines, and long after it could do the mayor any good. He even arranged for a wealthy friend to pay for the funeral.

On his last official visit to Washington, no longer constrained by having to maintain a working relationship with the Reaganite Republicans, the mayor attended a drug conference and finally let Reagan's "drug czar," William Bennett, have it. He had always thought Bennett an incompetent fool who theorized about inner cities from the comfort of a suburban den. Now, in front of a roomful of urban mayors, he told him so.

Upon returning to New York, the mayor turned his guns on the realtors he had been so often accused of coddling. He demanded that they finally make good on the linkage agreements from which so many had reneged or ignored. Linkage, in essence, meant that for every glittering condo a Donald Trump created in Manhattan, he was obliged to create low income housing in the Bronx. The problem was that the realtors rarely bothered to do so—especially in the freewheeling eighties, with a friend in City

Hall. The greatest linkage project of all, the zillon-dollar Battery Park City, had so far not coughed up a nickel for low income housing.

Now, unexpectedly, the mayor turned on them. All through the eighties, the Zeckendorf Corporation had destroyed wide swaths of Single Room Occupancies, traditionally the last resort of down-and-outers. Now their executives found themselves at the ground breaking of a new SRO building at one of their prime locations on Forty-Sixth Street. As the mayor made a speech, their grumbling was almost audible from the podium—in the eleventh hour, the son of a bitch was turning into a pillar of morality.

To the forces of international repression, the mayor was merciless. Perhaps remembering the visit of the Chinese youths to his office on primary day, the mayor renamed the traffic island in front of the Chinese Embassy Tiananmen Square. It was a bald and remarkable insult to the diplomats who sat inside.

On November 5, David Dinkins defeated his Republican opponent, as expected, and the Koch Administration entered its lame duck finale. The last official acts were all more of the same, the behavior of a kindly grandfather more than a bitterly departing politician. He demanded, and got, salad bars put in the city's prisons, notorious for their lack of nutrition. He filled the city's school programs with entitlements for special kids, which emerged at the end as his pet project. It was as if, childless himself, he was drawing all the city's Tiny Tims to his bosom.

Finally, and most surprisingly of all, he abandoned his resistance to the homeless. Now, any city housing project would have to set aside some spots for them, no matter how loudly the community leaders complained that it would shred the "fabric" of their neighborhoods.

All of this behavior was shocking to everyone, and only the ones who had known him the longest could guess at his motives. Perhaps this was his nova, the white-hot burst of the star before it dies. He was using it to show what might have been, what the ideological son of Adlai Stevenson, unfettered by political realities or his own personal demons, might have wrought.

On December 31, his last day in office and the last day of the 1980s, the mayor paid a morning call to a police precinct in Queens. He had vowed to visit them all before leaving office, and this was the last one on the list. A long blue line of fifty stood at rigid attention as the mayor got into his limousine to leave.

When he returned to City Hall for the last time and walked into the vast rotunda, the payback for his loyalty was all around him. The Police Department Emerald Society pipers were arrayed on every level of the curving staircase, filling the old hall with their beautiful ancient bleating. The mayor wept uncontrollably. Apart from sharing with him the sound of their ancestors, they were forgiving him at last for the dumb remark in Northern Ireland.

The next day, he sat shivering on the platform outside City Hall during the inauguration of David Dinkins. As Dinkins began his remarks, former Mayor Koch remembered his own first inaugural. He had arrived at the ceremony on a public bus, a symbolic move of which he was quite proud, especially in light of Dinkins' gaudy stretch limousine. The new black mayor and his wife were like Lotto winners moving into a mansion.

He chastened himself. He ought to try to be the good loser. He tried to sustain another line of thought, but it was too goddamn cold! Why, he had always wondered, did politicians consider overcoats a sign of weakness at inaugurations? He made a mental note never again to vote for someone who didn't have the sense to dress for the weather.

Now he found his thoughts turning to his last inauguration, a freezing day four years earlier. How dreadful it had been. On this very platform he had sat among Brutus and Cassius—Donald Manes and Stanley Friedman and all the other thieves who had sold New York City out in Queens diners and in the men's rooms of funeral homes. All of which reminded him of the turtle. At one point, Henry Stern had given him a stone turtle from a Central

Park fountain for his bedroom at Gracie Mansion. Ex-mayor Koch wanted to be sure to return it. This was the measure, he thought wanly, of how paranoid he had become. God forbid that anyone should think he was going to try to take the goddamn turtle with him into private life.

The ceremony ended, and the coatless politicians gratefully left the cold air of the park to the spectators. The mayor found the formal reception dull and left early. The Dinkins people, for all their angry black rhetoric, were mild and vaguely technocratic.

It had been months now since Ellen McCarthy had returned home from Long Island to find her Waterford crystal vase gone, as well as a small brass clock. Both had been gifts from her mother. On her pillow she had found Larry Locke's blue crocuses, brown at the edges. When she finally discovered the shards of the vase in the garbage, she was able to reconstruct the events. It was a clear portrait of Larry, the destructive romantic.

Usually, after episodes like this, he would arrive a day or two later and stand in the doorway shaking his head and smiling rue-fully, like a child with muddy shoes. This time, however, days passed and he did not come. The crocuses soon joined the shards of glass in the trash, spring turned to summer and finally to au-tumn, and she knew he would not be back. The brass clock was never found.

Periodically, reports filtered back to her through the vast net-work of poverty professionals. Apparently he had been offered a job by Dean Morton of St. John's Cathedral as the superinten-dent of the small shelter run by the church. He took the job, be-came quite ill, and soon quit. This came as no surprise to Ellen. Often he had expressed his contempt for shelters of any kind. He felt the keepers and wardens to be parasites, even lower forms of life than the inmates. No wonder he would take the claustropho-bia of such a situation into his body and get sick.

When winter came and no further word arrived, she began to worry and set out to find him. The Upper West Side was the most fruitful place to start, because he was last seen there, and because it contained the largest concentration of homeless people in New York. As pigeons flock to places where people fling bread crumbs, so do the homeless hover around the liberals of the Upper West Side, not just for money, but for an encouraging smile. This was the homeless underground, where information was passed from mouth to ear, like birds sitting on a wire.

Trying to find a homeless man, Ellen discovered, taxed not only her patience but her vocabulary. Was Larry a cocoa-colored man, a chocolate-colored man, or a dark honey-colored man? His name was of no use; in a subculture where many of the citizens are wanted for child support, or worse, names are withheld. Ultimately she described him by imitating him—the flurry of his hand gestures when he perceived an injustice, the gloomy, stolid brooding.

"Ah! I know the cat you mean!" a vagrant outside of Zabar's said finally. He went on to describe a cappuccino-colored man with curly hair and a crooked smile, and the look of an Indian. Ellen nodded. The man said that Larry was in fact due outside of Zabar's in half an hour. He was apparently trying to organize the homeless of the Upper West Side into a campaign for pennies. The storekeepers had stopped accepting pennies in bulk, and that was sometimes all the currency the homeless had. This was Larry's new crusade.

"Should be here around eight. You want to wait?"

"No thanks."

"It's warm in the bookstore." He pointed to a place called Shakespeare & Company next door.

"I don't think so," she said. She handed the man a dollar and left. It sounded as if Larry's spirit was intact, and that was all she cared about. The love affair did not interest her anymore, nor did the cause. She would continue to report to work and do her job as well as she could. But, she thought, you don't have to sleep with them, and you don't have to change the world. If the coffee is strong and hot, and you can look them in the eye without flinching, that would have to be enough. You only had to smile if you felt like it.

———

The mayor's people worried much about his transition to private life. There was no family to cushion the blow, and he had been padding about the immense mansion on the East River for so long that his tiny Greenwich Village apartment, which he had retained throughout his time in office, might now seem like a monk's cell.

But new digs were found, and the adjustment to civilian life was not as jarring as his friends had feared. The man had carried an exhausting burden for a long time, and he was laying it down somewhat gratefully. Now there was—hallelujah—time to *read*! And read he did, everything under the sun, but first the river of commentary that accompanied his fall from power. "Like a warrior beaten from the fields," wrote Murray Kempton, "Koch would not leave but lingered in the woods beyond."

"His great trouble," wrote another columnist, "was that he was so alone, with no one to see him in his underwear, or tell him when he was acting like a jerk."

"He was an ethnic comedian," said a third, "bored by his material but unable to transcend it."

All of it hurt, but he was able to dismiss it as elitism and even jealousy. The real reviews, the ones he would cherish, came from the thousands of letters that poured in from middle-class families in Brooklyn and Queens—his people. "I worry about you," read a letter from Flushing. "Now don't get into trouble with your big mouth, and don't eat junk food!! I love you, Ida Shapiro."

Junk food would not be a problem for the ex-mayor. His tastes had refined considerably after twelve years of being able to eat for free in the best restaurants on earth. For his intimate dinner par-ties, he now shopped at Balducci's, an epicurean Disneyland a block away from his new apartment. He haunted the place—ogling, tasting, sniffing, buying. Occasionally, however, even Bal-ducci's was inadequate, especially when the mayor wished to serve Jewish food. On these occasions, *everywhere* was inadequate except Zabar's, the Upper West Side palace of herring and whitefish and sable and lox.

And so, on the first Passover following his retirement, in the raw early spring of 1990, the ex-mayor schlepped uptown. He cre-ated a stir wherever he went, and Zabar's was no exception. People were amazed by how tall he was in real life, and how very quiet. But there he was, burdened down with a loaf of challah and an armload of artery-clogging goodies and waiting in line to pay, just like everybody else.

On his way out the door, the former mayor's eye was caught by a panhandler. There was something familiar about the man, even through the matted grime. So sure of this was Ed Koch that he re-entered the store and spoke to one of the countermen he knew, a grizzled *alte kakka* named Gus. It was a sad story, said Gus as he hacked up the sturgeon in front of him. Apparently the poor fel-low had been a black political figure at one time, or something like it. For Zabar's, he had been nothing but a pain in the ass, hanging around the store and squawking about pennies, trying to force the store to take them. Finally they had had to get tough with him; either he behaved himself or they would call the police. That was the last thing the guy wanted, because Zabar's was a fab-ulous panhandling spot. Who wouldn't want to be where thou-sands of Jews were emerging from a store with pockets full of change and hearts full of religious conviction?

So he agreed to stop hassling people and they let him stay, but lately he had seemed to be going downhill fast. He'd gotten very skinny and very dirty and was losing his teeth. Other employees had seen him smoking crack around the corner, and everyone thought that was part of the problem.

The former mayor absorbed the sad tale, wished Gus a Happy Pesah and left. Outside, again in the presence of the panhandler, he could not control the mensch in himself. "You know," he said, "You need some dental work."

The man stared at him with no expression.

"I hear that at one time you did political work. I think that's a very noble calling."

Again the man did not reply. Against his better instincts, the former mayor reached into his pocket, found a quarter, and placed it in the man's hand.

"Happy Pesah," he said, adding for the edification of the Gentile, "May the Lord's vengeance pass over your house, as it passed over the Jews' houses in Egypt."

Truthfully, he felt a bond with the pathetic vagrant. He was going home to begin the preparations for a lush seder, but it wouldn't take place until the following night. Tonight, and for many nights afterward, he would be alone in the dark city.

Larry Locke watched the large man disappear into the night. The quarter in his hand now joined three others in his pocket. Together with a dollar bill, four dimes, three nickels, and sixty-one pennies, that made three dollars and sixteen cents. Another eighty-four cents would enable him to score a hit of crack from José around the corner, then get a cup of coffee and one of those chocolate glazed doughnuts. Beyond that he had no plans.

———

The reconstruction of 850 Longwood Avenue was due to conclude almost eighty years to the day from the moment the first tenant moved in. On that day in the cold early spring of 1910, some two weeks after Albert Brackman and James Meehan had cut the ribbon in their top hats, a well-to-do Ukrainian couple was due to arrive with their baggage and their servants.

Albert Brackman rose early, gave his brown mare an extra feed of oats, and put the tack on her even before his own breakfast. He didn't want anything going wrong, didn't want a leather strap busting on him at the last minute and making him late.

But everything had gone smoothly. A spring snow had fallen, a wonderful track for the blades of his sleigh. The mare had been newly shod with cleats, and they bit smartly into the frosty earth as horse and driver flew across Longwood meadow. Brackman arrived at the building just as James Meehan was going down into the basement to have a look at the boiler. Architect and builder descended together. Early complaints about heat would spread quickly, and they needed no negative publicity if they were to rent these expensive apartments.

The boiler was fine, however, and by the time Martin Milintoff arrived with his entourage, the building was a wonderful, toasty spot from which to contemplate the fields of white. Brackman and Meehan repaired to the tavern down the road and drank until their wives wondered where they were, and then for a while after that. That night, the men had little sense of restraint or responsibility. They were celebrating the birth of a child.

So, too, in the early spring of 1990 did the moment arrive for Eve Miranda to consider the matter of tenants. As she sifted through applicants, a timid assistant pointed out that the loan from the city's Housing Preservation and Development office carried with it certain conditions. One of them, written into law by Ed Koch before he stepped down, was an uncharacteristic concession to the homeless: any project accepting a city loan had to set aside some units for homeless housing.

Miranda was vexed. What about the fabric of the community? she protested to city officials. Its health was very, very fragile. They were barely holding out against drugs, prostitution, and a dozen other forms of depravity. Why were they being asked to introduce even more unstable elements into all this?

To this argument the city remained deaf. The law was the law.

And so, for a couple of bleak afternoons, Eve Miranda sat in her office morbidly depressed. Why had she bothered risking her neck to get rid of someone like Guiterrez? So a homeless crack addict could move right back in?

It was at this moment that she thought of the wandering black woman. After Eve had thrown her out of the bathtub a year earlier, she was rumored to have spent several months sleeping in the abandoned movie theatre across Prospect Avenue. Then she was finally chased out of there and took to the streets. The slim panhandling possibilities of Longwood Avenue defined the phrase "blood from a stone." Nevertheless she had remained in the neighborhood, doing God-knows-what in return for an occasional bed or meal or pint of wine. She had, in fact, become a local fixture, a rather pathetic one in the opinion of most.

But if Eve Miranda had to put a few homeless people in 850 Longwood, an old black woman was a preferable alternative to a violent crackhead. The only problem was that she had disappeared again. The preceding winter had been intense, and this suggested two grim possibilities: she had gone away or was dead.

Miranda began to make inquiries. There had been sightings, none of them recent. Finally one young woman pointed to an old building across Prospect Avenue, the ruins of a synagogue. Approaching it, Miranda thought the cornerstone odd, since it bore the name of an Irishman named McGraw.

The place was horrific. There was no roof at all, and by merely kicking open the door, Eve Miranda scattered a thousand screeching pigeons throughout the building's shell.

"Hello," she called.

No reply.

"Hello!" she cried again.

Nothing.

One last time she tried. "Anyone in here?!"

"Who the hell is that?" finally came an answer.

"Eve Miranda!!"

"I'm supposed to know who the hell that is?"

"I'm coming in . . ."

"You come near me I'll knock your goddamn head off. I got a brick in my hand."

Slowly Miranda approached the voice. Her eyes whirled in her head, first down to where she stepped, for fear of rats and rusty nails, then straight ahead, for fear of flying bricks. Finally she stepped through a charred door frame, and there sat Samantha Jones on a squalid mattress with a quart of Colt 45 in her hand.

"Hey, it's the old Señorita Dolores Del Rio. Man, you people is ugly. What the hell you want? Your chickens get loose?"

Eve Miranda struggled to control herself. She remembered now how offensive she found the old *negrita*.

"I want to talk to you."

"What you want to talk about?"

And so Eve Miranda explained slowly the situation to Samantha Jones. Samantha did not believe her and thought instead that this was a trick to imprison her or to get her into a city shelter. Miranda felt like she was coaxing a battered animal out of a corner. Finally, after a freezing hour of squabbling and screaming and accusations and assurances, Samantha Jones followed Eve Miranda out of the synagogue.

Arrangements were made for her to spend a week in a Fordham YWCA, pending some paperwork and the personal fumigation process insisted upon by Eve Miranda. One morning shortly afterward, Samantha Jones entered the renovated 850 Longwood Avenue. The vestibule was no longer marble but instead a far more serviceable gray plaster. The elevator was now fully functional, albeit with a profoundly changed design. An engine room had been built on the roof, and the descendant of the Bronx's first elevator was drawn up and down swiftly through steel casement.

Samantha Jones looked at it contemptuously and began to climb the stairs. By the time she neared the top, she was exhausted and in some pain. The winter had been brutal, and she felt ill most of the time now. There had been a doctor at the YWCA, but she preferred not to know what was wrong with her.

She finally reached the sixth-floor hallway, which was bright and newly painted in a salmon color. In her hand was a freshly cut key. She squinted at it, trying to match the number with the numbers on the door. She needed glasses.

Finally she found the room, which was at the end of the corridor. She opened the door, and immediately to her right was a small bathroom. She was crushed to observe that the tub did not have legs. It was not even a tub, but a sort of porcelain base for an efficiency shower. She sank onto a chair and absorbed the blow.

Her eyes scanned the room. It was just that, a room, and the smallest room in the building. She would later find out it was one of only two studio apartments. But it had an unusual feature. The window was an oval shape, high off the floor: if she stood on her tiptoes, she could see the hill of Kelly Street.

The Number 2 train to Gun Hill Road rumbled by, and Samantha realized that this would be an intermittent part of her reality. Putting that out of her mind, she sat on the bed, which was more like a cot with a thin, hard mattress.

She opened a soiled linen scarf that she had been carrying with her for some time and took out her box inlaid with mother-of-pearl, given to her long ago by her own mother. Whatever it was meant to contain it did not, since Samantha owned nothing but the box. Perhaps, she thought, she would keep her key in it.

She rose, went over to the door, and turned the latch.

Click. She tried the handle, and it was secure, immovable. She returned to her bed and reclined. It was getting dark. In the morning, the express trains would rumble by with more frequency, and the sun coming up over Kelly Street would probably waken her. But until then, through the long winter night, nothing would disturb her.

She was home.